THE COMPLETE IDIOT'S GUIDE® TO

Year-Round Gardening

by Delilah Smittle and Sheri Ann Richerson

ALPHA

A member of Penguin Group (USA) Inc.

I dedicate this book to Chaz Macdonald, my partner in life, otherwise known as the accidental gardener.
—Delilah

ALPHA BOOKS

Published by the Penguin Group

Penguin Group (USA) Inc., 375 Hudson Street, New York, New York 10014, USA

Penguin Group (Canada), 90 Eglinton Avenue East, Suite 700, Toronto, Ontario M4P 2Y3, Canada (a division of Pearson Penguin Canada Inc.)

Penguin Books Ltd., 80 Strand, London WC2R 0RL, England

Penguin Ireland, 25 St. Stephen's Green, Dublin 2, Ireland (a division of Penguin Books Ltd.)

Penguin Group (Australia), 250 Camberwell Road, Camberwell, Victoria 3124, Australia (a division of Pearson Australia Group Pty. Ltd.)

Penguin Books India Pvt. Ltd., 11 Community Centre, Panchsheel Park, New Delhi—110 017, India

Penguin Group (NZ), 67 Apollo Drive, Rosedale, North Shore, Auckland 1311, New Zealand (a division of Pearson New Zealand Ltd.)

Penguin Books (South Africa) (Pty.) Ltd., 24 Sturdee Avenue, Rosebank, Johannesburg 2196, South Africa

Penguin Books Ltd., Registered Offices: 80 Strand, London WC2R 0RL, England

Publisher: *Marie Butler-Knight*
Editorial Director: *Mike Sanders*
Senior Managing Editor: *Billy Fields*
Acquisitions Editor: *Karyn Gerhard*
Development Editor: *Julie Coffin*
Senior Production Editor: *Megan Douglass*

Copy Editor: *Nancy Wagner*
Cover Designer: *Kurt Owens*
Book Designer: *Trina Wurst*
Indexer: *Celia McCoy*
Layout: *Brian Massey*
Proofreader: *John Etchison*

Contents at a Glance

Contents

Introduction

Gardening has many rewards. Flower gardening feeds your soul, and vegetable gardening nourishes you and your family with wholesome, fresh produce. What could possibly be wrong with this picture? The harvest season is here and gone before you know it. Too often, you find yourself suddenly overwhelmed with more than you can possibly eat, freeze, dry, or can. And then there follow several long, fallow months.

In this book, you will discover innovative and inexpensive techniques for changing all-or-nothing gardening into a manageable year-round supply of fresh produce and flowers. We show you how to extend the season of spring vegetables into summer, how to grow and harvest summer vegetables in fall and winter, and how to overwinter hardy crops and ornamentals. With this book you can, at last, reap the rewards of gardening in all seasons.

How to Use This Book

The Complete Idiot's Guide to Year-Round Gardening is divided into six parts. Each addresses a different facet of gardening, from growing vegetables, herbs, and fruits to hardy perennials and tender ornamentals.

Part 1, "You *Can* Garden Year-Round," provides an introduction to gardening in every season. We explain essentials such as creating perfect growing conditions for every season and selecting plants that thrive in marginal growing conditions.

Part 2, "Gardening Basics: Before the Harvest," covers a garden essential—healthy soil. Discover how to determine whether your soil has the right balance of nutrients. And learn to raise garden plants from seeds.

Part 3, "Gardening Under Cover: Spring to Fall," helps you determine which garden design fits your needs. You will learn what a covered garden is and how to maintain it.

Part 4, "Gardening Under Cover: Winter," is about making the most of nature's least friendly gardening season. We revive interest in the ecological and economical root cellar. We also shed light on insulating covers that allow you to garden outdoors right through the winter.

Part 5, "Greenhouse Gardening: All Seasons," thoroughly explores the rewards of year-round greenhouse gardening. Learn the ins and outs of greenhouses, including heating and cooling options, helpful tools and gadgets, and beneficial insects and animals.

Part 6, "Gardening Basics: After the Harvest," casts an eye to next year's garden with a look at seed saving and garden cleanup. Finally, we wrap things up with how to pack and store your harvest to maximize freshness.

Extras

To help you find shortcuts, helpful information, and safety advice, we have scattered boxes throughout the book that will give you that extra edge when it comes to your own year-round gardening efforts.

Garden Guide

Here you'll find tips and tricks for simplifying and making your gardening experiences more enjoyable. These are things every gardener should know.

Green Thumb

In these boxes, you'll find horticultural information, techniques, garden lore, and other neat-to-know tidbits.

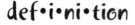

def•i•ni•tion

In these boxes, we explain technical gardening terms.

Safety First

These boxes explain important safety and health issues, and provide advice on what *not* to do.

An Important Safety Note to Readers

This book is not intended to be a substitute for an expert's advice. Readers should consult both an expert in the subject and their medical doctor before taking any action, and are responsible for the choice of and use of treatments and products included in this book. Readers should also read and follow all product label directions carefully.

The names of any products, ingredients, treatments, and organizations contained in this book are for information only. Inclusion does not connote endorsement by the authors or publisher, nor does omission of same indicate criticism or condemnation by the authors or publisher.

All recommendations are made without guarantee on the part of the authors or publisher, and the authors and publisher disclaim any liability in connection with the use of this information.

Acknowledgments

From Delilah: I would like to acknowledge those who made this book possible. Thanks to Alpha Books and Penguin Group (USA) for recognizing the timeliness of this topic and to my acquisitions editor, Karyn Gerhard, for enthusiastically encouraging my efforts every step of the way. Thanks to Julie Coffin for her excellent editing and gardening camaraderie, and to my co-author and fellow gardening enthusiast, Sheri Ann Richerson.

I owe much to my talented and tireless team of photographers, Donna Chiarelli and Thomas Wolf, of Donna Chiarelli Studio, whose styling and digital wizardry produced the images for this book.

Special thanks to my family: Chaz Macdonald, my personal help desk, for caring support and shooting additional photos for the book; to Duke for faithfully staying by my side as I wrote; and to the girls for their outstanding eggs and composting skills. My gratitude to my friend, muse, and pen pal, illustrator Mavis Torke; and to Steve Heller, manager of the Saucon Valley Barnes & Noble, and my friends and co-workers there for their interest and willingness to accommodate my schedule.

From Sheri: I would like to thank Tom Ogren and Janet Rosen, who were responsible for my involvement in this book. I would also like to thank my co-author Delilah Smittle, as well as Karyn Gerhard, Julie Coffin, Dawn Werk, and all the wonderful people at Alpha Books and Penguin Group (USA) who have worked on this book.

I would like to take a moment to thank all the wonderful people who were there throughout the writing of this book to offer support and guidance, including Rhonda, June, James, Chris, Lisa, Alice, Michelle, and Susi. Most of all, I would like to thank my patient, loving husband Jerry, who kept things going on the farm while this book was being written. Thank you all from the bottom of my heart.

Trademarks

Part 1

You *Can* Garden Year-Round

If you're skeptical, let us set you straight. You *can* garden year-round—even if you live in the North, even if you don't have a greenhouse, and even if you've never even grown a tomato in a pot! We tell you how, right here in Part 1. We explain how to fool Mother Nature and start crops very early in spring. Then we fill you in on how to keep those vegetables coming well into the autumn.

It's all about covering things up, in a basic sense. Some plants need covers to keep warm very early or very late in the year. Other plants want covers to keep them from getting too warm in the heat of summer. We tell you which plants need covers and when, and we tell you how to construct or install those covers, too. Gardening year-round is possible—yes, even for you! Part 1 gives you what you need to know so you can eat home-grown produce summer, winter, spring, and fall. Best of all, what you learn will save you work, time, and money.

Why and How to Garden Year-Round

In This Chapter

♦ Garden year-round, with or without a greenhouse

♦ Get a head start on the gardening season

♦ Extend your harvest

♦ Gardening year-round can save you time and money

Why would anyone want to trudge through the ice and snow just to grow a few vegetables in the dead of winter? The answer is simple: in addition to eating fresh-grown produce from your garden year-round, you are doing something that in itself is amazing. You are growing a garden when the weather outside is freezing cold. What can be more thrilling to a gardener than defying Mother Nature and coming away with the bounty to prove it?

Now is the time to learn exactly how to grow your own garden from which you can harvest year-round, even if you live where snow is on the ground in the winter. In fact, you can garden year-round regardless of where you live.

With a little experimenting, you'll be amazed at what you can accomplish with minimal investment. If you wish, you'll be able to fill your pantry, add to your income, and enjoy the beauty of cut flowers. So get out there, while the weather is accommodating, and get organized so you can join the lucky group of gardeners who have found a way to defy Mother Nature and garden year-round!

You *Can* Fool Mother Nature

Creating an artificial environment in which plants will thrive is not hard. A simple structure covered in clear plastic can raise the inside temperature enough to grow plants year-round. Fooling Mother Nature is easy; you can do it with virtually any plant and a covered garden structure such as a cold frame or greenhouse. The question you need to answer is: how far are you willing to go to grow what you want to grow all year long?

What does it take to fool Mother Nature? First, you need to know which hardiness zone you live in. Created by the United States Department of Agriculture, the hardiness zone map designates the climate areas in the United States. Each zone represents a 10°F difference in terms of the average coldest winter temperature. Knowing your hardiness zone is the first step to knowing which plants to grow, when to plant them, and when to harvest. Once you know all that, you can figure out how to extend the season or grow crops better suited to other hardiness zones. The second thing you need to fool Mother Nature is a structure—simple or elaborate—that protects plants from the elements yet lets in light.

The United States Department of Agriculture issued this map in 1990. By knowing what hardiness zone you live in, you can easily choose plants that are sure to thrive.

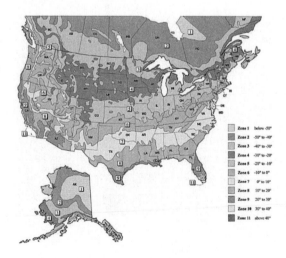

A *cold frame* is the simplest structure and requires very little in terms of construction or maintenance. A *greenhouse*, on the other hand, is larger, more costly to construct, and more complicated to maintain. A *tunnel house* is popular in cold climates because it extends the gardening season and does not require supplemental heat. In addition to extending the season, all three of these structures protect dormant plants from the cold, wet elements outside, allowing some to survive a winter that might otherwise cause them to perish.

def•i•ni•tion

A **cold frame** is a small, boxlike outdoor structure in which gardeners start or grow plants in pots. The sides may be constructed of wood, plastic, or bales. The top must be glass or plastic to allow light into where the plants are.

A **greenhouse** is a structure at least the size of a small room, with plastic or glass walls and roof. In a simple greenhouse, vents allow the gardener to control the interior temperature. In a more elaborate greenhouse, electric fans as well as heaters and automated watering devices are available to give the gardener full control of the environment. Plants are grown in raised beds or in pots.

A **tunnel house** is a plastic tunnel-shaped covering constructed over plants growing in the ground. The gardener may raise or lower the tunnel sides to control the interior temperature.

A simple cold frame made from straw bales and an old window insulates seedlings in early spring or protects mature plants in autumn and winter so you can continue to harvest.

(Donna Chiarelli Studio)

Some gardeners use compost and black plastic to help heat the soil inside unheated structures. But you can also use what we call a heat sink by placing containers of water in your greenhouses, cold frames, or tunnel houses. During the day the sun heats the water; then at night, the water releases heat as it cools. Water containers can be 55-gallon drums, milk jugs, or anything in between.

The easiest plants to start with are those that thrive in cool, moist conditions and a shorter day length. Aim for plants that you can start very early in the spring or in late summer. For the latter, some of these plants may seem to die back when temperatures are the coldest, but once the weather warms up again, you are likely to see new growth emerge.

The trick to fooling Mother Nature and successfully growing crops year-round is to find the right combination for your growing environment. Are you ready? Well, let's move on and learn exactly how to grow crops year-round!

Get a Head Start on the Growing Season

Planting seeds in a greenhouse, cold frame, or tunnel house gives you a head start on the growing season by allowing you to plant weeks earlier than you could outside in a garden. These structures offer the added benefit of not having to worry about being rained out of your garden. Inside these structures, conditions will be relatively dry, warm, and frost-free.

Methods

If you don't have a structure and don't want to build a structure, you can still get a head start by warming the soil or by covering your plants—or both. Starting from the bottom up, warm the soil by covering it through the winter with black plastic, compost, or a heavy layer of mulch. Thus protected, this soil will never get as cold as soil that is not covered. So when early spring planting time comes, this soil will be warmer sooner. Or working from above, cover early-planted seedlings with a row cover or frost cover. This lightweight polyester or polyethylene fabric lets some water and light through but insulates plants from extreme cold temperatures. If you choose a very lightweight row cover, simply lay it on your plants.

Garden Guide

If there's a chance that your early-planted garden will get snowed on, and if you are protecting that garden with a row cover, support your row cover with sturdy wires or plastic hoops. If you don't, the weight of the snow may crush your precious seedlings!

If you choose a heavier-weight cover, support the fabric with wire or plastic hoops and pull the fabric tight enough that it won't droop onto the plants when it gets wet. Secure the edges of the row cover with rocks or soil.

Row covers, suspended above the plants with hoops, are popular for keeping frost off plants grown out of season.

(Donna Chiarelli Studio)

Another way to get an early start is to wintersow some seeds, which takes advantage of nature's own cycle. Just think about it: what do the trees and wildflowers and weeds do? They drop seeds in late summer or fall. These seeds land on the ground, get rained on, and get snowed on. They freeze and thaw—or at least they get pretty chilly. And after all this abuse, they sprout in the spring.

Wintersowing involves placing seeds in moist growing medium in prepared containers—just like you would do when starting seeds normally (see Chapter 6). However, wintersowing happens in January or February. You set your seeds, in their containers, right out in the winter weather. The tops of the containers are open to provide a little air circulation and perhaps to let a little rain or snow in, so check periodically to make sure the growing medium doesn't dry out. Beyond that, the seeds will get wet, freeze, thaw, and do everything that seeds normally do. When the weather warms, the containers act like little greenhouses, providing a little extra warmth. And when the time is right, the seeds will sprout. If Mother Nature sends a late cold snap or a snowstorm, the containers protect the seedlings. You can wintersow many types of plants—both vegetables and flowers. (See Appendix D for wintersowing resources that include detailed instructions and lists of plants that lend themselves to wintersowing.)

Crops to Start Early

Cool-weather crops that do well when planted early include the following:

salad mixes	beets
carrots	potatoes
spinach	turnips
radishes	peas
scallions	leeks
watercress	

Your seed packets will guide you as to how early your particular varieties want to be planted. Seed-starting guidance is also readily available online, in a good seed-starting guide, from your mail-order seed source, or from the gardener you envy down the street.

After you get your garden growing weeks ahead of Mother Nature's schedule, you'll harvest produce weeks earlier than usual. If you're growing crops for profit, this can be an essential part of your marketing plan. If you're growing for your table, the earlier the crops come in, the more money you save on your grocery bill and the better you will eat.

An unheated greenhouse can help keep both cool-weather and heat-loving vegetables alive most of the year.

(Donna Chiarelli Studio)

Extend Harvests into Autumn and Winter

Let's say you've had a busy summer harvest. You ate and preserved the bounty from your garden as fast as you could. But it's going to freeze this week. Is it time to head back to the grocery store for your fresh produce? No! You can keep harvesting those fruits and vegetables well into autumn. You can even extend the harvest of some crops right into winter. The nice part is that to extend your harvest, you'll use the same techniques you used to start your crops in early spring.

Once you understand how extending the season works, you will want to experiment with many crops to see what works in your area. (See Chapter 2 for more about extending the harvest into autumn and winter.)

Green Thumb

The same cool-loving plants you started early in spring are the ones that work well for planting in late summer and harvesting in autumn and winter. However, you can also extend the season for heat-loving plants such as peppers, eggplants, and tomatoes.

Grow Flowers Year-Round

You can have flowers blooming year-round, even without the use of a protective structure. Of course, if you want a large variety of flowers in bloom all year, the best bet is to use a heated greenhouse. However, if you're interested in less complicated and less expensive options, you can extend your flowering season in other ways.

Growing flowers in an unheated covered structure, such as a tunnel house or unheated greenhouse, has many advantages over growing them outside. For one, many plants grow taller in a protected area. And plants will not suffer damage from wind, rain, hail, snow, or unexpected frost. If your goal is to grow cut flowers, erecting a structure in which to grow them would be to your advantage. You'll be able to plant earlier than normal, which means you'll have blooming flowers earlier than conventional gardeners. Also, because you'll have flowers blooming later in the season, you'll be the envy of all your friends and neighbors.

One thing to consider when choosing plants for greenhouse production is their resistance to disease. Avoid plants that are naturally prone to powdery mildew or other diseases. The conditions inside covered areas almost guarantee that these warmth- and moisture-loving diseases will affect plants, so it's best to save these plants for outdoor production.

You may choose to use your unheated structure as a year-round home for your flowers. If so, you'll want to read other chapters in this book to learn about watering, fertilizing, and generally caring for plants under cover all year. Or you may use your structure only to begin and end your season. Start seeds and nurture seedlings there in the early spring, and in the autumn, when temperatures begin to dip, transplant mature plants or pot them up and set them under cover.

Green Thumb

Believe it or not, some flowers will bloom during the winter months, even in northern climate zones and even without protection. Following are some pretty reliable winter bloomers: hellebores (*Helleborus*), heaths (*Erica*), heathers (*Calluna vulgaris* and others), witch hazel (*Hamamelis*), pansy (*Viola*), hardy cyclamen (*Cyclamen hederifolium*), snowdrops (*Galanthus*), winter aconite (*Eranthis*), gentians (*Gentiana*), larkspur (*Delphinium exaltatum*), and monkshood (*Aconitum*). Most of these plants will bloom outdoors between November and February. Experiment in your own yard to see what works well for you.

If you want to go further and use a heated greenhouse, you'll find, depending on the temperature of your greenhouse, you have no limit to what you can grow and flower year-round. Do remember that some plants will require additional lighting to flower during the winter if there are not enough hours of daylight.

Covered Gardening Techniques of the Past

For thousands of years, the only way to have something to eat was to collect it in the wild or grow it yourself. In cold climates this meant one of two things: either figure out how to preserve the harvest through the winter months or learn how to grow crops year-round.

def•i•ni•tion

A **cloche** is a bell-shaped cover, historically made of glass, that is put over a plant to protect it from frost, heavy rain, or hail.

The use of greenhouses—or at least protective structures made out of glass—goes back to the Romans. The Romans' techniques faded but then revived in the Middle Ages when glass pavilions were built to house flowers as well as fruits and vegetables. With advances in glass-making techniques, the glass *cloche* came into use and made it possible to protect just a few garden plants at relatively little expense.

A modern cloche, made from a plastic milk jug, can help you get a head start on the gardening season.

(Donna Chiarelli Studio)

In the late 1600s, glass greenhouses became relatively common, but only on European estates. They were not for the common man. Still, curious and learned people studied plant propagation, traded *species* of plants from all over the world, and generally expanded the body of botanical knowledge.

def•i•ni•tion

A **species** is a group of plants with common characteristics that set it apart from other plants of the same genus. A group of closely related species forms a genus, or plant family. Botanical plant names place the genus or family name first, followed by the species name. For example, in *Cyclamen hederifolium, Cyclamen* is the genus; *hederifolium* is the species.

Thanks in part to these early greenhouse growers, we now have proven methods that work. The guesswork is behind us, and we can enjoy the fruits of our labor year-round from our own covered gardens.

Save Money, Feel Good

By using time-proven techniques for year-round gardening, you'll save money and feel good. There's no need to reinvent the wheel; simply follow the model of our forefathers and walk in their footsteps.

Growing fresh produce year-round is a money saver in so many ways. Prices on fresh produce always go up once the product is no longer in season locally. If you're growing your own, you don't have to worry about the price hike, nor do you have to spend time driving to the local grocery store to buy produce. You simply walk out to your garden, pick the produce, wash it, and eat it. How much easier could it get?

Studies have shown that locally grown—and therefore, really fresh—garden produce is full of nutrients that can lead to better health. The longer produce sits on the shelf, the more nutrients it loses. Produce on your grocer's shelves is picked before its prime so that it won't be over-ripe when it reaches consumers. In addition, it is at least two or three days old by the time you see it on that shelf. By growing your own produce, you benefit from the ready availability of fresh, nutrient-rich fruits and vegetables. And of course, you benefit from the exercise you get while you maintain the garden. Even a small dose of year-round gardening yields healthful food and exercise—two ingredients for a healthy lifestyle.

The Least You Need to Know

- You can garden outdoors year-round.
- Some basic protective covers or structures allow gardeners to extend the harvest by starting seeds early.
- Those same covers or structures allow gardeners to prolong the harvest by protecting plants through the autumn and even into the winter months.
- Flowers also benefit from growing under cover.
- Fresh produce has more nutrients than days-old produce from a grocer.

Chapter 2

Creating the Perfect Conditions, Year-Round

In This Chapter

- ◆ Keep warm-weather plants happy when autumn temperatures begin to dip
- ◆ Help cool-weather plants thrive through the heat of summer
- ◆ Create the perfect growing environment year-round—in garden beds and in containers
- ◆ Heating, cooling, shade, light, and water play important roles in plant performance

The nights are getting cooler. You still have tomatoes in the garden. One especially chilly night hits, and the next morning your tomato plants look dead. You sense that the remaining tomatoes are not far behind, but wait! It doesn't need to happen this way!

In this chapter, we'll tell you how to extend the season and prevent those tomato plants—and other warm-weather crops, as well as flowers—from succumbing to that first frost. We'll also tell you how to keep cool-weather crops alive and producing outside of the usual early-spring growing season.

You'll have the power to create perfect conditions for your plants through all four seasons of the year, regardless of your local climate.

Growing Warm-Weather Plants Summer Through Fall

In most hardiness zones in the United States, growing warm-weather plants, such as tomatoes, peppers, and eggplants, during the summer months is not a problem. However, if you have a short summer or unusually cool temperatures, you may find that these heat-loving plants don't thrive or produce like they should. You know you can extend your harvest beyond the traditional July, August, and September routine, so here, we'll talk about a number of ways to keep those tomatoes—and other goodies—lined up on your kitchen counter.

Garden Guide

Heat-loving plants such as snap beans, cucumbers, eggplant, melons, okra, southern peas (cowpeas), peppers (both sweet and hot), pumpkins, squash (both summer and winter), sweet potatoes, and tomatoes thrive on summer warmth, both in the soil and in the air. You can extend their season by providing a little insulation in the autumn.

Creating the Perfect Conditions

To extend the productive lives of your heat-loving plants, a row cover may work for the first few chilly nights, but these plants will soon want even more protection. If you surround them with hay or straw bales or plastic panels and secure row cover over the top, you can effectively make a cold frame. Further insulate a small cold frame by wrapping it in a thick blanket at night to hold in the daytime heat. But be sure to remove the blanket during the day so the sun can warm up the interior of the cold frame again.

Or you can construct a tunnel over the plants with row cover held up by wire or plastic hoops. Heat-loving plants grown inside tunnel houses not only perform faster during the summer months but also last longer into the fall, thus increasing the amount of produce you harvest.

For some additional insurance inside your simple structure, lay out black or dark-colored plastic to help keep weeds down and to hold heat at the root zones of your plants. If you're planting in late summer, simply lay the plastic, poke holes in it, and place your seeds or transplants in the holes. If you're adding the plastic around mature plants, just roll it out next to the plants. In either case, make sure the plastic does not touch the stems of the plants. The plastic absorbs sunlight and then holds the heat in the soil. At night, the heat slowly dissipates into the structure.

Heating cables are another option to help you overwinter your plants. You can install these right under your beds. They keep the root zones warm, as well as the area immediately around the plants.

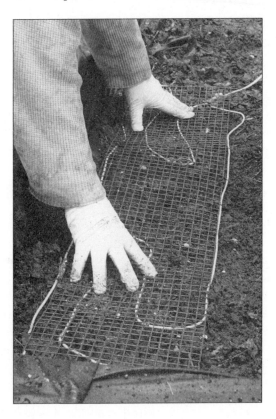

An easy way to heat soil in a specific area is by installing heating cables in a raised bed.

(Chaz Macdonald)

Safety First _____

Do not use an electric blanket outdoors or in an outdoor structure such as a tunnel house or greenhouse. Electric blankets are not made to withstand temperature extremes or to get wet. Using an electric blanket in such a setting is a fire risk.

One thing to remember when trying to stretch your harvest season is that you should never open your protective structure or lift your row cover early in the day. You'll let in cold air, and you don't want to do that! Wait until the sun has had a chance to warm up the interior of the structure, and you'll find that the plants have warmed up and are ready to have you handling them as you harvest.

Growing Cool-Weather Plants Summer Through Fall

Cool-weather plants, such as lettuce, cabbage, broccoli, and peas, are most happy when planted in spring and harvested before the heat of summer sets in. So does that mean you can't have any more fresh lettuce after June? Of course not. You can simply start a second crop in late summer and harvest it in the cooler autumn days. Cool-weather plants tend to bolt, or go to seed, in warm weather. When a plant bolts, it quickly sends up a tall flower stalk. Once that happens, the flavor of the crop declines. If you take a little extra care, your late-season harvest of salad greens and other veggies will be worth the effort.

Creating the Perfect Conditions

You can extend the season of your cool-weather crops in several ways. One is to grow these crops in a tunnel house. To create the right environment, install shade cloth along the length of the tunnel. Shade cloth is a synthetic fabric manufactured to let a certain percent of sunlight through. Using shade cloth over plants effectively keeps temperatures down. And cooler air and soil temperatures mean the soil will retain moisture better. For additional temperature control, raising the plastic or material on the sides of the tunnel house releases any built-up warm air. In a more elaborate set-up, a mist system inside a tunnel house—in addition to shade cloth—guarantees that the temperature will stay comfortable for your cool-weather plants. (See Chapter 8 for more specific information on using covers to keep plants cool in summer.)

If using a tunnel house seems a bit like overkill, another way to achieve success with cool-weather plants in the heat of summer is to use your shade. If you have an area that's shaded during the afternoon and evening, try planting cool-weather crops there. And remember that regular watering is still important. Keeping the plants as cool as possible in the summer months is the key to success.

A third way to keep these plants cool is simply to put a roof over them. Drive four stakes, T-posts, or fence posts into the ground and suspend shade cloth or a lattice across the tops of the posts. This "roof" provides shade but lets rainwater through.

By choosing a shady spot, you can grow salad greens and other cool-weather crops through the heat of summer.

(Donna Chiarelli Studio)

You can also extend the season of cool-weather plants by waiting until late July or early August to plant a second crop of seeds directly outdoors or transplant seedlings into the garden. The heat will cause the plants to grow rapidly, so you'll have to watch carefully to prevent the plants from bolting and setting seeds. Your goal is to give the plants a good start in the warmer weather so they're fully mature and ready for you to harvest when the temperatures begin to cool.

Growing cool-weather crops in summer and fall will take some experimenting, so keep a garden calendar and record both your successes and failures. With a little practice, you'll soon be able to grow cool-weather crops year-round.

Garden Guide

When choosing plants or seeds to grow slightly out of season, such as cool-weather crops to grow in late summer, check the seed packet for the number of days until harvest. This will help you gauge when to plant. Remember, you want the plants to be mature by the first frost.

Overwintering

It is possible to have fresh produce from your garden right through the winter months by *overwintering* your crops. Imagine having fresh salad greens in January!

def•i•ni•tion

Overwintering means keeping vegetable plants alive and producing through autumn and into winter.

If you live in an area that has extremely cold temperatures, you need to construct some kind of cover for your plants. So for example, you might use old storm windows or bales to make a temporary cold frame around the plants in the garden. Or you could install row cover over sturdy hoops. If you live in an area with mild winters, your plants may need only an occasional frost cover for protection.

These salad greens will stay warm under layers of bubble wrap and a tough, translucent tarp. The hoops prevent the weight of snow on the tarp from crushing the greens.

(Donna Chiarelli Studio)

The key to successfully overwintering any crop is to create the right microclimate. A microclimate is the climate of a small or restricted space, and in this case, we're talking about the microclimate around the plants you want to grow through the winter. Here's a rule of thumb: each layer of covering effectively raises your hardiness zone one and a half times. So for example, a gardener in USDA zone 4 who provides two layers of protection creates a microclimate equivalent to that of USDA zone 7.

Imagine being that zone 4 gardener—let's say you're in northern Iowa. Your plants, under those two layers of protection, feel as if they're in northern Georgia, even though it's January. Lucky plants!

In addition to creating a microclimate, another way to ensure success with any plants you intend to overwinter is to choose healthy and pest-free plants. Unhealthy plants or those loaded with pests are already struggling to survive, and stressed plants may not be able to survive the additional stress of winter, no matter how much help you provide.

Green Thumb

Many plants, such as Brussels sprouts, Jerusalem artichokes, and kale, taste better once they've been hit by a frost or two.

If you're trying to overwinter marginally hardy plants, such as banana (such as *Musa basjoo*), cold-hardy palm trees, artichokes, or cold-hardy cultivars of camellias, apply 3 inches of bark, pine straw, or leaves as mulch. Pine straw is the best mulch for tropical plants that you are overwintering in a zone or two lower than where they'd normally grow. The mulch helps insulate the root system and protects it from sudden temperature or moisture changes. For most vegetables, mulching is not a necessary step, but for many ornamentals, it's a good idea.

Provide the plants you want to overwinter with all the nutrients they need to thrive. Potassium is an essential nutrient that enables plants to survive when temperatures drop, as does sulfur. Both occur naturally in the soil, but if you know or suspect your soil is not very healthy, your plants might have a better chance at survival if you apply some organic material in autumn or use a complete fertilizer. Spraying an anti-desiccant on leaves will also help overwintered plants bear the low humidity of cooler winter months. The anti-desiccant seals the pores in the leaves so that the plant does not lose any moisture.

Watering plants in winter can be a bit tricky. Unless you live in a very mild climate, you won't be able to use your garden hose like you do in the usual gardening seasons. You may have to carry water in a bucket from an indoor faucet, so keep that in mind when you decide on a location for your overwintering plants.

Even though it's winter, your plants are still working hard for you, and they'll need water—ideally, an inch per week—to continue performing. When tending plants in winter, it's especially important to water them at their roots because water on foliage in an enclosed gardening structure encourages diseases.

Container Gardening

If you want to add colorful accents to a balcony, patio, courtyard, entryway, or a larger garden area, container gardening is the way to go. Think of outdoor containers as garden sculptures: they need to make a bold statement. They also need to hold enough soil for ample root room and moisture retention and be heavy enough not to topple over in a stiff wind. When it comes to outdoors, the bigger the pot the better, especially if you want to grow vegetables or ornamental combinations.

Safety First

Wet soil can weigh nearly 100 pounds per cubic foot. A damp hanging basket is weighty, so be sure to install a well-anchored bracket to keep it from falling and becoming a danger to someone.

Pots and hanging baskets are sized and sold in inches according to the diameter of the container's opening. A 12-inch pot or basket is a good starting size for outdoors. It's small enough to fit on a balcony but big enough to accommodate a tomato plant and a few herbs, several small vegetables, or a half dozen flowering plants.

Wood and concrete are good materials for large outdoor pots, such as half barrels and planter boxes. They're weather resistant so they can be left out year-round, and they're also heavy and most suited to permanent placement on a patio or in the garden.

Outdoor pots are also made of fiberglass or plastic. Fiberglass, the material of choice for many designer containers, is lightweight and durable, but expensive. Plastic is lightweight and inexpensive, but short-lived because sun exposure eventually makes it brittle and easily broken.

A half whiskey barrel provides plenty of room for a collection of culinary herbs and three Italian paste tomato plants.

(Donna Chiarelli Studio)

Durable, lightweight polyurethane foam pots insulate plant roots against temperature fluctuations, and in mild-winter climates, you can leave hardy plants out in them year-round. Foam pots are available in myriad shapes and colors including realistic replicas of antique terra cotta pots. I can testify that they're break-resistant and long-lasting—I have some on my patio that are 15 years old and still as good as new.

Green Thumb

With a little imagination, you can transform any container, from an old sink or garbage can to a galvanized washtub, into an outdoor plant container. When using found objects, group containers together by material or color for a cohesive look. Drill a few drain holes in the bottom of the container and line plant-toxic copper and galvanized ones with plastic sheeting or garbage bags before filling them with soil.

There's an art to planting a container, whether it's a pot or a basket, even if you plan to grow vegetables in it. Think in terms of creating a bouquet, and put the tallest plants in the center—or at the back of the container if you're placing it against a wall. Arrange the rest of the plants in pyramid fashion, working from medium-height plants surrounding the tallest ones down to the low-growing plants and cascading ones, which you should place around the rim of the pot.

A vegetable planter set up this way could have a tomato plant at the center or back surrounded by medium-height herbs such as basil, and then creeping thyme and cascading Greek oregano around the rim. An ornamental pot might contain tall flowering cannas or a hibiscus at the center surrounded by trailing purple heart vines and asparagus ferns. By all means, mix and match—dress up a vegetable or herb container by tucking in a few flowering plants, especially edible flowers such as calendula, flowering chives, lavender, nasturtiums, and violets. These will look as pretty sprinkled over a salad as they do in your containers!

When considering vegetable and fruit plants for containers, let size and shape of the mature plants guide your choices. Look for plants with naturally compact or, conversely, trailing shapes. Also, watch for signs at the nursery; some nurseries mark certain varieties as "container varieties."

Here are a few of the many choices of vegetables, herbs, and flowers for baskets and containers.

bush beans	eggplants	melons, especially small-fruited varieties
cucumbers	green onions	peppers

salad greens	strawberries	sweet potatoes
swiss chard	tomatoes: patio, cherry, grape, and paste varieties	

Herbs in general perform well in containers because their needs for root room, fertilizer, and—for some—moisture are modest. When shopping, match the size of the mature plant to the size of the container.

basil	chives	cilantro
dill	fennel	marjoram
oregano	parsley	rosemary
sage	thyme	

A vast number of annuals, perennials, and even houseplants perform outdoors in containers from spring to fall. Be bold and experiment with foliage and flowers, being careful to combine only all sun-loving or all shade-loving plants in one container. Then place your containers or baskets according to their light needs. These are some container favorites:

alyssum	asparagus fern
banana	begonia
calendula	canna
chrysanthemum	coleus
dusty miller	geranium
hydrangea	impatiens
lavender	marigold
nasturtiums	ornamental sweet potato vines
pansy, violet	petunia
purple heart vine	primula
snapdragon	zebrinia
zinnia	

Caring for Container Plants

Root room, moisture, and fertility are limited by the size of the container and the number of plants it contains. You can, and should, pack plants tightly into window boxes, containers, and baskets for a lush display. But remember to water and fertilize, with a half-strength solution, often—daily during hot weather—because containers dry out quickly, especially in the sun.

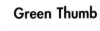

Green Thumb

Avoid using dark-colored pots outdoors unless you live in a cool-summer area or can keep them in the shade. Dark pots absorb and hold heat from the sun, which can "cook" plant roots to death.

After plant roots fill the container, water runs off the surface rather than sinking into the soil, so you may think you're providing adequate water, but in reality, not much is sinking in. I've learned, through experience, the best way to water pots and baskets, which are small enough to pick up, is to soak them up to the rim in a bucket or tub of water—overnight, preferably. When fully saturated, pots and baskets can go longer, sometimes up to a week, between waterings.

Patio pots and barrels contain a larger volume of soil and hold moisture longer than smaller pots and baskets, but you should still check them every other day or so and water as needed. To test, stick your finger into the soil: if it feels moist 2 inches below the surface (up to the second knuckle), it does not need water.

Garden Guide

Mix moisture-retaining additives, such as compost, aged manure, or moisture crystals, into small containers and those destined for sunny locations. Moisture crystals are dried, translucent polymer granules that absorb moisture and release it slowly to plant roots. You can buy them from garden centers and catalogs.

Minimal maintenance is necessary to keep container plants performing at their peak. Pick ripe fruit and vegetables, and deadhead flowers to keep plants from going to seed and looking ratty. Be on the lookout for occasional weeds, and shape plants with gangly growth. You rarely have to repot summer container plants, but you may want to keep a few extra bedding plants handy for replacing ones that die for one reason or another.

Grow your container plants in a nutrient-rich, moisture-retaining potting mix. If you need a lightweight mix for baskets or window boxes, use a light commercial potting mix containing peat moss and *perlite,* or make your own by mixing potting

def•i•ni•tion

> **Perlite** is a lightweight, gritty, porous, white material made by heating volcanic rock. Perlite reduces the weight of potting soil while increasing air circulation and drainage.

soil half and half with perlite. For standing (rather than hanging) containers, We prefer this homemade soil-based mix:

1 part potting soil or pasteurized top soil

1 part finished compost or composted manure

1 part coarse sand

2 parts perlite

We don't advise leaving clay pots outside in freezing weather because the moist clay can freeze, then break. But you can leave cast iron, cement, plastic, fiberglass, and polyfoam pots out over winter. If they contain hardy shrubs or trees, insulate the pot itself by wrapping several thicknesses of bubble wrap around the pot and securing it with clear weatherstripping tape. Set the pot up on bricks for good drainage.

Covering Container Plants

You'll want to cover your container plants to protect them from extreme weather. In early spring when you set out individual potted plants, you can protect them from the cold by setting a commercial cloche over them. Or use the classic homemade version—a translucent plastic gallon-size jug with the bottom cut out and the cap removed. Popping the top off allows hot air to escape during the day without compromising nighttime heat retention.

To protect larger containers in spring and fall, drape floating row cover or an old bed sheet over the plants in the evening to keep them from being frosted. And be sure to remove the cover in the morning.

If a container is in an exposed location, loosely wrap burlap around the exposed plant to protect the plant from wind burn. Leave the burlap open at the top so the plant can receive sunlight because even in winter, evergreens photosynthesize.

The Least You Need to Know

◆ Shade and water play a big role in helping cool-weather plants survive the heat of summer.

◆ You can keep heat-loving plants alive and thriving into fall under cover.

- Cold frames, row cover, and tunnel houses can protect both your cool-weather crops and your heat-loving crops, depending on the season.

- You can grow fabulous containers full of flowers, herbs, *and* vegetables with just the right mix of soil, water, and fertilizer.

- If you provide the protection, your overwintered plants will produce fresh food for you all winter long.

Part 2

Gardening Basics: Before the Harvest

This part is mostly about dirty things—soil, compost, and fertilizer. If you're a gardener, though, you don't think of them as dirty because you know they are the essentials—the building blocks of every garden. We tell you how to decide what your soil needs and how to fix its problems (if it has any). We also tell you how to mix up some fantastic "black gold"—compost that's better for your plants than almost anything. And we help you figure out whether you need to use fertilizer, when to use it, and what kind to use.

Finally, with those building blocks in place, we get down to the business of gardening. And where better to start than planting seeds? We tell you what ones are the best to try, when to plant them, how to take care of those tiny seedlings, and when it's safe to transplant them to your garden.

3

Start with the Soil

In This Chapter

♦ Healthy soil is essential

♦ Plants need nutrients to thrive

♦ Raised beds can make gardening easier

♦ The importance of keeping your under-cover soil healthy

Growing a great garden takes more than just popping a few plants into the ground. It takes healthy soil that is alive and full of nutrients. And it takes proper watering as well.

Yes, you can create healthy soil. By simply adding plenty of organic matter, making sure your ground drains well, and mulching, you will be well on your way to creating the perfect gardening environment. So jump right in; learn what it takes for your garden to thrive; and then sit back and reap the rewards.

What Is Healthy Soil and Why Is it Important?

Healthy soil is alive! Good garden soil is teeming with beneficial micro-organisms and lots of earthworms, too. Healthy soil is *friable*, full of oxygen, and well supplied with all 17 of the nutrients necessary for successful plant growth.

def•i•ni•tion

Friable means "easily crumbled." Friable soil neither sifts through your fingers nor clumps up into a solid ball when squeezed in your hand.

The soil in your garden is your basic building material. Good healthy soil is the foundation upon which all your gardening success depends. Just as we cannot build a great house on a weak foundation, we cannot have marvelous, abundant, healthy gardens unless we start with first-class soil.

So what if your soil isn't much to start with? Don't despair; you can do many things to improve your soil. In this chapter, we explore different ways to turn ordinary soil into the primo good stuff—the rich, loamy kind of soil every gardener longs for.

Qualities of Healthy Soil

Healthy soil has five qualities: good drainage, friability, adequate nutrients, correct soil pH, and humus. For your soil to be top-notch, all five qualities must be present.

Good drainage is the first quality of healthy soil. If soil doesn't drain properly, plant roots become waterlogged, and the plants do not thrive. When soil doesn't drain properly, tiny channels in the soil remain filled with water instead of air, and plants won't thrive no matter what you do. If soil drainage is poor, plant roots will not go down deep. As a result, plants will suffer excessively during the slightest dry period because their shallow roots won't have access to water.

How do you know whether your soil has adequate drainage? Try this test. Dig a hole 1 foot deep and fill it with water. It should drain right away. If it takes more than 10 minutes for the water to drain, then you don't have adequate drainage.

The second quality of healthy soil is friability. If you pick up a clump of soil and squeeze it, does it break up into many little parts? If so, your soil is friable. It will allow air and water to pass through. Soil that lacks friability will either clump up in your hand or simply sift through your fingers.

Nutrients is the third quality. To grow and thrive, plants need water, the right temperature, light, and the right amounts of nutrients. Plants need large amounts of *macronutrients,* such as nitrogen, phosphorus, and potassium, and smaller amounts of *micronutrients*—also sometimes called "trace elements"—such as zinc, selenium, iron, and molybdenum.

def•i•ni•tion

Macronutrients are nutrients plants need in large quantities. Of these macronutrients, the primary ones are nitrogen, phosphorus, and potassium. The secondary macronutrients— still vital to plant health but needed in lesser quantities—are calcium, magnesium, and sulfur.

Micronutrients are nutrients essential for plant health but needed in only very small quantities. Sometimes called minor elements or trace elements, the seven micronutrients are boron, copper, iron, chloride, manganese, molybdenum, and zinc.

Different cycles of growth need different nutrients. For example, a lawn, which is made up mostly of green leaves, needs abundant nitrogen because it is the nutrient mainly responsible for rapid leaf and stem growth and for maintaining the color green. Few soils have the perfect balance of nutrients each plant needs for optimum growth, but there are many ways we can guarantee that our soil does provide what our plants need to thrive.

The fourth quality of healthy soil is the correct soil pH. pH is the measure of a soil's acidity, based on a scale of 0 to 14. On the pH scale, 0 is extremely acid, and 14 is the top of the chart for alkalinity. The number 7 is considered neutral. Some plants, such as blueberries, cranberries, and azaleas, grow best in acidic soil with a pH of around 5. Most garden plants, however, thrive in a pH range between 6 and 7. If soil is too alkaline, we add soil sulfur or gypsum to it to even it out. If soil is too acid, we add limestone to get it into balance. (See Chapter 5 for more specific information about feeding and fertilizing your soil.)

Garden Guide

There's no need to have an expensive soil test done on your garden soil if all you want to know is the pH of the soil. Soil test kits and soil pH meters are readily available for the home gardener. Find them at most retail garden centers.

The fifth, final quality is the presence of humus, the organic matter in soil. Humus is the result of the decomposition of leaves and other plant material that takes place naturally in the soil. We'll talk more about humus later in this chapter.

How Nutrients Benefit Plants

First, let's get one thing clear: fertilizer is not plant food, no matter what it says on the bag! Using sunlight, plants make their own food—sugars and starches—through the process called *photosynthesis*. The macro- and micronutrients in the soil act like vitamins and minerals for a plant; they are needed in addition to the food the plant makes during photosynthesis.

def•i•ni•tion

Photosynthesis, from the Greek meaning "making things with light," is the process by which plants use energy from the sun to turn water and carbon dioxide into starches and sugars. The starches and sugars act as "food" for the plant. Oxygen, a by-product of photosynthesis, is released into the air.

Macronutrients

Nitrogen (N), phosphorus (P), and potassium (K), are the three macronutrients all plants need and which gardeners are most likely to buy in a bag of fertilizer. These three are always expressed in the same order—N, P, and K. On all commercially sold fertilizers, organic or inorganic, the amounts of N, P, K are expressed as numbers, and these numbers are percentages.

Nitrogen is abundant in some soils, especially soils rich in humus, but is lacking in other soils. Most soils in the Midwest have abundant nitrogen, whereas soils in the South and in the West tend to be low in nitrogen.

Nitrogen leaches from soil when it is watered or when it rains. If you irrigate your plants often, you may need to add nitrogen. Because of this leaching action, plants grown in containers always need supplemental nitrogen.

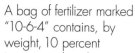

Garden Guide

A bag of fertilizer marked "10-6-4" contains, by weight, 10 percent nitrogen, 6 percent phosphorus, and 4 percent potassium. Filler or carrier material makes up the rest of the bag's weight. This filler material helps users distribute the fertilizer evenly.

Nitrogen makes plants grow fast; it makes them grow green and tall. Plants growing in nitrogen-poor soil grow slowly and their older leaves turn yellow. Too much nitrogen encourages leaf and stem growth at the expense of fruit. Tomato plants, for example, that get too much nitrogen grow very large but have few tomatoes. Good organic sources of nitrogen include chicken manure, blood meal, and rabbit manure.

Plants need phosphorus for the growth of roots, flowers, seeds, and fruits. Plants that grow in phosphorus-poor soil make few flowers, and their fruits are small. Root crops such as potatoes, carrots, radishes, turnips, beets, and parsnips require abundant phosphorus for optimum production. Bulb plants, such as daffodils and tulips, also require plenty of phosphorus. Phosphorous doesn't move quickly through the soil, as nitrogen does, and doesn't leach out as fast as nitrogen. This means, though, that to get phosphorus down to the roots of plants, sprinkling fertilizer on the soil surface may not get the job done. Phosphorus is best applied in the planting holes when planting seeds or bulbs or when transplanting seedlings. Good organic sources of phosphorus are bone meal, compost, and all types of manure.

Adequate amounts of potassium are necessary for all types of plant growth, but in particular potassium is needed for strong stems. Adequate or high levels of potassium also tend to impart some extra winter hardiness to plants and makes it possible for them to overwinter when the temperatures drop. If your soil is low in potassium, spread wood ashes on your soil. Like phosphorus, potassium doesn't travel well in the soil, so it's best to apply potassium when planting or transplanting.

Calcium (Ca) is another macronutrient, but one that's considered a secondary nutrient. Soil lacking calcium does not support good crops. For example, lemons grown in calcium-deficient soil get a soft, dark spot on the end of the fruit. Much the same thing occurs with tomatoes grown in calcium-deficient soil; they rot on the ends, a condition called blossom end rot. Calcium is abundant in lime and in gypsum. If the pH of your soil is acidic (6 or lower), you might benefit from adding some lime to your soil both to add calcium and to bring your soil pH closer to neutral (7). If your soil is neutral or slightly alkaline (having a pH of 7 or above), then instead of lime, use gypsum to add calcium to your soil. Gypsum is also useful for breaking up tight clay soils.

Green Thumb

Save your eggshells; they are a great source of calcium. Wash them out, dry them, crush them, and then put them around the base of plants that are happy to have a little extra calcium, such as tomatoes. You can also add eggshells to your compost.

Magnesium (Mg), another secondary macronutrient, is part of the chlorophyll in green plants and is essential for photosynthesis. Manures, compost, dolomite limestone, and fertilizers with trace elements are good sources of magnesium.

And the last of the secondary macronutrients is sulfur (S), which is needed for root and flower growth. Adequate sulfur in the soil also makes plants more winter hardy and resistant to cold. Some fertilizers contain sulfur, and sulfur can be purchased as soil sulfur—usually used to make a soil more acidic. A good, inexpensive source of sulfur is gypsum.

Though we've given information here about what to add to soil that's deficient in these secondary macronutrients, note that unless a plant or crop has very particular needs, adequate amounts of these minerals are usually in the soil. Having a deficiency of one of these minerals is not a common occurrence.

Micronutrients

The micronutrients plants need to grow are boron, copper, chloride, iron, manganese, molybdenum, and zinc. Only very small amounts of these nutrients are needed, and too much of any of them, especially copper, chloride, or boron, can cause problems. As with the secondary macronutrients, having soil deficient in a micronutrient is rare. The exception would be soil in a field that has had the same crop planted in it for two or more years in a row. Certain plants "use up" certain nutrients in the soil. This knowledge is what led to crop rotation, in which farmers plant corn one year and soybeans the next, so as not to wear out the soil. The micronutrients that plants need in order to thrive are best supplied through good compost, fish emulsion fertilizers, and most types of composted manures.

Your plants also need three nonmineral nutrients: hydrogen, oxygen, and carbon dioxide (CO_2). By supplying your soil with plenty of organic matter, you ensure there's enough carbon dioxide in the soil. Plants get hydrogen from water (H_2O). Where do they get their oxygen? From the ground, believe or not. That's why you need to make sure your soil is friable—that there are enough air spaces—yes, oxygen—in the tiny spaces among the soil particles. Besides adding gypsum, compost, and organic matter to your soil—all of which help make the soil more friable—you should add mulch. Mulch improves the friability of soil by encouraging the presence of earthworms, and the tunnels the earthworms make through the soil provide space for additional oxygen. The worm castings add to the general fertility of the soil. A good thick mulch holds in water, prevents weed growth, and keeps the soil cooler when hot and warmer when cold.

Types of Soil

In soil science, there are hundreds of different kinds of soil. But for our purposes, we can divide soil into three types: sandy, loamy, and clay. Sandy soils have the largest particles and drain the fastest. Loamy soils have medium-size particles and the greatest humus content of the three types. Clay soils, with the smallest particles, hold water well, but for plants that don't like to have wet roots, that's not good.

Each type of soil has pros and cons, but generally, loamy soil is considered the finest. For commercial fruit growing, the very finest soils are sandy-loam soils—fertile, friable, and well-drained.

Green Thumb

Certain plants grow best in particular soil types. For example, the best blueberries grow in acidy, sandy soils. The best corn grows in loamy soils. And the highest yields of grapes come from sandy-loam soils. With fruit trees, apples grow best in sandy or loamy soils, but plums and pears thrive in clay soils.

Overcoming Soil Problems

To overcome soil problems or to improve your soil, what you need to do depends on what type of soil you have in your garden. So let's take a look at each of the three soil types and how you might improve them.

Improving Sandy Soil

Sandy soil usually drains fast and warms up quickly. Because the individual particles are so large, there is plenty of air space between the particles, so these soils are usually quite friable and easily worked. The main problems with this type are that it may lack needed nutrients and it's prone to drying out too fast.

To keep sandy soil from drying out, cover it with some kind of mulch. To increase nutrients and improve water retention, add organic matter. Compost, horse or cow manure, peat moss, and any other kind of organic matter will improve sandy soil. During the growing season, sandy soil may need more fertilizer than other kinds of soil. If you use organic fertilizers, you'll help build up the beneficial microorganisms in the soil in addition to "feeding" your plants.

A thick layer of old hay or straw used as mulch best covers sandy soils lying fallow or not being used. If you have sandy soil and a fallow garden area, plant a green manure crop, such as clover, or alfalfa. Let it mature, and turn it under in the autumn to add organic matter to your soil. You can accomplish the same thing over the winter with a cover crop. In northern climes, hairy vetch and rye are among the few hardy enough to plant in late summer and survive the winter. In more southern areas, clovers, vetches, medics, field peas, oats, rye, and wheat all work as cover crops. Whether you try this strategy in summer or winter, the crop suppresses weeds while it grows and then supplements your soil after you till in the mature plants.

Improving Loamy Soil

Loamy soil is the ideal soil to have. It is usually rich, friable, easy to work, quick to warm up, and well-drained. These are those dark, rich, loose soils that grow the best crops. Few of us are blessed with good loamy soil, but by working with what you have, you can make your own soils more like loamy soil.

Loamy soils require the least fertilizer, but you may need to monitor the soil pH. It might be necessary to add lime to sweeten an acid loamy soil or to add some gypsum or soil sulfur to make a slightly alkaline loamy soil more acidic. Remember, the best pH for most garden plants is between 6 and 7.

Improving Clay Soil

Clay soil can be very heavy and hard to work. People sometimes add sand to clay soil, thinking it will loosen it up, but don't do it! Adding sand to clay soil doesn't work.

To improve clay soil, add large amounts of organic matter and large amounts of gypsum. Some good farmers add a ton or more of gypsum, every year, to the clay soil in their fields. The gypsum adds calcium, and the gypsum binds to the clay particles and makes the soil looser and easier to work.

Garden Guide

Avoid walking on clay soil when it is wet. And, likewise, do not move any kind of heavy machinery on wet clay soil. Doing so will compact the soil, robbing it of air.

Gardeners should never—and we repeat, never—work clay soil when it is wet! Working clay soil when it's wet is a sure way to compact it, which makes it harder, stiffer, and less friable. Working any soil when it's wet is not a good idea, but with clay soil it is a flat-out bad idea. Let clay soil dry out before you plow, dig, or cultivate it.

Adding organic matter to clay soil improves the soil's drainage in addition to improving its friability and nutrient levels. Also, simply digging small ditches through clay soil helps drain it, as long as each ditch ends up at a lower spot than where it started so water drains away or can be pumped away if need be. Some gardeners dig small ditches to the lowest spot available and then dig a hole that is at least 3 feet deep in that spot and put a sump pump in it. You want to make sure the sump pump is deep enough so it does not freeze and burst. Another solution is to drain excess water to that same low spot and then plan a garden there specifically for water-loving plants.

Most of us, though, don't want to have exposed ditches running through our gardens. Open ditches don't appeal to our sense of aesthetics, and keeping the ditches clear requires annual maintenance. Another way to make a drain through heavy clay soil is to dig a trench through the garden to a drain area and then fill in the trench with rocks and gravel. Commonly, gardeners then place old planks or pieces of plywood over the rocks and gravel and cover it all with soil. Over time, excess water in the soil finds its way into the rock-filled trench and flows downhill to the drain spot.

A slightly more elaborate, long-term, and aesthetically pleasing solution is to use tiling to drain the area. To tile an area means to lay perforated pipe beneath the surface of the soil to promote the drainage of excess water. Note: we call this "tiling" because it used to be done with red clay drain tiles. Now tiling usually involves plastic pipe rather than what we normally think of as anything that resembles a "tile." Large hardware stores and farm supply stores carry plastic drain tile. This drainage tile, either flexible or rigid PVC pipe, is perforated—it has holes all along one side.

Water always moves downhill, so the first thing you need to do—whether you decide to dig ditches or tile your garden area—is to identify the lowest part of your yard or garden, an area to which you can drain excess water. Keep in mind that it's best to keep your own water on your own land, so to speak. In other words, don't dig a drainage ditch to the edge of your property line without first talking to your neighbor about the water you intend to drain onto his land.

To install tiling, dig a trench 2 to 4 feet deep toward an outlet where you can drain the extra water. Place the pipe in the bottom of the trench, making sure it is angling downward, with the holes on the bottom, and cover the pipe with soil or stones. Excess water will find its way into the pipe's holes and then run downhill to the drain area. If you are concerned about soil plugging the holes in the drain, you can cover the pipe with filter cloth.

Tiling an area is a big job, but it can solve drainage problems for the remainder of your gardening years. It is almost impossible to over-drain heavy clay soil. However, too many drains placed too close to each other may eventually make it next to impossible for plants' roots to get a good deep soak.

The perfect garden soil is attainable, no matter where you live. Remember: the key is to create friable soil full of organic matter. Creating the perfect garden soil by adding organic matter won't happen overnight but will take several years to achieve. However, every year you will notice small improvements in your soil.

To Cultivate or Not

To cultivate is to prepare soil for crops and gardening by breaking up the soil. Years ago, almost all gardeners and farmers alike cultivated the soil in both spring and fall to kill weeds and to break up the soil. And in truth, cultivating also makes the garden look nice.

Today, though, attitudes about cultivating have changed. Farmers and gardeners worldwide are switching to low-till or no-till methods. Gardeners are giving up the practice of cultivating in favor of mulching. A good, thick mulch can do the same things cultivating used to do. The mulch suppresses weeds, holds in moisture, and softens or loosens up the soil. And you have to admit, a nicely mulched garden bed looks great.

But sometimes, cultivating may still have some advantages. If the garden is very weedy, cultivating is a good way to kill those weeds. If you are sowing tiny seeds, such as those for carrots or onions, directly into the garden bed, it may make sense to cultivate the soil so the seedbed is very well broken up. And for gardeners who love to get a good workout, cultivating the soil certainly provides plenty of exercise.

Techniques for Cultivating

Rototillers are one of the most popular ways to cultivate soil. They come in a variety of sizes, from large and pretty unwieldy to not much bigger than a small electric sweeper. The size you need depends on your task. If you're breaking sod for a new garden bed or if you have heavy clay soil, you probably need one of the big, unwieldy ones to do an adequate job. If you're not up to the task, there are people who would be happy to do this job for you—for a fee, of course. If you have loamy or sandy soil, you won't need such a heavy-duty tiller. Whatever the size of the machine, the mechanics are the same. The rotating tines of the tiller stir up the surface of your soil. The depth of the stirring depends on the tiller and on settings—at least on some models—that you adjust.

Double-digging can do more for the soil than a tiller. Not only can you dig deeper, but by mixing up the soil, you'll bring nutrients deep in the soil to the surface, making them more accessible to your plants' roots.

Double-digging typically needs to happen only once—when you initially prepare a garden site. Think of this as sort of peeling back the covers of your new garden. Follow this procedure:

1. First, decide how wide you want the garden to be. That distance (we always suggest about 4 feet) will be the length of the trench you are about to dig.

2. Dig a trench 1 foot deep and 1 foot wide along the width of your future garden. As you remove the soil, put it into a wheelbarrow.

3. In the bottom of the trench, use a garden fork or spade to "stir up" the soil even further—at least another 8 inches would be great. Don't remove this soil; just loosen and stir.

4. Put several inches of organic material, such as compost, into the trench. Stir this up with the loosened soil.

5. Now dig another trench right next to the first. Place the soil from the second trench into the first trench.

6. Repeat steps 3, 4, and 5 until you have double-dug the entire garden space.

7. After you dig, loosen, and amend the final trench, use the soil in the wheelbarrow to fill in the trench.

No matter what method you use to break up the soil, another important part of cultivating is weed management. You can hoe the weeds, use a tiller or small cultivator, or pull them by hand. The less you disturb the soil, the less you disturb the earthworms' air tunnels. And the earthworms' air tunnels are a good thing! For that reason, after you plant your garden, removing weeds by hand or using a thick layer of mulch to suppress weeds is generally considered less disruptive than hoeing or cultivating.

Virtues of the No-Cultivation Method

Garden soil that is healthy, has plenty of humus in it, and is covered by thick mulch may not need to be cultivated at all. To plant seeds, scrape back a small section of mulch and place the seeds in the soil. As the seedlings grow and get some size to them, redistribute the mulch closer to the new seedlings.

Some garden enthusiasts insist that no-till is best simply because of the earthworms. Choosing *not* to till means you do not disturb the ground, so earthworms and their pathways are not destroyed. Earthworms help make the soil fertile by redistributing organic material in the soil. They also leave behind their castings, which are a popular—and extremely fertile—organic fertilizer.

Chickens

Because chickens scratch at the ground with their feet, they make great cultivators. Some gardeners put them in an area where they wish to plant a new garden so they can tear up the soil and eat the insects and weed seeds. Also, if you till your garden, put some poultry in that area for a short time to eat insects and weed seeds that you brought to the surface.

Chickens can help keep your garden pathways clear of weeds and insects.

(Donna Chiarelli Studio)

Chicken tractors are popular with many gardeners who want to control the area to which their chickens have access. Chicken tractors are basically portable chicken coops that a tractor can pull to a new spot. They come in all shapes and sizes, and the chickens are contained inside, which provides a level of control for you and a level of safety for them. Placing a chicken tractor in a spot where you want to start a new garden bed or revitalize an old one is an effective way—and labor-free for you!—to break up the turf or get the soil worked up.

Raised Beds

Growing plants in good *raised beds* is a real pleasure. In a raised bed, the soil warms up fast in the spring, stays friable, and is easy to work, and the drainage is fast and sure. Plants thrive in raised beds, and raised beds are easier for the gardener to work in, too.

A raised bed can be of any length, but the width of a raised bed is most important. Four feet wide is about the perfect width. If a bed is four feet wide, almost anyone can reach the center of it without ever having to step into the bed itself. If no one ever steps or stands in the bed, then the soil will never be compacted. When the soil stays loose, it's easier to work, and roots grow stronger and faster in it.

def•i•ni•tion

Raised beds are areas for growing plants that have been mounded up or contained within timbers, rocks, or landscaping stone. The resulting bed area is higher than the ground around it, which promotes good drainage.

The height of a raised bed varies and depends, to some extent, on materials available and gardener preference. In some situations, a very tall bed is practical. If you were building raised beds for people in wheelchairs to use, for example, you'd want to make those beds about two feet tall.

Most raised beds are raised only 6 to 10 inches. Beds built with 2×8 redwood or cedar lumber last the longest because both woods are naturally rot resistant, even when in contact with soil and water. You can use pine or other less expensive lumber or peeler cores (a roughly 4×4 rounded "log" left over from the veneer-making process). Lumber other than redwood or cedar won't last as long, but it may hold together for 10 years or so. You decide whether to go with a long-lasting but larger up-front investment (redwood or cedar) or a less lasting but less expensive option (pine and others).

Safety First

Don't use old railroad ties to make a raised bed for any plants that are edible! These old railroad ties were soaked in creosote, and the creosote eventually leaches into the soil and gets into the plants. Creosote is a toxic substance.

Likewise, don't plant vegetables in an old tire filled with soil. Old tires decompose, and vegetables grown in them may well take up any number of toxic substances from the tires. If you use an old tire for a raised bed, grow only ornamental plants in it.

Materials Needed

Many home gardeners have built their own raised beds. If you're able to bend and lift and have some common power tools, you'll be able to do it, too. Here's what you'll need for one rectangular raised bed:

- lumber or peeler core in the amount required for your 4-foot-wide raised beds

- 4 pieces of rebar long enough to reach beneath the frost line in your area—generally 2 or 3 feet

- carpenter's square

- heavy hammer or sledge hammer

- circular saw (optional)

- hacksaw (to cut rebar)

- electric drill and drill bit slightly larger in diameter than the rebar

- landscape fabric (enough linear length to line the insides of your lumber)

- staple gun and staples

Building a Raised Bed

With those materials and with a plan in your head—or better yet, sketched out—you're ready to begin.

Notching the ends of land-scape timbers with a circular saw before assembling a raised bed allows you to lock timbers together securely at the corners.

(Donna Chiarelli Studio)

Drill a hole through stacked timbers at each corner. Use the carpenter's square to make sure the corners are square.

(Donna Chiarelli Studio)

Drive a piece of rebar through the predrilled holes at each corner.

(Donna Chiarelli Studio)

Cut enough landscape fabric to line the inside of the raised bed. Staple the fabric to the top edge of the timbers to prevent soil from washing out through cracks and joints in the timber walls.

(Chaz Macdonald)

Fill your finished raised bed with a mixture of half compost and half good garden soil or topsoil and rake smooth. Or if you want to plant root vegetables, such as carrots, beets, or turnips, fill the bed with equal parts of compost, soil, and coarse sand.

(Chaz Macdonald)

Soil Under Cover

When choosing soil to use under covered areas such as tunnel houses, greenhouses, or cold frames, remember the better the soil you start with, the greater your success will be. Just as soil in raised beds or containers needs to be topped off with fresh compost, so does soil under cover. You can use mulch under cover, as well, to help the soil hold moisture and to keep the roots of the plants warm or cool, depending on the season.

The Least You Need to Know

- The soil in your garden is the foundation material essential to an abundant, fruitful garden. The healthier the soil is, the more bountiful your harvest.

- Healthy soil has five qualities: good drainage, friability, the correct pH, plenty of nutrients, and humus.

- There are three main types of soil: sandy, loamy, and clay; loamy soil full of organic matter is the perfect garden soil.

- You can improve each type of soil so it is easier to work and better for your plants.

- Gardeners may or may not choose to till garden soil to control weeds and/or make it workable for planting or transplanting.

- Raised beds make gardening easier and can be filled with the perfect blend of organic matter and soil.

Compost: Black Gold

In This Chapter

- ◆ Help the environment and get free plant nutrients
- ◆ The right ingredients for compost
- ◆ The perfect way to compost for every situation
- ◆ Improving air circulation produces compost faster
- ◆ Worms can do your composting for you

Information on composting is readily available, but you don't need to go hunting for it because right here we provide a beginning-to-end how-to on composting. You *can* compost, no matter where you live or how much space you have—or don't have. In this chapter, we'll take the guesswork out of composting; we'll clarify the difference between slow and fast composting and explain how to use compost year-round for soil warming and cooling. And you'll learn how valuable compost is as a fertilizer for your garden or your container plants.

So get ready! It's time to learn how to turn kitchen scraps, weeds, leaves, newspapers, teabags, and other compostable materials into black gold for your garden.

Why Should You Compost?

Composting is the process of allowing formerly living materials to decompose or break down. But what are these "formerly living materials"? They include livestock manure; weeds; leaves; grass clippings; and kitchen scraps, such as fruits, vegetables, and coffee grounds. The decomposition part of composting is a natural process that occurs every day. Humans help by "putting things together," which is just what the Latin roots of *compost* mean.

Composting makes sense. It saves money—because you don't have to buy fertilizer. It saves the environment—because you keep things out of the waste stream that don't need to be there. And it's good for your plants—because all the little living organisms in compost improve your soil and make things grow. Do you need any more reasons? Well, okay, that's the short version. Keep reading to get the whole story.

Environmental Benefits

Using compost to improve your soil helps to eliminate puddling and runoff. For example, if you have improved your clay soil, the increased amount of organic matter will allow rainwater to soak in and travel through the soil, rather than to puddle on the surface or simply flow away. Soil enriched with compost also holds fertilizer better, thus eliminating the chance that fertilizer will run off after a hard rain and pollute a stream or harm wildlife.

Green Thumb

According to the U.S. Environmental Protection Agency, yard waste and "food residuals" make up 24 percent of the municipal solid waste stream. That's a lot of compost that we're throwing away!

Once your soil is compost enriched, you'll have no need for synthetic fertilizers because the compost will provide everything your plants need to thrive. You'll need fewer pesticides, as well, because your super-healthy plants will be less susceptible to infestations.

Another advantage of using compost in your garden is that it allows you to get a head start on the planting season. Just imagine extending your harvest so that you buy less produce at the grocery store. That means better, more nutritious food for you and less packaging material (from the produce you didn't buy) going into your trash.

Creating compost is all about not wasting precious natural resources and finding a better, more environmentally friendly way to garden. Simply put, it's cool to compost.

Benefits to Plants

Composting benefits plants by adding nutrients to the soil. The healthier the soil is, the better your plants will grow. Adding compost to your soil may even enable you to grow plants that wouldn't grow there otherwise.

Well-made compost contains both macronutrients and micronutrients, many of which aren't found in human-made fertilizers. Compost slowly releases these nutrients, essential to plant and soil health, into the soil, a process that can take months or even years. What's important is that the compost, once integrated in the soil, is there to get the job done.

And compost acts as a soil buffer, helping the soil maintain the correct pH. Compost has the ability to neutralize alkaline and acid soils to the pH level that most plants prefer.

Safety First

Composting is a wonderful way to create a source of organic nutrients for your plants. However, you should take a few safety precautions. When turning a compost pile, wear either washable or disposable gloves and a dust mask. When you're done working, wash your hands immediately. The fungus that may grow in compost can cause respiratory problems or aggravate them if you already have issues. Some people have allergic reactions to compost as well.

Composting Basics

One of the most important parts of creating compost is choosing the right ingredients. As with any recipe, adding too much or not enough of an essential ingredient makes a difference in the outcome of the product. If you add the right ingredients, layer them, keep them moist but not wet, and avoid putting in ingredients that could sour your compost, you'll end up with a product—finished compost—far superior to anything on the market, no matter how much money you might be willing to spend.

It's All About Decomposition

In order for raw materials, such as grass clippings, livestock manure, and kitchen scraps, to turn into ready-to-use compost, the materials must decompose or break down naturally. When we make a compost pile, our goal is to make the best mixture possible (by adding the "right" ingredients) and to speed up the natural decomposition process (because we're impatient).

The materials in your compost pile will rot—there's no question about that. The key is to provide the food, water, and air the microorganisms need to do the decomposing as efficiently as possible. The water and air are easy. Your pile will be outside, so it'll get rained on. And there's air all around, of course. So what about the food?

The right ingredients for a compost pile fall into two categories, the "browns" and the "greens." Brown materials are high in carbon and provide energy. Green materials are high in nitrogen and provide protein for the microorganisms.

Brown Materials

The most common browns to add to your compost pile are these:

- leaves
- woodchips and sawdust
- hay and straw
- paper, paperboard, and cardboard
- eggshells, coffee grounds, and tea bags
- soil

Leaves are the most common brown materials and they are also easy to get. Go out and rake all the leaves you can find. Ask friends, family, and neighbors if you can have their leaves. Most people will be more than happy for you to take them; some will even rake and bag them for you.

If you're a woodworker, if you've had a tree cut down, or if you cut your own firewood, you might have a plentiful supply of wood chips and/or sawdust. Both are good brown materials to compost, but they come with two words of caution. First, compost them separately, if possible. Wood materials take a while to break down, and while they do so, they pull nitrogen from the soil, which means the nitrogen is not available to the plants that need it. If you have wood chips or sawdust, let these materials sit in their own compost pile for a whole year before you distribute the compost or incorporate it into your main pile of other browns and greens.

The second word of caution is this: do not compost sawdust, wood chips, bark, or branches from walnut trees. All parts of a walnut tree contain a substance that inhibits growth in many plants, and the substance does not break down or go away in a compost pile. If walnut were composted, the finished compost would contain the same growth-inhibiting substance.

Hay and straw are both excellent additions to the compost pile. Even better than hay is spoiled hay because the weed seeds are more likely to be nonviable. Hay is higher in nitrogen than straw, but straw is higher in carbon. For that reason, straw is viewed as an even better addition than hay. Choose straw that's been used as bedding or has gotten wet. Straw is quite slow to decompose, which is another reason why it's such a great additive. The action of remaining straw particles decomposing helps open up the soil structure after you have added the compost to your soil.

This open compost pile, at the edge of a garden, has a layer of browns—mostly leaves—on top.

(Donna Chiarelli Studio)

Add paper, paperboard, and cardboard to your compost pile, but cut it up into small pieces first. Worms love shredded paper, and using this material will encourage them to make a home in your compost bin. When choosing paper to shred, avoid papers that are high gloss or highly colored. Also, avoid cardboard with a glossy or waxy finish or with plastic tape on it.

Eggshells, coffee grounds, and tea bags are another example of a free material that does wonders for the compost pile. Eggshells contain high amounts of calcium; the drawback is they take a long time to decompose. Do not throw whole eggs into your compost pile because the rotting eggs will attract pests. For best results, crush only the shells and add them to the pile. Coffee grounds are high in nitrogen and can really get a compost pile cooking. Finally, don't forget to toss your used tea bags into the pile.

Green Materials

The best and most common greens for your compost pile are:

- grass clippings
- hedge trimmings
- kitchen scraps, mostly fruit and vegetable peelings
- livestock manure

Grass clippings will likely be your number-one source for green compost materials. Use clippings from your own lawn, and ask your neighbors for theirs, too. But do not save clippings if you've recently applied fertilizer or weed killer to the lawn. And if you garden organically, you may want to limit your grass clippings to only those that have never been treated with chemicals.

Hedge trimmings are another great source of green materials. Boxwood and privet come to mind as common household shrubs that often get an annual trim. Small cuttings from these and other shrubs break down easily, but shred larger branches before adding them to the pile.

Vegetable and fruit peelings are great for a compost pile. If you're worried about critters finding them, simply dig them into the center of the pile and bury them. It's best to use raw, uncooked peels in your compost as cooked fruits and vegetables may contain other ingredients, such as oil, that slow down decomposition. If you do compost cooked fruits and vegetables, do so in a covered compost pile.

And livestock manure is the other main source of compost greens. Many farmers will be more than happy to have you clean out their barns and haul the manure away. Some great manures to use are goat, sheep, rabbit, chicken, horse, and cow. Less common but equally useful are alpaca and llama. Again, if you garden organically, ask about the animals' diets. Fresh manures are famous for containing weed seeds and fly larvae. When adding fresh manure to your compost pile, cover it tightly with a tarp or plastic and keep it that way for about a month to help kill the fly larvae. Many farmers have a manure pile behind the barn, and manure from there—rather than fresh from the barn floor—would be partly aged already, which helps minimize the weed seed and fly problem.

Air and Water

The microorganisms need air to help the decomposition process. To provide air, turn the compost pile once a week. By turning the pile, you allow air to reach different parts of the material. The easiest way to turn compost is to create a second pile so you can just flop the material from the first pile onto the second. When you're done, the bottom of the old pile will be the top of the new.

Water is the other vital ingredient. Do not allow your compost pile to dry out. But don't soak it with water, either. If it seems a bit dry, give it a quick spray with a garden hose or empty one watering can onto the surface. Depending on where you live and the climate, you may need to give your pile a sprinkling as often as once a week.

If your compost pile is covered, you will still need to keep an eye on it so it does not dry out. Instead of removing the entire cover, uncover a small section and check it. If the pile is damp, simply cover it up. If it needs watered, remove the entire cover and sprinkle it the same way you would an uncovered pile, then place the cover back on the pile.

Activators and Additives

A compost activator helps speed up the composting process, especially if you are trying to compost things such as tree branches, which are slower to break down than many other materials. A compost activator can also help maintain a perfect pH balance in your compost pile. Most compost activators contain ingredients such as kelp, dried blood meal, and calcium. It is a good idea to read the ingredient label to see what is in each one. Some are organic and some are not. There is no need to spend a lot of money to buy a top-of-the-line commercial activator; a generic commercial activator will work just as well. You can buy compost activator at most garden centers or garden departments in home improvement stores.

In addition to commercial activators that are specifically designed to accelerate the composting process, you can use other materials, some of which you may already have on hand. From the feed store, cottonseed meal or soybean meal work just as well as commercial activators in most cases. If the compost is not intended to be purely organic, a great inexpensive activator is ammonium sulfate. If you use this, sprinkle it on twice a year. Another option is to use kelp or even cracked corn as activators. Remember that if you garden organically, you may need to add an activator that is certified organic.

While a compost activator helps speed up the decomposition process, an additive simply adds to the bulk of the compost pile. There is nothing magic about an additive. Some great additives for the compost pile include prepackaged manure, which is a great way to go if you do not have access to fresh manure. Often at the end of the growing season you can find bags of manure, topsoil, potting soil, or other prepackaged soil additives such as kelp or dried blood meal on clearance. This is a great time to stock up. If you don't have a compost pile set up but come across a great deal, simply set the bags aside, unopened in a shady spot. The manure will turn into compost in a few months, and then you can use it straight from the bag if you wish.

Making Compost

When it comes to making compost, you can quickly turn brown and green waste into black gold. By quickly, we mean you can start composting and have finished compost for your garden within one growing season. Or you may choose to take the slow route and let nature work her charm for a year or two.

When making compost, you should know what the temperature of the compost pile is, especially if you're in a hurry to get things going. Temperatures inside a pile can vary quite a bit, reaching as high as 160°F. The hotter the pile gets, the faster it breaks down into compost, but the ideal temperature is between 110° and 140°F. To check this temperature range, you can buy a composting thermometer or an outdoor thermometer with a wire to bury in the pile.

Fast Compost

If you want to get on the fast track to making compost, remember that shredded or chopped materials break down faster than large chunks of materials. Avoid adding branches to your compost pile unless you chop them up or your compost pile is quite hot.

It can take anywhere from two weeks to several months for your compost pile to be ready to use. To speed up decomposition, turn it at least once a week. Why turn it? Remember those critical ingredients for decomposition—air, water, and food? By turning the pile, you aerate the material in the pile, thus speeding decomposition. A pile of tightly packed materials decomposes more slowly than one that is loosely packed. Also, make sure the pile remains hot enough to keep the raw materials breaking down quickly. To keep a pile hot, turn it on a regular basis. The more air that is incorporated into the pile, the hotter the pile will get and the faster the material will break down.

Slow Compost

Creating slow compost is the easier way to go. Simply choose an area that is out of the way, in full or part sun. Layer your green and brown materials and decide whether you wish to cover your pile or not. The main reason you would cover your pile is to keep flies away if you are using fresh manure or to conceal the pile from your neighbors' view. The only thing left to do after that is to keep the pile moist and wait for it to turn into compost. If you cover the pile, be sure to check it at least once a week to see if watering is necessary. Remember, the pile must stay moist to break down properly. Using this method, the process of going from raw materials to usable compost could take up to two years. The composting action is that much slower because the pile does not get turned.

Some gardeners find it convenient to have several slow, or cold, compost piles in various areas of their yards. One pile might be easily reached from the vegetable garden, and another might be near a flower garden. Or one might be in a place where the gardener wants a new garden bed. Creating a compost pile is a great way to kill the grass and weeds in an area and to enrich the soil before you even start the garden.

Bins, Piles, Sheets, Underground

There are many ways to confine compost. You can buy a contained, heated composter to keep in your kitchen. You can buy a worm bin and have vermicompost, which is when worms help turn kitchen scraps and yard waste into compost. There are small, portable, premade compost bins and large barrel-shaped compost bins you spin by hand. You can build a compost bin out of pallets, or you can simply make a pile on the ground.

Compost bins come in many size and shapes, so you'll be sure to find one just right for your situation.

(Donna Chiarelli Studio)

Fancy compost tumblers that turn by hand really don't do any more than a compost pile on the ground. They simply look nicer, keep the compost contained, and, once you have a finished product, are easy to dump into a wheelbarrow.

A cheaper alternative is to make your own compost bin out of wooden pallets; you can even get pallets for free by calling around to lumber yards, factories, or retail stores in your area. You'll need five pallets to create a two-compartment, *m*-shaped compost bin, which is the best configuration. You'll also need six T-posts.

Simply lay two pallets on the ground side by side. These will form the back of the bin—or the top of the *m* shape. Drive one T-post right where the two pallets meet. Then drive another T-post at the other edge of each pallet. Stand each pallet up and tie it to the T-posts with wire. The top of your *m* is complete. To make the first leg of the *m*, lay a pallet down at the left end of your back wall, perpendicular to the wall. Drive a T-post at the front edge of this pallet. Stand the pallet and tie it to the post. Do the same at the far right end. Then set the final pallet in place in the middle of the *m*, drive the last post, and secure the last pallet.

Use one compartment to hold new materials. As these materials begin to break down, use a compost fork to move them into the second compartment to finish the decomposition process. When you need fertilizer or mulch for your garden, take the finished material from this second compartment.

Sheet composting, or putting a thin layer of compost materials over an area, is a great way to create a raised bed area. Simply mow the area you wish to plant in, lay down cardboard or a thick layer of newspaper, and start your compost pile. You can frame your pile, if you wish, with wood, concrete, or other materials you have on hand. If you're in a hurry, instead of putting raw material on top of the cardboard, cover it with finished compost. Then spread leaves or wood chips on top to allow decomposition to take place.

Garden Guide

A compost fork is better than a regular garden fork because the tines are thinner and more widely spaced. The tines are also curved, which facilitates scooping and containing loose material. It also helps keep chunky material from getting stuck in the tines.

You can do sheet composting in your flowerbeds with materials that have not broken down into compost, such as leaves, wood chips, or other types of mulch. However, there are some disadvantages to using this method. One drawback is that you can't use kitchen scraps if you are using a single layer of leaves or wood chips around your plants. Also, you should understand that using this method of composting will not destroy weed seeds or plant pathogens because the pile does not heat up.

Underground composting is yet another method available to people who do not want a large compost pile in their yard or who do not have room for such a pile. To compost underground, dig a hole 6 inches deep. Add 5 inches of brown and green materials and cover this with one inch of soil. That's all there is to it. The material will break down underground, and a year later the area will be ready for you to plant in.

Curing Compost

Compost that has finished all its natural reactions—in other words, that has finished breaking down—is cured. Compost that's not fully cured has cultures, or good bacteria, that continue to be active; therefore, the compost is still in the process of breaking down. It is okay to use compost that's not fully cured as long as it isn't hot. Compost that is too hot can "cook" plants' roots. The only time hot, unfinished compost should be used is to warm the soil in the spring if there are no plants or seeds already planted in the area.

How can you tell whether compost is "done" or not? Compost that has a slight organic aroma may not be fully cured. An easy way to finish the process quickly is to put small amounts of the compost into gallon-size buckets with holes in the bottom of them and let them sit for several weeks. When the aroma fades, the compost is cured. You may want to finish your compost using this method if you have a hard time turning the pile. It is sometimes easier to dump a bucket of compost than to turn a large pile.

The curing process, which takes place in your compost bin, can take four to eight weeks. During this process, the compost pile should have a temperature between 80° and 110°F. The appearance of the compost tells you when it's cured; it should look dark and crumbly. You'll also notice it no longer heats up when you turn it.

Finished compost is dark, crumbly, and easily scooped or shoveled.

(Donna Chiarelli Studio)

Screening Compost

If you're using unfinished compost, you may have to screen it depending on how unfinished it is. If there are many large pieces of material still in the mix, you should screen it. To screen compost, lay a screen with half-inch openings over a wheelbarrow or bin. Scoop or shovel your compost onto the screen. Stir or rake the compost on top of the screen or jiggle the screen to encourage the small particles to sift through. Return the larger particles to the compost pile to finish breaking down. There's no reason to screen compost if it is truly composted because completely broken-down compost does not have large pieces of material in it.

Compost as Cover

Using compost as a soil cover offers many advantages. Compost is often spread on top of soil for one of two main purposes. The first is to warm up the soil in the spring to get a head start on the gardening season. The second is to cool soil and conserve moisture. But compost does so much more than just heat and cool the soil.

Compost Cover to Heat Soil

Compost can warm up your soil so that you can plant seeds or transplant seedlings into the ground sooner than you would otherwise be able to. Put the compost on soil first thing in the spring to help heat it up and prepare it for planting. If your soil is already tilled or if you are using a no-till method, you can place the compost directly on top of the soil.

Compost Cover to Cool Soil

You can use finished compost like mulch and spread it in the garden to help keep the soil cool by preventing sunlight from hitting the soil. Compost also helps keep soil cool by retaining moisture. When might you want to keep the soil cool? When you're trying to extend the season of cool-weather crops, such as salad greens, cabbage, broccoli, and peas (see Chapter 2), cooler soil will help keep those plants happy. A 3-inch layer distributed around these plants—but not actually touching their stems—should do the trick.

Compost Cover as Fertilizer

Compost not only makes the perfect mulch, but it's also the perfect fertilizer. A great reason to use compost in your garden as a top dressing for plants is because of the nutrients it contains. As the compost incorporates itself into your existing soil, you won't need synthetic fertilizers. Your soil structure will improve, and all the necessary macronutrients and micronutrients will be in your soil waiting for your plants' roots to take them up.

Vermicompost

The earthworm has amazing strength when you consider that it has the power to move a stone that weighs 50 times its body weight. Earthworms also ingest soil and organic matter equal to the amount of their body weight each day. The waste that earthworms excrete is known as worm castings or vermicompost. Vermicompost is an excellent tool for improving the soil.

The real beauty of vermicompost is that the worms do all the work.

(Donna Chiarelli Studio)

Earthworms are important in the compost pile and in your garden soil for their ability to aerate the soil. By aerating, these tiny creatures assist the microorganisms with the decomposition process. And as you already know, decomposition is a good thing when it comes to compost.

You can encourage earthworms to take up residence in your compost pile in a variety of ways. One of the easiest ways is to include shredded newspaper in your pile. Then find some worms in your yard, or buy some earthworms locally, and add them to the pile. Earthworms love newspaper. They'll work for you by breaking down the newspaper, by depositing castings or "worm manure," and by aerating the pile. (For more information on using worm castings as fertilizer, see Chapter 5.)

Another way to encourage earthworm activity in your compost pile is to add kitchen scraps. Earthworms need a constant supply of fresh organic matter to thrive, so simply place the new materials on top of the pile and let the worms do the work of incorporating them into the compost.

If you have a limited amount of composting space in your yard, consider worm composting, also known as vermiculture. With worm composting, you can create compost anywhere, even in your garage. Vermiculture, or composting with worms, is often done indoors because it allows year-round composting to take place. In fact, because most people who practice vermiculture feed their worms a diet that consists mainly of kitchen scraps, the garage is a great location for these types of compost bins.

Green Thumb

A single worm produces castings equal to its own weight every day. In a year, worms in an acre of land plow through 50 tons of soil. Those same worms produce 5 tons of castings during that year as well.

The worms in a compost bin—or vermiculture bin, as they are called—start out with a layer of bedding such as shredded newspaper, chopped leaves or other dead plant material, a handful of sand or soil, and kitchen scraps. The worms eat the kitchen scraps and turn out worm castings, which can be used directly in the garden.

The Least You Need to Know

- ◆ Compost is made from an equal mix of "green" and "brown" materials.

- ◆ Composting keeps reusable materials out of the landfill and creates nutrient-rich fertilizer or mulch for your garden.

- ◆ You can compost wherever you live.

- ◆ You can make slow compost in a year or two by allowing nature to take its course.

- ◆ You can speed up the composting process to produce usable compost within one growing season.

Chapter 5

Feeding and Fertilizing

In This Chapter

- The importance of nourishing your plants
- Understanding—and correcting—your soil's pH
- The benefits of organics
- The pros and cons of manufactured fertilizers

You want to give your plants the best possible chance to survive and thrive, and that's where feeding and fertilizing come in. In this chapter, we'll tell you how to determine and provide the best nutrients for your plants and discover the essential role soil pH plays in helping or hindering plants as they try to absorb nutrients already in the soil and in the supplements you provide. In addition, we'll look at the pros and cons of organic versus manmade fertilizers and offer tips on gardening in an eco-friendly way.

So get ready to get your hands dirty! Your plants will thank you for it.

The First Fertilizers

It's easy to think they've always been around, but human-made fertilizers didn't appear on the gardening scene until the wake of World War II. Before then, gardeners provided natural plant nutrients such as organic matter and manure mixed with mineral sources, such as shells and bones and wood ashes.

Green Thumb

The most famous kitchen middens have been unearthed in the British Isles, but they've also been found in Europe, Japan, South America, and even Florida. Most are along coastlines and rivers, which accounts for the large numbers of nutrient-rich shells from edible shellfish.

According to archaeologists, prehistoric gardeners sorted their trash and threw the organic scraps into kitchen middens or compost piles. One day, one of these stone-age gardeners noticed that discarded vegetable seeds sprouted and grew better in these piles than anywhere else. (Think of those volunteer tomatoes thriving out in your compost pile.) So they moved their community gardens into the middens, built fires nearby, and used the sites as outdoor kitchens, harvesting and cooking their dinner right on the spot.

Putting Your Soil to the Test

Those early gardeners were on the right track. They knew that it took more than just putting seeds into the soil. They understood that adding things to the soil helped their food crops produce more or better food. So you can use their knowledge to your—and your garden's—advantage. But before you even think about what fertilizer you're going to use, you need to know which nutrients and how much of each your soil needs.

Although all soil contains both the macronutrients and micronutrients that plants require (see Chapter 3), few of us are blessed with perfect soil. So you need to test the soil to find out what it does contain. Laboratories, agricultural colleges, and Cooperative Extension offices may have soil-test kits for you to buy. (For a list of soil-test sources, see Appendix C.) You can locate one of these sources by searching online or looking in your phone directory.

After you get a kit, here's what you do. Collect a few tablespoons of soil from various parts of your garden and mix them together in the envelope supplied in the kit. Then simply send your sample to the lab to be chemically analyzed. The lab will send you a report that states the pH or the soil's level of acidity or alkalinity, the type of soil, and the percentages of various nutrients it contains. A good test also recommends what nutrients and the amount of each you should apply to balance the soil's fertility and pH.

You also can buy do-it-yourself kits online or from garden centers, but results won't be as accurate or detailed as those from a laboratory. For example, an over-the-counter test may list nutrients you need to add to your soil, but not the amount needed. If this is the case, follow the application directions on the product's packaging. Before investing in a kit, chat with that neighbor down the road with the fantastic garden. If that neighbor has had no particular soil complaints, chances are that your soil is also pretty good, and you can get by with an over-the-counter soil test kit.

Understanding Your Soil's pH

Old-timers used to call acid soil "sour" and alkaline soil "sweet" because before soil tests were available, gardeners actually *tasted* the soil to gauge its pH. (Do *not* try this at home!) Happily, soil testing is more scientific now, and the pH scale more accurately describes the level of acidity or alkalinity.

Why does all this matter? The pH level affects solubility of plant nutrients, making them less available to plants the farther the pH gets from the neutral point on either end of the scale. One of your most important goals in garden improvement is working to neutralize your soil's pH.

Garden Guide

I treasure my pH meter, a small plastic box mounted on a metal spike, I found at a local garden center. When I stick the spike into garden soil, a potted plant, or even a bucket of fertilizer water, the meter displays the pH level. This battery-free meter has served me for many years, unlike a soil test, which provides valuable guidelines for improving soil but only one-time pH results.

Fortunately, many plants are fairly flexible and can thrive in soil that, give or take a point, hovers around the neutral 7 on the pH scale, with many being comfortable in the pH range between 6 and 7.

This simplifies things for me and for other gardeners from the Midwest to the East, where acid rain regularly lowers (i.e., acidifies) the soil pH. We can get by with a soil test every 5 or 6 years (or not). But if you garden in the West or Southwest, where the naturally alkaline soil makes attempts to neutralize it temporary at best, you need to test your soil every other year and amend soil annually to help maintain a more neutral pH.

Altering Your Soil's pH

To correct the pH balance of soil, the most-used additive is compost, which improves and neutralizes the soil. Work in a 3-inch layer or more—more is better in most cases.

To acidify soil, add peat moss or garden sulfur and work it in according to test results or package directions. Unfortunately, acidifying soil is not a one-time deal because peat moss neutralizes as it breaks down and sulfur sifts through the soil, gradually being overpowered by the soil's natural alkalinity. So you'll need to repeat the process as often as tests indicate.

To increase alkalinity, add powdered limestone to the soil according to package directions. Note: this is rarely needed in a vegetable garden. But it is most often done to lawns east of the Mississippi River because lawn grasses prefer a slightly alkaline soil, whereas lawn *weeds* prefer acid conditions.) Lawns that are limed annually in fall become naturally thick and weed-free over time, reducing or eliminating the need for man-made weed-and-feed products.

To Test or Not to Test

The soil-test report you receive will tell you which and how much of each nutrient you need to apply to your soil. But if this sounds complicated and overwhelming and you think your soil is of average fertility, save yourself the trouble of testing by getting fertilizer advice from successful neighborhood gardeners. You can also simplify your fertilizing chores by buying an all-in-one bagged fertilizer. Applied according to instructions, it can only add to the nutrients already in your soil.

NPK: Fertilizer Ingredients

Let's review the macronutrients because they are the primary ingredients in any fertilizer. Nitrogen (N) promotes deep green foliage color and rapid, early, and green growth. Phosphorus (P) aids healthy root growth, seed growth, and winter hardiness. And potassium (K) is necessary for disease resistance, strong stems, and plentiful yield.

And remember that the numbers on the fertilizer bag represent the percentages of these three nutrients—NPK, in that order. If a fertilizer contains equal amounts of these three ingredients, such as a 10-10-10 analysis, it is a *complete fertilizer*. If it has only one or two of the nutrients, it is an *incomplete fertilizer*. The larger the numbers, the more concentrated—and often more expensive—the fertilizer. If you choose to fertilize, you should probably use a fairly weak formulation with a balanced formula— a fertilizer that contains equal parts of the three macronutrients.

def•i•ni•tion

> A **complete fertilizer** is one that contains all three of the primary macronutrients—nitrogen, phosphorus, and potassium.
>
> An **incomplete fertilizer** is one that contains only one or two of the three primary macronutrients.

Premium fertilizers contain the secondary nutrients calcium, magnesium, and sulfur, along with some of the seven trace elements—copper, boron, iron, chlorides and chlorinides, manganese, molybdenum, and zinc. Plants need these only in minute quantities, so reserve these fertilizers for correcting nutrient deficiencies specifically identified by a soil test.

Read fertilizer packages carefully, and pay attention to the analysis—those numbers that indicate the percentages of N, P, and K. It doesn't really matter whether the package says "azalea food," "rose food," or "vegetable food." What matters is the analysis. You don't need to buy a special food for each type of plant you want to fertilize.

Human-Made Fertilizers

Human-made or synthetic fertilizers come in a wide variety of strengths, using the same NPK analyses that we've talked about. Human-made fertilizers also come in several forms, including water-soluble powders or liquids, both of which are diluted with water and either poured on the soil or sprayed on foliage. These fertilizers are fast-acting and often used as a plant pick-me-up. Time- or controlled-release forms are capsule-like solids that release nutrients slowly. To apply, you broadcast, or spread, them over the soil. Granules are small nuggets that you apply over soil, like the capsule variety, to release nutrients fairly slowly.

Safety First

To ensure that there's no fertilizer residue on food at harvest time, do not apply any fertilizer to food plants within two weeks of harvest.

The most important thing to remember with human-made fertilizers is that it's easy to overdo and it's easy to waste. Applying too much can actually harm plants, causing weak growth susceptible to pests and diseases. So follow label directions carefully. Also, some fertilizers can be damaging to plants if the undissolved product touches foliage or roots. To be on the safe side, you may want to dilute human-made fertilizers to half strength before applying. Remember: your soil already contains most of the nutrients your plants need, and you're adding the fertilizer to give them a little extra boost. Even at half strength, the fertilizer is still providing that boost, and you ensure that you're doing no harm at the same time.

Organic Options

If you're thinking of going the organic route, you're not alone because organic fertilizing is as popular now as ever. Applying mineral and organic nutrients, such as shell grit and bone meal, composted manure, blood meal, and other organic fertilizers (see the following table), to the soil's surface is a good way to recycle byproducts of mining, lumbering, and food processing. And because the organic nutrients slowly work down into the soil, it's hard to damage plants by overdosing or "burning" plant tissues, which can occur with human-made fertilizers if they are not properly applied.

Local Organic Fertilizers

Here in semi-rural eastern Pennsylvania, "the mushroom capital of the world," we garden in an area blessed with natural fertilizers. Surrounded by traditional farms and horse stables, we can buy a variety of manures (sometimes they're free for the taking) as well as a local specialty called "spent mushroom compost," which is a fertile concoction of straw, manure, and mineral nutrients that's used only once by commercial mushroom farmers and then sold by the truckload to local gardeners.

You likely have similar resources where you live. Each geographic region of the country has a nutrient-rich garden specialty, whether it's cottonseed meal in the Southeast or kelp in coastal areas. You might get your bounty directly from a farmer or from a garden center. Don't hesitate to ask questions of other gardeners to find out where their local sources of organic goodies are.

Fertilizing in Slow Motion

Perhaps the only drawback to dense, slowly dissolving organic fertilizers such as bone meal, wood ashes, and minerals is that it can take several months for them to dissolve and become available to plant roots. You can compensate for this by planning ahead and scattering them over the soil in the fall after you clean your garden. Over the winter, the nutrients will gradually find their way into the soil, thanks to the rain and melting snow. Once in the soil, beneficial bacteria slowly break them down, making the nutrients available to the garden plants you set out the following spring. (For more on how beneficial bacteria work, see Chapter 4.)

Useful tricks for applying solid fertilizer during the growing season are top dressing or side dressing. If you choose top dressing, spread solid fertilizer across the surface of the garden as mulch. With side dressing, apply fertilizer between rows of crops or in a circle around individual plants. With either method, don't let fertilizers touch the plants. Direct contact of fertilizer with plant tissue can "burn" the plant tissue.

Manure and Other Organic Fertilizers

Manure is among the oldest and best organic fertilizers and was used at least as long ago as 2300 B.C.E. in Mesopotamian gardens. Manure is a good source of macro-nutrients and also conditions the soil by aerating it and improving its ability to retain moisture.

In Chapter 4, we talked about the benefits of adding rotted manure (from herbivores only, please) to your compost pile, so here, let's talk specifically about manure's nutrients. Horse and cow manure are among the most nutrient rich, both having an analysis as high as 1.3-.9-.8. Poultry and rabbit manure are a bit stronger, measuring as high as 2.8-2.8-1.5. (Note that the analysis is approximate because it varies according to the animals' diets.)

How do these manure nutrient analyses affect your plants? Well, if you're interested in boosting the blooming potential of your flower garden, you would want to choose poultry manure for your compost pile because it's relatively high in phosphorus. And as you know, phosphorus promotes flowering and fruiting.

Now let's consider worm castings, which are in a league of their own. They have an analysis of around .5-.5-.3, but they're fully composted and ready to use from the get-go, meaning they won't burn your plants. Worm castings contain a full compliment of trace minerals, making them an organic super plant food. In addition to nutrients, worm castings contain *humic acid*, which stimulates plant growth, and their high organic matter content helps the soil retain moisture.

def•i•ni•tion

Humic acid is a byproduct of plant decomposition that makes plants grow better. This fast-acting, dark brown liquid isn't a fertilizer, but it buffers the soil pH and makes it easier for nutrients to move within the soil and for plant roots to absorb nutrients. Humic acid occurs naturally and is also manufactured and packaged in commercial plant tonics.

Use worm castings as a tonic by sprinkling moist or dry castings (the consistency is similar to top soil or coffee grounds) on the soil sparingly any time during the growing season. Use about 1 tablespoon per plant of any size. Doing this twice during a growing season feeds a plant for six months. (See Chapter 4 for more about composting with worms.)

There are many other excellent organic fertilizers, and in fact, any organic material contributes some nutrients to your garden. Here are some good options, along with their approximate nutrient analyses. Mix and match these fertilizers according to your soil test results or your plants' individual requirements.

	Nitrogen (N)	Phosphorus (P)	Potassium (K)
Alfalfa hay	2.5	0.5	2.0
Blood meal	13.0	1.5	0.8
Bone meal, steamed	4.0	12.0	0
Chicken manure, dried	2.8	2.8	1.5
Cottonseed meal	6.0	2.0	1.0
Cow manure, dried	1.3	0.9	0.8
Horse manure, fresh	0.6	0.3	0.5
Peat moss	2.3	0.4	0.8
Rock phosphate	0	38.0	4.5
Straw	0.6	0.2	1.0
Wood ashes	0	1.8	5.0

Garden Guide _____

Wood ashes are a good source of potassium, but they can be harmful if applied during the growing season because they're so concentrated that they can chemically burn plant tissues. For safe use, either sprinkle ashes between layers of compost and age for at least three months before using in the garden, or sprinkle ashes lightly over the garden in the fall, after you harvest, and let them decompose over winter.

The caustic qualities of wood ash are beneficial in one case: by sprinkling a ring of ashes around the perimeter of your garden, you can exclude slugs, which can't survive crossing the line.

Pouring on Liquid Fertilizer

Most of us enjoy a good nosh (or we wouldn't grow food plants in the first place, right?), so it makes sense for us to use expressions such as "plant food" and "feeding our plants" when we set out to fertilize them. But the truth is that plants don't eat; they sort of drink. They slurp up nutrients dissolved in groundwater through fine root hairs that grow along the ends of their anchoring roots—think of those little white hairlike roots you peel off a carrot before eating it.

So to fertilize plants in a way that makes sense to them, let's change our metaphors from eating to drinking and learn to mix a cocktail of plant nutrients that your plants can absorb through their thirsty root hairs. Scientists call this process osmosis. But don't worry, it's easy and not too scientific.

Nutritious Compost Tea

Compost tea has a couple big advantages over solid organic fertilizers. This liquid fertilizer (compost steeped in water) is fast-acting for two reasons. First, its nutrients are already in solution (liquid form) and are therefore readily available for roots to take up. Second, if compost tea is applied to plant leaves, they absorb the solution, which can bring about seemingly instant plant rejuvenation (see DIY compost tea recipe that follows).

Compost tea is an excellent, eco-friendly, fast-acting fertilizer. More importantly, the

def•i•ni•tion _____

Compost tea is a liquid fertilizer made by steeping finished compost in water. The strained solution is applied to plants or soil as is any liquid fertilizer.

beneficial organisms that convert organic material into compost in the first place also give off compounds that repel foliar, or leaf, diseases. Some of these organisms remain active even in finished compost and continue to produce these compounds. Plants showered with compost tea repel leaf diseases and are generally healthier, growing thicker leaves, which are difficult for disease-carrying sucking insects, such as aphids, to penetrate.

DIY Compost Tea

The old standby recipe for compost tea calls for steeping a cloth bag containing a shovelful of compost in a five-gallon bucket of water until the solution is the color of tea. Then remove and dispose of the bagged compost, dilute the solution by half, and use a watering can to sprinkle it over plants.

That concoction is good, but let me introduce you to an improved method in which you'll inject air and nutrients into the mix to feed and multiply beneficial organisms, producing an even more effective brew.

Living Compost Tea

1 5-gallon bucket

5 gallons of water

2 pieces of twine

1 small aquarium pump and 4 feet of air tubing (available at discount and pet stores)

1 small rock

1 shovel of finished compost

2 TB. molasses

2 TB. fish emulsion (sold at garden stores)

2 TB. white or cider vinegar

1 old pillowcase or burlap bag

Watering can with sprinkler head

1. When your local weather source predicts three dry days in a row, set up your compost tea factory near an outdoor electrical outlet. Fill the bucket with untreated water (if using treated municipal water, let it stand overnight to allow any chlorine to evaporate).

2. Attach one end of the tubing to the pump's air nozzle. Using a piece of twine, tie the loose end of the tubing to the rock to weigh it down. Then drop the rock and tubing into the bucket. Set the pump on the ground near the outlet and plug it in.

3. Stir in molasses, fish emulsion, and vinegar.

4. Gently scoop the compost into the pillowcase or bag, tie it with a piece of twine, and lower the bag into the bucket. Allow the mixture to bubble and steep overnight.

5. The next day, unplug the pump and put it away. Remove the compost (return it to the compost pile). Pour the solution into a watering can, and sprinkle it over the foliage of food plants or ornamentals. (This is a great tonic for roses.)

Use the compost tea within 24 hours so your plants will get all the beneficial organisms while they're still active.

Aside from an aquarium pump and air tubing, you need look no further than your pantry, garden shed, and compost pile for the ingredients for Living Compost Tea.

(Donna Chiarelli Studio)

Let your bucket of compost tea steep and aerate overnight before sprinkling it over plants.

(Chaz Macdonald)

Other Liquid Organic Fertilizers

Other liquid organic fertilizers include fish emulsion and powdered seaweed, or kelp. Fish emulsion is a thick, brown concentration of fish waste that supplies ample nitrogen (approximately 5-1-1). Some commercial brands smell fishy, while others are deodorized (check the label if this matters). Dilute it, and spray on foliage or pour over the soil, but use it sparingly in the garden because it is expensive and can attract cats and other creatures.

Seaweed concentrate has an analysis of about 1-0-1, but it's rich in trace elements, is especially good to get seedlings off to a strong start, and is vegan-friendly (some of my nonmeat-eating gardening friends forgo using animal-based fertilizers in their gardens). Like fish emulsion, seaweed is pricy, so you should dilute and spray it on foliage as a tonic.

What's Right for You?

Now that we've looked at several options available to boost the nutrients in your soil and give your plants a little extra help, what's right for you? Should you go organic, like so many others are doing? Or should you rely on the synthetic, or human-made, fertilizers? That's a decision only you can make, but here are some final thoughts.

Organic fertilizers are fairly straightforward and safe to use. Many human-made fertilizers, on the other hand, require careful handling and application.

It's a given that organic fertilizers are made from living or once-living things; that's what makes them organic. A manufactured fertilizer can be labeled as organic even if part of the product is synthetic. To muddle things a bit more, the use of the word *organic* varies according to the laws of each state. So to be absolutely sure, you need to know your state's laws. And then you need to take your time and read package information and ingredient lists carefully.

Remember that the ingredients—the macronutrients—in the fertilizer are the same, whether the product is organic or synthetic. You just have to decide how important the *source* of those nutrients is to you and your gardening efforts.

The Least You Need to Know

◆ Before you apply that first drop of fertilizer, determine your soil pH (acidity or alkalinity) to see what it needs and what it doesn't need.

◆ The primary macronutrients—nitrogen, phosphorus, and potassium (NPK)—provide balanced nutrition for your plants.

◆ Both organic and human-made fertilizers come in solid and liquid forms and contain the same nutrients, so individual gardeners have to decide which type and form is best for them.

◆ Compost tea is a fast-acting, natural, easy-to-make fertilizer you can give your plants.

Chapter 6

Seeds to Seedlings

In This Chapter

- ◆ Starting plants from seeds is an essential part of gardening year-round
- ◆ Timing seed sowing to weather conditions helps succession plantings thrive out of season
- ◆ Tips for planting and caring for seeds to ensure sprouting and strong growth
- ◆ Whether an in-ground or raised-bed garden is best for you

In this chapter, we start at the beginning: planting seeds. Starting plants from seeds is such an important and rewarding aspect of gardening! So we want to cover the fine points of starting seeds—indoors and out—and transplanting seedlings into the garden. We'll also tell you how to water seedlings, fertilize them, and protect them from the elements.

But first steps first: let's find out how to get those seeds and seedlings off to a strong start. So gather your seed catalogs and settle in for an enlightening read to find out how starting your own seeds will help you garden year-round.

Basics of Seed Starting

Now you may wonder, why should I take the time to order seeds from a catalog when I can find potted seedlings everywhere—at garden centers, at discount stores, and even at grocery stores? One of the most important reasons to start your own seeds is strictly a matter of choices. If you buy seedlings from a local source, your selection is pretty limited. However, when you order seeds, you can choose from a vast selection and suit your own particular taste, whether it be for large or uniquely colored flowers; flavorful and exotic or medicinal herbs; the newest vegetable hybrids; or maybe old, colorful, or tasty *heirlooms*. And if you start your own seeds, you can save costs.

Another reason has to do with dollars and cents. If you, like so many of us these days, are cultivating a thrifty streak, you'll be delighted to learn that even with today's inflated prices, you can cut your gardening (and grocery) expenses drastically by starting your own seeds. Consider this: one commercial bedding plant in a 4-inch pot or a 6-pack of seedlings can cost as much as or more than a packet of 100 seeds. Seed starters reap huge savings by cutting out the seedling "middleman."

To take things a step further, when you buy seeds of *open-pollinated plants*, future sowings can be yours for free. Just let a few plants go to seed at the end of the season and save some seeds to grow the following year.

def•i•ni•tion

Heirlooms are varieties of flowers, vegetables, and small fruits selected over many generations for superior traits. These old-time garden favorites boast robust flavor, exceptional color, and stable storage qualities. Seeds from heirloom plants produce a plant just like the parent plant. By contrast, seeds from a modern hybrid plant are sterile or produce a plant different from the parent plant.

Open-pollinated plants are pollinated naturally by wind, birds, or insects. Due to haphazard parenting, you can expect a few offspring—about 1 percent—to be unlike your variety, but these are easily removed from the garden.

Whether you're planting a leathery, white-skinned, nickel-size lima bean or fine, black, dustlike begonia seeds, the dormant bundles of life called seeds are just waiting to encounter the moisture, heat, and light that you provide to trigger them to sprout and grow into plants. Regardless of size or appearance, a seed is a dormant, embryonic plant, complete with root, stem, and seedling leaves called cotyledons. Each seed also contains a kernel of nutrition, called an endosperm, which nourishes the embryo until the seed can sprout in soil.

If you are sowing seeds you've collected from your own garden plants, invest in a seed-sowing guide (see Appendix D). Even if you are sowing packaged seeds, one of these guides is a wise investment because it provides detailed growing instructions and troubleshooting advice not usually included on seed packets.

Timing

Starting a new batch of plants from seeds every other week lets you space out your garden crop throughout the growing season. Called succession planting, this practice lengthens your harvest season. But more importantly, starting your own seeds lets you time new crops to harvest in summer, fall, and even into winter. You can enjoy flowers and vegetables long after local stores sell out of bedding plants. And fresh-picked produce is better tasting and more nutritious than preserved food. Succession planting cuts down on those huge harvests that come all at once, forcing you to can and freeze food in a frenzy—usually on a hot day in August.

Garden Guide

Don't get so caught up in the notion of seed starting that you rule out buying seedlings. Think of them as convenience plants that fill an important niche in your year-round garden. Bedding plants are good candidates for containers or small gardens (you may not have room for 100 seedlings) and for filling vacant spots in your garden if your homegrown seedlings succumb to a late frost, hail storm, or other natural disaster. And you can buy a few starter pots of finicky plants, such as eggplant (heat-demanding insect magnets that challenge any gardener!), before investing time in coaxing a lot of them from seed.

Types of Plants to Grow

There are three distinct categories of plants: annuals, biennials, and perennials. The differences are not as much in how the seeds germinate and grow but in the overall length of the plants' lifecycles.

Annuals grow, flower, and set seed in one season. Most vegetable plants and many herbs and flowering plants are annuals. Lettuce and spinach are good examples of annuals. Old-fashioned flower favorites, such as marigolds, zinnias, and sunflowers, are also annuals. Each year, gardeners plant the seeds of these plants, and the plants grow, blossom, produce fruit or seeds, and die back.

Biennials produce leaves and roots the first year, and then flower or produce fruit and go to seed and die at the end of their second season. Examples of edible biennials include parsley, Swiss chard, cabbage family members, and root vegetables such as turnips. Because they live two years and are generally cold hardy, biennials can survive wintering in the garden (with protection in freezing climates) and some can be harvested from fall into spring. Flowering biennials such as clary sage (*Salvia sclarea*) produce showy leaves the first year, and then flower and set seeds the following year.

Perennials live from 3 to 50 years or more. They reproduce by seed and some also by underground or ground-hugging stems called runners, or new plants called plantlets that sprout at the base of the old ones. Asparagus and rhubarb are two of the few perennial food plants, but there are many perennials for the flower garden. Peonies are examples of especially long-lived perennials as they grow happily for decades next to driveways and old, abandoned farmhouses.

Special Handling

Some types of garden seeds need special handling to induce *germination*. Some, such as those of morning glories and nasturtiums, have hard seed coats that you need to open or at least crack before sowing to allow moisture to penetrate. This process is called *scarification*. The easiest way to scarify seeds is to rub them gently across a nail file.

def•i•ni•tion

Germination is the process of a dormant seed sprouting and growing into a seedling.

Scarification is the process of scratching away a small amount of a seed's hard outer coat so moisture can reach the plant embryo within to induce sprouting.

Other seeds, such as morning glories, dried beans, corn kernels, and parsley seeds, need to have their seed coats softened by presoaking. Steep them overnight in warm water—about 80°F—before planting. To keep the water warm, set the bowl where you germinate your seeds on a heat mat or on top of a water heater.

Seeds of some warmth-loving plants, including cucumbers, squash, pumpkins, and melons, germinate best when they're presprouted. Spread the seeds across a dampened paper towel, roll the towel up, and seal it in a plastic bag. Keep the bag at optimum temperature for sprouting (again, that seed-sowing guide will come in handy). Check the towel daily. When roots emerge from the seeds, plant the sprouted seeds in 4-inch pots of moist seed-starting medium and grow according to packet directions.

Green Thumb _____

Seeds can carry a few difficult-to-control plant diseases such as alternaria blight, anthracnose, and bacterial wilt. If you collect and save your own seeds (see Chapter 18), disinfect them before planting. Soak seeds in 125°F water for a half hour. Drain and add cool water; then drain again and plant immediately. Commercial seeds are treated and certified disease-free before packaging.

Some seeds, generally those of woody shrubs, vines, and trees, need a dormant period, usually over a cold winter, before they will germinate. To reproduce these conditions, gardeners use *stratification*, where they place seeds in a moist growing medium and refrigerate for a specified length of time, depending on the type of seed.

def•i•ni•tion _____

Stratification is a period of refrigerated storage required to induce germination in seeds that naturally drop to the damp ground in autumn and overwinter before sprouting in spring.

Indoor Seed Sowing

Starting seeds indoors is a common way to give your garden a head start in the spring. By starting seeds and raising seedlings inside, you get a batch of strong, healthy seedlings of whatever variety you chose from the seed catalogs. While other gardeners are spending money on whatever seedlings are available at the garden center, you have the satisfaction of knowing your handpicked varieties are right in your basement or your dining room.

To sow seeds indoors, the minimum materials you need are the seeds, of course, containers, and a seed-starting medium you can mix yourself or purchase ready-made. With those three basics and a south- or west-facing window, you're ready to start seeds indoors. If you want to take a little more control of the process, you can get covers for the containers, heating mats to warm the containers, or grow lights so you're not dependent on daylight from whatever windows you have. With these materials, you can grow a container full of healthy seedlings and get a jump-start on this year's garden.

Containers

Containers for seed starting can be as varied as your imagination can conjure. Gardeners have successfully sown seeds in milk cartons, empty butter and yogurt containers, rusty tin cans—even egg cartons and egg shells! And then, of course, there are the trays, or flats, at the garden center made specifically for starting seeds.

Green Thumb

Save your store-bought seed flats and pots—you can reuse them until the plastic turns brittle and breaks from age. Stack and store them at the end of the season, and then, to keep from exposing seedlings to soil-borne diseases, clean and sterilize them before sowing seed the next season.

To sterilize flats and pots, soak them for half an hour in a tub filled with a solution of one part bleach to nine parts water. Rinse them with a spray nozzle on a garden hose and let them dry in the sun. Exposure to ultraviolet sunlight kills bacteria and other pathogens.

If you'd prefer a nonplastic option, consider peat pots, which are biodegradable pots made of compressed peat moss. If you're sowing plants with especially delicate roots, peat pots are desirable because you can plant the entire pot rather than transplant the seedling out of the pot. When planting, tear away the pot's rim and bottom to help the seedling's roots find the soil. Solid peat pellets, pots made by shaping newspapers around a mold, and soil blocks formed in a press all work in similar ways. The advantage of these methods is that all are biodegradable, but the disadvantage is that you have to purchase new supplies each spring.

Whether you choose homemade or store-bought, reusable or biodegradable, your seed-starting containers need a few drainage holes, the right quantity and kind of seed-starting medium, and the right number of seeds per container.

Soil

Experts recommend sowing seeds in a commercial or homemade sterile, soil-free mixture made up of half peat moss and half *vermiculite* or fine, clean sand packaged at hardware or home stores as "children's play sand." This mixture protects seedlings from fungal diseases, but it doesn't provide any nutrients. So every time you water, use half-strength plant food, which provides most, but perhaps not all, of the nutrients the seedlings need. Also, this method may encourage algae growth on the surface of the growing medium.

I reserve this sterile mix for difficult-to-germinate seeds. For starting most vegetable and flower seeds, I prefer to use a mixture of equal parts of garden or commercial top soil and finished compost. I fill my pots half full with this mixture, sprinkle about a half-inch thick layer of vermiculite on top, and sow the seeds in that. This method provides a sterile environment (the vermiculite) for sprouting, and the seedlings then send roots into the soil/compost blend where they are protected and nourished by the antibiotic qualities of the compost, and they adapt to the garden soil they'll grow in for the rest of their lives. I have never lost a seedling with this method.

def•i•ni•tion

Vermiculite is a lightweight, tan, granular material created by heating mica chips until they expand. Vermiculite isn't as heavy as soil and improves drainage, air circulation, and water and fertilizer retention in soil.

To make sure you have no pathogens or insect eggs in the seed-starting soil you took from your garden, sterilize it in an outdoor grill. I recommend a grill rather than your oven because soil stinks when heated. Spread a 4-inch-deep layer of soil in a pan (an inexpensive loaf cake pan works well). Cover the container with foil, and insert a meat thermometer. Heat the soil in a closed grill until the thermometer registers 180°F. Maintain this temperature for 30 minutes and cool. The cooled soil is sterile and ready to use.

If you'd rather use convienient and reliably sterile potting mix, you can buy it in bags and even plastic-wrapped bales at any garden center, hardware, or discount store. Read the label before buying, because some contain slow-release nutrients, and others require you to fertilize sprouted seedlings with half-strength fertilizer with every watering. When using commercial potting mix, be sure to premoisten it with warm water, because the peat moss it contains tends to repel cold water rather than absorb it when it is dry.

Planting the Seeds

Traditionally, experts have recommended broadcasting a packet of seeds over a large, shallow seed-starting tray filled with seed-starting medium. I used to do this for all the seeds I started, but it taxed my patience and, worse, sent seedlings into transplant shock each time I moved them. Transplanting disrupts the plants' roots, which slows growth at best, causes wilting, or kills the plant at worst. If you start your own seeds, some amount of transplanting is unavoidable, but there are some ways to get around it, too.

I still use the broadcast and potting-up method for seeds too small to pick up, usually flower seeds. However, I've settled on a seed-starting method for bigger vegetable seeds that saves valuable time in spring when I have so many other gardening tasks to do, such as winter yard and fish-pond clean-up and preparing the garden for planting.

Garden Guide

> To minimize transplant shock when moving seedlings to their permanent outdoor home, move medium along with the plant's roots when transplanting. Also, transplant on a cloudy day or in the evening. If that's not possible, shade the transplant. Keep the soil and air around it moist by covering it with a clear or translucent cover, such as a plastic bag or a milk jug with the bottom cut out, until the plant adjusts to its new environment.

I sow one seed in each corner of a square 4-inch plastic pot or a peat pot filled with my own seed-starting mix. I choose square pots because research has shown that plant roots are less likely to circle, or grow in a circular pattern, in a square pot. Circling roots are bad news because they have a tendency to continue growing that way even after you put the plant into the ground. If the roots continue to grow inward, the plant can't take in nutrients and won't grow properly. Square pots also fit neatly into the shallow, rectangular plastic trays garden centers sell.

Sowing four seeds per pot ensures that at least one will sprout and grow. When the seedlings emerge, I use a pair of scissors to thin them and cut off the weakest two. I cut rather than pull because pulling disturbs the roots of the keepers. Then I allow the remaining two seedlings to grow undisturbed in the same pot for 6 to 8 weeks until it's time to plant them in the garden. After a couple of weeks in the garden, if both are still growing, I snip off the weaker of the two to prevent crowding.

Garden Guide

> Always label each pot of seedlings or each flat (if the flat contains all the same kind of plant) with the name of the plant and the sowing date. Use a permanent marker and plastic labels, which are available at garden centers and discount stores. Or recycle an old window blind by cutting the slats into whatever length suits your needs. When you transplant the seedlings, use the same label to mark each seedling or row of seedlings in the garden.

Indoor Timetable

How much of a head start do your indoor seedlings need? Here are a few popular garden plants and their optimum indoor sowing times. I've arranged them in order, starting with those crops that need to be sown the earliest (for the last frost date in your area, see Appendix D).

Plant	When to Sow
peppers	8–12 weeks before last frost
eggplant	6–8 weeks before last frost
onions	6–8 weeks before last frost
tomatoes	6–8 weeks before last frost
broccoli	5–6 weeks before last frost
cabbage	5–6 weeks before last frost
lettuce	4–5 weeks before last frost
cucumber	2–4 weeks before last frost
melons	2–4 weeks before last frost

For successive crops, start seeds weekly during the range of weeks indicated. Check your seed packet directions for the best sowing times for specific varieties. Most seed packets also indicate the best time for transplanting the seedlings outdoors.

Note that the last frost date varies significantly from location to location. This date—the average date of the last winter frost in a given area—is the last likely day, statistically, on which temperatures might dip below freezing and harm tender young plants. Though averages and statistics can guide us, there are no guarantees, of course. The actual last frost might occur days earlier than the average date or weeks *after* the average date. The only consolation (weak though it may be) is that if you get hit by a late frost, you won't be alone. The other gardeners in the neighborhood will also be out crying in their seedlings. But when you sow successive batches, you will have seedling replacements ready to go into the garden.

Soil-Warming

Germinating seeds need to be kept warm. Even cool-loving crops, such as cabbage and broccoli, which grow best when outdoor temperatures are in the 60s, germinate best in soil that hovers around 80°F. Although a few germinating seeds require temperatures as high as 90°F, that much heat will kill most seeds. To learn the optimum temperature for the seeds you want to germinate, check the directions on the seed packet, consult a good seed-starting guide (see Appendix D), or search online to find germination temperature recommendations.

You may have a warm spot in your house, such as the top of a water heater or other appliance, where there's room to set one or two flats of seeds. Set a room thermometer there for several days to make sure the temperature stays at the level your seeds need to germinate.

If you want to make sure your seedlings are receiving proper, consistent heat, invest in a propagation heat mat, a waterproof plastic or rubber mat that encases thermostatically controlled heating cables. When plugged into an outlet, the mat provides consistent, gentle bottom heat to seed flats and pots. A propagation heat mat is especially handy if you want to start your seeds under grow lights, which gardeners typically set up in a cool area, such as a basement, potting shed, or garage.

To monitor the temperature in your seed-starting pots or trays, you may want to use a soil thermometer, which you can purchase for about $10 at a garden center or from a garden catalog. Give it a good 10 minutes of contact with the soil to allow it to register the soil's temperature. Later, when you think it's time to transplant your seedlings, you can use the same thermometer to check the temperature of your garden soil.

A soil-heating or propagation heat mat aids germination by keeping the growing medium at the consistent, warm temperature seeds require for optimal germination.

(Donna Chiarelli Studio)

To use a propagation heat mat, set it next to a sunny window or on a shelf under grow lights, plug it into an outlet, and set planted seeds or seedlings on it. When seedlings develop several sets of adult leaves, move them off the mat to a sunny spot at room temperature.

(Donna Chiarelli Studio)

Germinate in Light or Dark

Most flower seeds and some vegetable seeds require light to germinate—more or less light, depending on the type of seed. Consult your seed packets or your favorite seed-starting guide for instructions on whether to cover seeds and, if so, how deeply. If a seed requires total darkness to germinate, it must be buried in soil. As a rule of thumb, dark-germinating seeds should be buried three times their diameter, so the bigger the seed, the deeper you plant it.

If a seed requires full light to germinate, sprinkle the seeds over the surface of the seed-starting medium and mist them lightly to moisten and help them make good contact with the growing medium.

If seeds need light, but not necessarily full light, they'll need just a thin layer of material covering them. Sow seeds over the surface of the seed-starting medium, and then sprinkle a light dusting of vermiculite or clean sand over them.

Plant big seeds, such as beans, corn, and squash, between half an inch and 1 inch deep. My favorite method for these is to put on a pair of disposable gloves and poke a hole in the growing medium with my index finger to the depth of my first knuckle. Then I drop the seed into the hole and gently fill the hole in with gloved fingers.

Garden Guide

An old kitchen sieve or sifter is a great tool for sprinkling seed-starting medium, vermiculite, or sand over seeds that need to be lightly covered to germinate.

A few seed packets will direct you to germinate in complete darkness. The jury is out as to whether this is absolutely necessary, but there's no harm in this method. Plant these seeds as directed, and then drape a folded black plastic trash bag loosely over the seeded flat or pots to exclude the light. Check on them daily, and remove the bag as soon as the seeds germinate.

The following table gives examples of some types of flower seeds that have differing light requirements for germination.

Seeds That Need Full Light to Germinate	
begonia	coleus
impatiens	petunia
portulaca	snap dragon

Seeds That Need Some Light to Germinate	
cleome	cosmos
flowering tobacco	stocks

Seeds That Need Darkness to Germinate	
asparagus fern	borage
pansy	sweet pea

Gardeners have successfully raised seedlings on sunny windowsills for hundreds of years. If you don't have a wide windowsill, you can set up a temporary seed-starting station on a folding table next to a south- or west-facing window. When the seedlings emerge, rotate the pots daily to keep them from leaning toward the window and growing crooked.

If you don't have an available window, if you don't revel in somewhat messy pots of soil in your living room, or if you don't want to leave things to chance, set up a grow light in your basement, garage, or a garden shed. You'll see fancy, expensive grow lights on the market today and even all-in-one carts with shelves and lights ready for you to assemble. However, nothing tops a 4-foot-long fluorescent "shop light" from the hardware store. It will set you back about $12 and usually comes complete with two cool-white tubes and a length of chain from which to hang the fixture.

For seeds that require light to germinate, set your pots or trays on a table or shelf and suspend the light 6 inches above the pots. When the seeds sprout, watch the seedlings to see which way they grow. If they stretch toward the lights, lower the light to about 4 inches above the leaves. If the seedlings lean to one side or the other, the light is too close, so raise it a couple of inches. Readjust as needed. You want the seedlings to grow straight and tall, with stocky stems.

Garden Guide _____

Check your seedlings to see if they're getting enough light. Compare the distance between leaves. If new leaves have more distance between them than older ones near the base of the seedlings, then the plants are reaching (starving) for light. Move the seedlings closer to the light source, whether it be a window or a grow light.

If you use a grow light, there are general guidelines as to how long to run the light. However, see how your seedlings grow and adjust the time as they need it. Buy an inexpensive lamp timer, plug the grow light into it, and set the timer to keep the light on for 16 hours. If your seedlings look a bit thin and pale, increase the time to 18 hours. Some schools of thought recommend running the light 24 hours a day to give seedlings a strong start. The key to this method is to move the seedlings out from under the light and into natural daylight just as soon as they have two sets of adult leaves so they can adjust to a normal night-and-day routine.

Watering Techniques

Watering delicate seeds and seedlings is a tricky business. To keep them alive, you need to keep the seeds, the seedlings, and the growing medium moist at all times. How moist? That's a good question because the right level of moisture is critical. If the growing medium dries out during germination, seeds will stop growing, and you'll lose the entire batch. On the other hand, if the medium stays wet, the seeds will rot and never sprout at all. Aim to keep the potting medium about as damp as a wrung-out sponge.

How you go about watering seeds and seedlings is equally important. Warm water is a must because peat-based seed-starting medium does not absorb cool water well. Cool water will also chill seeds and seedlings, causing a growth setback.

Do not water seeds and seedlings from overhead with a watering can, cup, pitcher, or anything else. Even if your pouring device is fitted with a sprinkler attachment, pouring water on seeds or seedlings delivers water with enough force to push seeds too deep into the growing medium or to cause seedlings to clump together and grow into a tangle.

Bottom watering—putting water in an outer tray instead of pouring on top of the growing medium—is the best way to water seeds and seedlings because it doesn't disturb seeds and ensures that seedlings' foliage remains dry. Keeping the leaves dry deters fungal leaf infections that thrive on damp foliage. To bottom water, make sure seed flats or pots have drain holes. Then set them in a shallow, waterproof tray and add tepid water to a depth of half an inch.

Bedding-plant flats without holes are nearly perfect water basins for bottom watering, but they're thin and tend to flex, break, and leak. The best trays I've found for this purpose are sturdy, shallow cat litter trays I discovered at the local dollar store. They have provided years of service.

Another slightly different method of bottom watering is to use a capillary mat. This mat is a piece of synthetic fabric that absorbs moisture and then releases it slowly to potted seeds or seedlings that sit directly on it. You can buy this material from garden catalogs and online sources (see Appendix D), or make your own.

To make a capillary mat, follow these directions:

1. Cut a double thickness of a knit fabric (an old synthetic blend T-shirt works well) to fit in the bottom of a solid tray or flat. Lay the fabric in place and dampen it.

2. Drill a small hole in the plastic lid of a wide-mouth container, such as a peanut-butter jar. Fill the jar with water, and screw on the lid.

3. Turn the jar upside down, and set it on the fabric.

4. Set your pots of seeds or seedlings on the prepared mat.

5. Water will slowly wick from the jar into the fabric mat as the pots absorb water from the mat.

6. Refill the jar when the water level is low. If algae grows on the mat, remove it and soak it in a 10 percent bleach solution; then rinse the mat and place it as before.

If you discover your growing medium has dried out, using a hand-held mister to moisten the surface with warm water will help the medium quickly wick up the water you add to the tray below. You can buy a mister or spray bottle at garden centers and discount stores, but a well-rinsed spray-cleaner bottle also does the job.

Covering Seeds

Seeds and seedlings need to develop in a warm, humid environment. After sowing and watering, cover the seed pots and flats with clear plastic bags. Food storage bags are big enough to cover single six-packs; clear plastic trash bags or dry-cleaner's bags are big enough to accommodate an entire flat. Stick garden labels or short stakes into each corner, and add a couple to the center of the flat to keep the plastic off the surface of the growing medium. Circulating air is important to prevent fungal infections, so leave the end of the bag open and check daily to be sure the medium is moist but not moldy. If you spot mold, remove the bag until it disappears. When your seedlings grow one set of true leaves, remove the covers so the seedlings can adjust to room conditions. True leaves are the first set of adult-like leaves that develop *after* the initial set of seedling leaves.

Garden Guide _____

Damping off is a fungal disease that attacks and kills seedlings in one day. Infected seedlings turn black at the soil line and collapse. To prevent the disease, avoid overwatering and wetting foliage. Also, provide circulating air by running a small fan over seedlings. Dispose of infected seedlings and the growing medium in which they grew.

You can purchase clear plastic covers sized to fit standard plastic seed flats from garden centers and garden catalogs. These are convenient but fragile and somewhat pricey. Their biggest disadvantage is that, unlike roomy plastic bags, they allow only a couple of inches of head room, so you must remove them shortly after the seeds sprout.

Thinning, Transplanting, and Hardening Off

In spite of all your efforts, some seedlings will grow close together, and you'll have to thin out the weaker ones to allow the stronger ones to develop without competition. Use a small pair of scissors (I use pointed grade-school scissors.) to snip off weaklings at soil level, and leave at least half an inch between the remaining seedlings.

When seedlings growing in community pots have two sets of true leaves and sturdy stems, it's time to transplant them into individual 4-inch pots where they'll grow for 4 or 6 weeks until you plant them in a permanent container or in the ground.

Even if you've already thinned out the weaklings, community-grown seedlings will still be growing in close proximity. So your challenge during transplanting is to lift seedlings from the growing medium and pull them apart without damaging the roots.

For this job, the best tools are fingers, a large knitting needle, and a table knife, fork, and spoon. My personal favorites are a vintage place setting with pointed handles that are perfect for poking seedling-size holes in growing medium and detangling fine seedling roots. As you transplant, always remember this: never hold a seedling by its stem. Accidentally squeezing or bending the stem can be fatal. Instead, grasp a seedling by one of its leaves to lift and move it.

Grasping seedlings by the leaf prevents gardeners from accidentally breaking fragile stems during transplanting.

(Donna Chiarelli Studio)

Here's how to transplant your community-grown seedlings:

1. Cover your work surface with newspapers for a sterile, easy-to-clean area.

2. Count your viable seedlings, and fill enough 4-inch pots with moist potting medium to hold two seedlings each.

3. Using the pointed end of a spoon handle, knitting needle, or pencil, make a hole about half an inch deep in two opposite corners of the pot. Set the pots aside while you prepare the seedlings.

4. Insert the table knife between clumps of seedlings and slice down to the bottom of the flat and around each clump. Lift one clump with the tines of the fork and set it on your work surface.

5. Use the knitting needle or a pencil point to pick the growing medium away from the roots of the seedlings. Then lift one seedling at a time, by grasping one of its leaves between your fingers.

6. Lower each seedling into a hole in one of the pots you prepared in Step 3, and gently push growing medium into the hole to fill in around the roots.

7. Repeat this process until you have transplanted all seedlings. Then move the seedlings to a sunny windowsill or back under your grow lights until the seedlings have several more sets of leaves and are ready to move outdoors.

Hardening off is the final stage of raising seedlings. Without this step, fragile seedlings will not survive the fluctuating temperatures, wind, and rain they encounter outdoors. Either set the seedlings outside each day and bring them back inside at night, or set them in a cold frame, unheated greenhouse, or some other partly shaded, protected place.

def•i•ni•tion

Hardening off is the process of setting indoor-started seedlings outdoors in a protected place so the seedlings can gradually adjust to outdoor weather conditions.

Hardening off seedlings in an unheated greenhouse gradually acclimatizes them to garden conditions.
(Donna Chiarelli Studio)

Moving Transplants to the Garden

Prepare your seedlings (and purchased bedding plants) for transplanting into the garden by removing them from their containers. Gently squeeze or loosen up each soil ball with your fingers to dislodge the roots somewhat and to help them travel out into the soil. If you started seeds of delicate-rooted plants in peat pots or pellets, skip this step because you should avoid disturbing their roots.

Here's how to transplant your hardened-off seedlings into the garden:

1. Use a trowel to dig a hole in well-prepared garden soil, making the hole the same size as the seedling's root ball.

2. Fill the hole with water and wait for it to drain away.

3. Then set the seedling's root ball into the hole, and gently fill in around it with garden soil, pressing gently to firm the soil around its roots.

4. Sprinkle water around the planted seedling to moisten surrounding soil.

5. Repeat this process to plant all seedlings.

Green Thumb _____

Tomato plants have the ability to root all along their main stem, so when transplanting tomato seedlings into the garden, bury them deeply—up to the lowest set of leaves—to help them produce an abundant root system.

Outdoor Seed Starting

Starting seeds indoors gives you a head start on your growing season and succession plantings. But you'll always have plants you must *direct sow* outdoors. Some, such as nasturtiums, beans, and peas, have fragile roots that are easily damaged during transplanting. Root crops such as carrots need to send taproots deep into the soil. Planting carrots in a pot can stunt that tap root. Vining plants, such as cucumbers, squash, and melons, sprout and grow quickly. So if planted in a pot indoors, they'd become a tangled mess before you could get them outdoors and into the garden.

def•i•ni•tion _____

To **direct sow** is to sow seeds directly into soil outdoors exactly where you want the plants to grow.

The beauty of direct sowing is that it eliminates the time-consuming tasks of starting seeds indoors, hardening them off, and transplanting them. There's also more room in the garden than in your house, so you can plant—more seeds!

Timing and Soil Preparation

Timing direct sowing outdoors can be tricky. If you sow the seeds too early, they can rot in cold, wet soil. Or if weather is temporarily mild, seeds may sprout and then get nipped by a late frost. On the other hand, if you're trying to stretch the spring season into summer by sowing cool-loving lettuce or spinach seeds in June, the warm soil temperature will keep the seeds from germinating.

The moral of this story is that you can't trust your last frost date. If your local weather is stuck in late winter after the last frost date or if it decides to skip spring and go directly from winter to summer, you have to adjust your planting dates or compensate with seed- and seedling-protection techniques.

Latitude also dictates when you sow your seeds. In the North, where the growing season is short and sometimes on the cool side, you must start warmth-loving annual flowers and vegetables indoors to give them time to mature before fall frosts. But happily, if you're a southern or West Coast gardener, you can skip this step and direct-sow impatiens, peppers, and tomatoes right in your warm garden soil in early spring or in late summer for early-winter harvests.

If you are new to gardening, find out when to plant various seeds in your area by doing one of the following:

◆ Ask a local garden center employee.

◆ Ask your local Cooperative Extension agent (see Appendix D).

◆ Ask the successful gardener down the block.

◆ Conduct an Internet search and locate an authoritative regional gardening website.

◆ Consult a regional gardening book.

The first time around, preparing garden soil can be taxing. But you have three ways to start a new garden: stripping sod and then tilling, building a raised bed (see Chapter 4), or using the lazy bed method, which is a bermlike raised bed with no borders. Whatever method you choose, the end result is a loose, crumbly, fine-textured soil that's easy to dig and easy for seedlings to root and grow in. And after the first year, if you're careful not to compact the soil by tromping on it too much, you can sow seeds with little preparation.

Garden Guide

To keep from compacting garden soil as you work, either create beds shallow enough to reach across or stand on a piece of plywood at least 2 feet square to distribute your weight across a larger area of soil. If you have a big garden, use two pieces of plywood—one to stand on and the other to move ahead as you work so there is always a board to stand on.

Sow seeds in well-worked soil. And make sure the surface stays loose and crumbly. Hard rains or overwatering can crust the soil's surface, preventing adequate oxygen from reaching germinating seeds and making it difficult or impossible for seedlings to break through the soil. One solution is to sprinkle sand over the seeds instead of soil to keep the soil from crusting over. Or you can cover your seeds with soil as usual, and then cover the beds with floating row cover fabric, which forms a barrier against driving rain and hail and transmits rain gently to the soil by filtering it through the fabric.

Black Plastic, Cold Frames, and Hot Beds

If your weather is not cooperating with your planting schedule, you can provide temporary protection for seeds and seedlings and still get your garden off to a good start in spite of Mother Nature.

In unseasonably cold weather, you can prewarm the soil in a planting bed by covering it with black plastic sheeting, which is sold in rolls at garden centers and in garden catalogs. If you want to plant a small area, you can use large black plastic trash or leaf bags. Simply lay the plastic down where you want to plant, and weight down the edges with soil, bricks, or rocks.

Once a week, lift the plastic and insert a soil thermometer. When the soil reaches the ideal temperature for the seeds you want to sow, it's time to plant. To sow small seeds such as lettuce or spinach, remove the plastic (save it to use again elsewhere), and scatter your seeds in the chosen area.

For heat-loving plants, such as tomatoes, peppers, squash, and melons, leave the plastic in place all season. To sow these plants, cut x-shaped slits in the plastic, fold the flaps back, and sow a few seeds in the exposed soil. The beauty of this system is that the plant roots bask in warmth and the fruits stay clean because they rest on plastic instead of on damp soil.

Seeds sown in an unheated cold frame or greenhouse have the benefit of soil warmed by the sun's rays plus protection from wind and storms. Either start the seeds in trays or pots or direct sow in the ground inside these structures. Then transplant seedlings to the garden when the garden soil is warm.

If it's unseasonably cold and you have access to electricity in your outdoor seed-starting area, you can add bottom heat by setting a propagation heat mat under potted seedlings or burying a soil heating cable in an in-ground bed. A soil heating cable is a plastic-coated electric wire attached to a thermostat. Placed under soil in seed-starting beds and plugged into a grounded outlet, it warms the soil to the ideal temperature for germination. We talk about raising plants in cold frames and greenhouses in Chapter 8.

Sowing and Spacing Techniques

When direct sowing outdoors, always heed the spacing directions given on the seed packet. It surely will seem that you're spacing the seeds too far apart, but you must space them widely to allow plenty of room for the mature plants to grow without crowding each other.

To sow seeds individually, hold a few in the palm of a closed hand. Work them out of your palm with your fingers, one at a time. Use your thumb and forefinger to drop them into planting holes or along a furrow—a long, shallow trench that you've dug for seed sowing.

There are two basic styles for direct sowing seeds. The traditional method is to sow them in rows. A newer idea is to broadcast seed over a square intensive plot no wider than you can reach across. (For more information on row and intensive gardens, see Chapter 7.) Row sowing is good, especially for new gardeners, because when the seedlings come up in a neat row it is easy to distinguish them from the weeds. Intensive gardens also work well. Simply scatter seeds across your planting area and sift soil over the seed to the depth recommended on the seed packet, or scratch gently with a rake to cover the seeds to the proper depth.

Simplify row sowing by creating a combination measuring stick and furrow maker. Here's how:

♦ Buy a piece of lightweight 1-inch diameter galvanized conduit pipe, which is sold at hardware stores. It comes in 8-foot lengths, but most hardware stores will cut to any length you desire.

♦ Next you'll need two different, highly visible colors of waterproof plastic tape (I used red and blue), also sold at hardware stores. Use pieces of tape to ring the pipe at 6-inch intervals, alternating the two colors. The reason for this spacing is that most garden seeds and bedding plants are planted 6 inches, 12 inches, or 18 inches apart. You'll be able to tell at a glance, by counting the colored rings, how to space your seeds or seedlings along the pipe.

♦ To use the device, lay it where you want to plant—on well-worked soil that's been raked smooth.

♦ Step on the pipe just hard enough that it makes a perfectly rounded furrow about half an inch deep. Then move the pipe beside the furrow. Place seeds in the furrow, spacing as recommended. With your fingers, push soil from either side of the furrow to cover the seeds, and pat the now-covered furrow gently to ensure that the seeds are in contact with soil.

- If you're setting out bedding plants, dig planting holes beside the appropriate colored ring and plant your bedding plant as directed earlier in this chapter.

- Repeat the process for the next row, using the measuring rings on the pipe to space each row, as recommended on the seed packet.

Watering Outdoor Seeds

Water direct-sown seeds and seedlings gently. A watering can fitted with a fine sprinkler head, called a rose, works for a small area. For bigger beds, use a garden hose fitted with a nozzle on a gentle sprinkle setting or with a water breaker. A water breaker is a wide nozzle with many small holes that delivers a gentle shower. As you water the beds, stand as far away as you can and still hit all areas with the water, and wave the nozzle slowly back and forth to keep from pummeling the soil and washing seeds away. If you covered your beds with row cover, uncover them before watering or lift one side so you can be sure you're watering the beds evenly, and then recover after watering. If your seedlings are surrounded by plastic sheeting, save water by waving the business end of the hose over just the planted areas.

Mature plants can easily go a week, sometimes two, without water, but if germinating seeds dry out, they'll never sprout. You must check your beds daily and water as often as needed to keep the soil surface moist. During hot spells, this could be daily or every other day. On the other hand, you mustn't overdo it because seeds will rot in wet soil.

Garden Guide _____

If vulnerable seedlings wilt due to sun exposure or dry soil, try to revive them. Cover them with a piece of plywood propped up on bricks to block out the hot afternoon sun. Or cover them with an old sheet draped loosely over wire or plastic hoops to keep the sheet from touching the seedlings. Keep the soil moist and leave the protection in place until the seedlings recover.

Fertilizing

Seeds do not need fertilizer to sprout, but once they emerge, seedlings benefit from dilute feedings. Water seedlings with half-strength liquid fertilizer every other time you water. As seedlings mature, they should grow well without fertilizer in good garden soil (see Chapters 3 and 4). If you have any doubts about your soil fertility, fertilize mature garden plants monthly according to commercial fertilizer package instructions, or side dress them with compost as we explained in Chapter 4.

Thinning Direct-Sown Seedlings

When sowing seeds outdoors, you should sow two or three seeds in each planting hole to make sure at least one comes up. Keep your scissors handy to snip off the weaklings, keeping only one seedling to a hole, to avoid crowding. To make sure your chosen seedling can go it alone, snip when the strongest one has at least one set of adult leaves and a sturdy stem. If you planted winter squash, which is not as prolific as its summer squash cousins, consider leaving two seedlings to double your harvest from each planting.

Protecting Seedlings

One way to protect seedlings is to place mulch around them. Mulching around seedlings helps the soil retain water (which reduces the amount of time you spend watering) and protects the seedlings from mud and soil-borne pathogens that can splash onto them with rain or watering. Floating row cover will do all this and more, protecting seedlings from cold, heat, strong sun, storms, and weeds (see Chapter 8).

The Least You Need to Know

◆ Growing open-pollinated varieties gives you free plants in future seasons.

◆ A seed-starting guide is invaluable because it supplies more detailed growing instructions than seed packets.

◆ Weigh your region's last-frost date against local forecasts to determine when to sow seeds and set out seedlings.

◆ Scarify, presoak, or stratify seeds to aid germination.

◆ Seeds need warmth and varying degrees of light to germinate.

◆ Bottom watering prevents dislodging seeds and seedlings.

◆ Hardening off helps seedlings adjust to outdoor garden conditions.

Part 3

Gardening Under Cover: Spring to Fall

Let's do a quick review. First, we convinced you that you *can* garden year-round. Then we shared how to build a great foundation for your garden—soil, compost, and fertilizer. Then we planted seeds. Now we're actually growing a garden!

In Part 3, we tell you how to get the most out of your garden by designing it well and by covering it to protect your plants from weather and bugs. We cover all kinds of covers—from a milk jug to an unheated, uninsulated greenhouse and everything in between.

Learn how to maximize the produce you get from your garden throughout the spring, summer, and fall growing seasons. You've never eaten so well!

Chapter 7

Garden Design Options

In This Chapter

♦ Garden designs for any type of garden

♦ Garden covers for every season

♦ Natural mulch covers

♦ Ornamental options

We're all familiar with the gardens of our youth. The big rectangles with the neat and orderly rows of corn and beans and tomatoes feel comfortable to us. Gardening under cover, however, calls for something other than large rectangles. In this chapter, we'll explore the garden design options available. We'll show you how intensive gardens make good use of little space, and you'll discover the benefits of in-ground and raised beds.

You might want to grab a pencil and paper because this chapter is going to inspire you to start sketching your garden design right away. So let's go!

Overview of Under-Cover Gardening

Long before the invention of floating row covers, vegetable-garden design evolved. Its beginnings were rooted in farming practices. Fields were, and still are, plowed in long, unprotected rows with wide paths between them because plows are hard to turn around. But to make the best use of protective covers such as floating row cover and clear plastic, which come in standard lengths and widths, we need to take a space-saving approach to garden design.

Row Gardens

To garden under cover, we need to look at a more efficient use of land. We need to arrange our gardens so we can easily cover the maximum number of plants with a single width of protective floating row covers, bug netting, or clear plastic.

Garden Guide _____

If you need to protect only one or a few plants, you can make a small cover by inserting two hoops in the ground at right angles in a cross-shape or umbrella-like arrangement. Cut a piece of row cover, clear plastic, or insect netting large enough to cover the hoops and extend to the ground, where you can anchor the material by setting rocks or bricks on the edges.

You can also form a ring around the plant with a piece of wire fencing or chicken wire and drape the protective covering over this framework.

Single rows of plants are easy enough to cover because you can push each end of a supporting hoop into the soil of the path on either side of a row and drape the fabric or plastic cover over them, suspending it just above the plants to allow room for them to grow without touching the covering. If your rows are longer than the covering, simply overlap it with an additional length, clipping the two together with clothespins or alligator clips. But you can cover two or three rows with the same piece of material if you place the rows close together, or plant intensively in block-shaped beds.

The traditional row-and-path design of vegetable gardens has been handed down from farming practices and is not the most space-efficient design for smaller modern gardens.

(Donna Chiarelli Studio)

Pathways

Your grandfather's vegetable-garden design is not the best one for us these days, because many of us have small gardens tucked into urban or suburban yards. The wide-path row design gobbles up space, and you and I could fit one or two more rows of plants in that space! By minimizing the number and especially the width of garden paths, you can save space, reduce labor, and grow and cover more plants.

Instead of a 3-foot-wide path, aim for one just wide enough for one person carrying a weeding or harvest basket to turn around in. Somewhere between 12 inches and 2 feet wide should be adequate.

In addition to narrowing garden paths, you can decrease the number of rows. In other words, don't space out *each* row of plants, but rather, plant two rows of beans, for example, relatively close together. You'll still have access to both rows of beans—one from one side and one from the other. If you're planting a crop that isn't as bushy as beans, such as carrots or radishes, you can plant three or even four rows and still reach all plants from one side or the other. And when you want to cover the seedlings or plants to protect them from hard rain or insects or excessive sun, it'll be relatively easy to construct one cover over several rows of plants, instead of having to make an individual cover for each row.

Garden Guide

Pathways in conventional row gardens are usually bare, hard-packed soil or mown lawn. Both are fairly high maintenance; the gardener either has to weed or mow. As an alternative, cover your garden paths with flattened cardboard boxes, which are biodegradable, topped with clean straw to suppress weeds.

At the end of the season, rake up the partly decomposed cardboard and straw and cover unused beds with it, or use it as a winter mulch around plants in your ornamental garden.

Leaving garden soil unplanted—as we do in garden pathways—is like laying out a welcome mat for weeds. So if you adopt a closely planted, space-saving garden design, you'll pull the rug right out from under those weeds.

Intensive Gardens

The intensive garden, sometimes called a square-foot garden, is an improvement over the traditional row garden for small-space gardeners. These gardens are laid out in

4-foot-wide squares, and a path borders each side of the square, allowing the gardener to reach the center of the growing bed from any of the four side paths. By combining four squares with a cross-shape path in the center, you have an attractive, formal vegetable garden design.

Green Thumb

The style of vegetable gardening in which plants are grown close together in highly fertile soil is often called French intensive gardening. King Louis XIV's head gardener at the Palace of Versailles developed this method, but it was popularized by market gardeners who worked small plots around Paris until they were crowded out by urban development at the turn of the twentieth century.

Covering square beds with a protective covering is similar to spanning several rows in a traditional row garden. To do this, cut a full 10-foot length of row cover in half to create two 5-foot lengths, each the right length to cover one 4-foot garden square.

At one edge of the garden bed, set one end of a hoop in the soil at the corner of the bed and the other end in the soil at the center of that edge of the bed. Set a second hoop at that center point, and then out to the other corner of the bed. Do the same thing at the opposite side of the bed. Now cover the entire garden bed with a piece of row cover, netting, or plastic supported by the two sets of hoops. Hold the covering in place by putting bricks or rocks along the edges of it at the edges of the paths.

The controlled geometry of the beds and borders of an intensive or square-foot garden gives this style a lot of curb appeal. When looking at the neat square plots, your eye follows the paths, giving a look of symmetry to the planting beds, even when they are brimming over with floppy herbs, wayward tomatoes, and exuberant squash vines meandering into the pathways.

Plant in Squares or Rows

We have two possible planting schemes for an intensive garden. For a random, cottage-garden look and for ease of planting, subdivide a 4-foot garden bed into 1-foot squares and broadcast small seeds, such as those for salad greens or carrots, within each subsection. Or for larger garden plants, such as tomatoes and peppers, plant one plant per 1-foot square.

The second scheme combines elements of the American row garden and the French intensive. With this method, you sow or set out seedlings in rows spaced 6 inches or 12 inches apart. In my garden, I have 4-foot squares, and I plant each square with rows because it's so easy to spot weeds when my seedlings are lined up in neat rows.

In-Ground and Raised Beds

The remaining options for covered garden design are traditional in-ground beds or building raised beds. In-ground beds are initially the easier route because after you till and improve the soil (see Chapters 3 and 4), you can plant directly in the ground. In-ground beds are the logical choice if your garden is large, on level ground, and has well-drained, fertile soil. Wire or PVC hoops can be cut to length to span rows or planting blocks, and easily inserted along the edges of prepared beds to support protective covers.

In this raised bed, the gardener has constructed a low tunnel to protect one row of plants from insect pests.

(Donna Chiarelli Studio)

Raised beds, on the other hand, also have many virtues. In addition to containing the best soil possible, the tall sides of raised beds make them easier to tend than in-ground beds, whether you kneel or stand. Raised beds begin life virtually weed-free, and it's easy to keep up with the occasional weed seed dropped by birds or blown in on the wind. And finally, because you can reach all parts of the beds without stepping into them, you never compact the soil and never have to till a raised bed; it's ready to plant early every spring. When you insert hoops at the edges of raised beds, the bed frames brace the hoops, creating sturdy supports for protective covers.

Ornamental Gardens

Ornamental gardens containing perennials, vines, shrubs, and trees are not really subject to the same design rules as food gardens, because these permanent plantings are less intensively cultivated. A few well-placed stepping-stones or mulch protects flower-bed soil from compaction and allows access to an ornamental bed for the few times each season you need to go in to weed, prune, set out, or divide plants.

There are two dominant styles of ornamental garden design: formal and informal. Formal ornamental gardens are laid out in squares with intersecting pathways, very similar to an intensive food garden. Plants are repeated from square to square for symmetry. But unlike a food garden in which you need to reach the center of the bed from all sides, you should size the squares in an ornamental garden to fit its plants. A mixed bed of shrubs, small trees, and perennials needs to be fairly large to accommodate these spreading plants when they mature.

The informal ornamental garden can fit a suburban backyard or cover acres of ground. It has a restful, naturalistic design, with meandering paths that invite a person to slow down and take in the view. In an informal garden, achieve symmetry by repeating colors and plants at strategic bends of the path.

Green Thumb

For a naturalistic look, mimic the way plants spread in nature and plant perennials in drifts. A drift is a group of the same kind of plants closely spaced in the center and more widely spaced toward the edges of the group.

An old saying about planting perennials goes "the first year they sleep, the second they creep, and the third year they leap." Loosely translated this means newly set out perennials and young woody plants need to be babied their first year while they establish a healthy set of roots. After planting, cover the soil with a 4-inch-thick layer of organic mulch, such as finished compost or shredded bark, to shade the roots and maintain soil moisture.

Garden Guide _____

When placing marginally hardy plants, look for compatible microclimates in your yard. A microclimate is an area with growing conditions that differ from most of your yard. It can be a heat pocket next to a south-facing brick house or rock wall, a cool spot at the base of a hill where cold air puddles, the consistently moist soil near an outdoor water faucet, or the alkaline soil where lime leaches from a cement walk or driveway.

While you wouldn't want to hide your beautiful perennials, if your ornamental garden contains marginally hardy plants, temporary covers can save them from excessive heat, cold, and pest damage. Many perennials are hardy, but gardeners develop passions for certain plants and are famous for pushing hardiness limits. Similarly, if you plant in early spring, summer, or fall, you can cover young plants with floating row cover to shade the foliage and deflect chewing insects.

We've already said that you should clean up your food garden in fall. For a perennial garden, save that clean-up until spring. It's important to leave dead foliage on the plants over winter to insulate the plants' crowns against freeze damage. If you have marginally hardy perennials, cover their crowns with several inches of dry, fluffy mulch, such as straw or dead leaves, held in place with an overturned bushel basket or burlap weighed down by bricks or rocks. Check the plant tag or a reliable garden guide for a plant's USDA Hardiness Zone rating and the AHS Heat Zone rating (see Appendix D).

The Least You Need to Know

- Intensive gardening protects plants with less cover and less work.

- Formal garden design gives visual structure to sprawling plants.

- Overcome problems of infertile soil and poor drainage with raised beds filled with good garden loam.

- Raised beds warm up fast for early spring planting and provide support for protective covers.

- Winterproof dormant perennials with a covering of fluffy, natural mulch such as pine straw or shredded, dried leaves.

Chapter 8

Tunnels, Wraps, and Other Covers

In This Chapter

- ◆ The advantages of gardening under cover
- ◆ Tips for gardening under cover outdoors year-round
- ◆ Row covers, cloches, cold frames, and unheated greenhouses
- ◆ Cooling covers for summer gardening

Gardening under cover allows you to extend the harvest season to get a head start on spring or garden longer into fall—maybe even into winter if that's what you want to do.

To get this head start in spring, you need to warm things up, so in this chapter, we'll tell how to warm up that soil and create a cozy place for tender seedlings to grow so you can keep a whole garden, or just a few special plants, warm and safe from finicky spring weather. And what about the heat of summer—how can you combat that? We'll show you how to make shade for those plants that just can't stand the heat.

Heating things up—cooling things down—is all this really worth the effort? Yes, it definitely is if you want your garden to grow more produce for a longer period of time. And the good part is, after you read this chapter, you'll know how to help your garden plants through the seasons. So let's venture into tunnels, wraps, and other covers!

Warming Garden Covers for Spring

Remember what happened last week—last month, last year, or whenever—when someone left that tarp or that kids' wading pool out on the lawn for a couple of summer days? When someone finally moved it, all the grass was dead underneath! Why was the grass dead? Because it got cooked. The sun's rays beat down on that plastic and heated it up, and naturally, the grass and the soil underneath heated up as well. Even at night, that plastic held most of the heat in, even though the air temperature cooled. There was simply no escape for the hot air, so the grass turned brown and looked dead.

What a disappointment that burned grass was! But you can put that same process to work for you—when you want it and where you want it. You can use it to warm up the soil in spring so you can plant your seeds or set out your seedlings earlier than you would otherwise be able to. You can take advantage of the sun's warmth, and with a few relatively simple materials, you'll soon be the gardener on the block whom everyone envies. They'll see you out harvesting your salad greens before theirs have hardly even sprouted, because you'll know about covering your soil or your plants to keep them warm and cozy.

Soil Covers

If you plant seeds or set out seedlings in spring, it will happen sooner or later; it happens to every gardener. The weather turns surprisingly chilly, and the meteorologist issues a frost warning. Your young plants are definitely at risk. And you've worked so hard to get your garden started early! What can you do? The answer: bring on the sheets and blankets! Simply lay the covers over your plants. If plants are especially fragile or if your blanket is on the heavy side, you'll need to prop the cover up somehow. Anything will do in a pinch—sticks you've been meaning to pick up from the lawn, your garden trowels, or lined-up plastic nursery pots.

In the morning, lift the covers off the plants, but wait until the air has warmed up a bit. If it really did freeze, don't remove the frozen covers. They'll be stiff and heavy, and you'll likely damage the plants just trying to move the covers. Wait until later in the morning when the covers have thawed. Or if the cold snap is severe and the covers don't thaw that day, leave them on for a day or two until they do thaw.

*Place old blankets over plants
or seedlings in the event of
an unexpected spring frost.*

(Donna Chiarelli Studio)

Black plastic has been a very popular product for warming the soil for years. Just like the tarp or the pool in my earlier little scenario, the plastic heats the soil when the sun's rays hit the plastic, and then the plastic holds much of the accumulated heat in at night. To use plastic as a soil warmer, stretch it out in the desired area. If you have snowy winters, do this in a prepared bed in late autumn. Or if your winters are not necessarily snowy—and for less wear and tear on your plastic—you can wait until early spring. Secure the edges with dirt, bricks, rocks, or landscape pins about a foot apart to prevent the wind from picking up the edge of the plastic.

Another way to heat up the soil is to add a 3-inch layer of compost. Think of it as a blanket for your soil—the compost warms by slowing the natural release of heat from the soil. At night, when the outside temperatures drop, the compost acts like an insulator, holding the heat in the soil.

Spread compost over a prepared bed and leave it uncovered over the winter. Or you can distribute the compost and then cover it with black plastic for additional heating power. Either way, you'll be improving your soil as well as helping it warm up sooner in the spring.

How do you know when the soil is warm enough? You take its temperature, of course. Put a soil thermometer (available inexpensively from garden centers) into the soil under whatever soil cover you've chosen. Soil temperature preferences can vary from crop to crop. Warm-weather plants such as tomatoes, eggplants and peppers prefer a soil temperature of 70°F. Cool-weather crops such as kale, lettuce, radish, spinach, and peas prefer soil temperatures of 40°F.

Soil thermometers are wonderful tools for monitoring the soil temperature around your plants.

(Donna Chiarelli Studio)

Row Cover

After you heat up your soil and plant your seeds or set out your transplants, it's time to think about row cover. In early spring, row cover helps collect heat and holds it close to your tender plants during that up-and-down spring weather. You can simply lay row cover over your plants; in that case, it's called floating row cover. However, it's better to create low tunnels by supporting the row cover with hoops. This tunnel construction creates an air layer that heats up during the day and holds heat during the night. Hoops range in height from 12 inches to 36 inches. As with a black plastic soil cover, secure row cover along the edges with soil, bricks, rocks, or landscape pins.

Garden Guide

Pay attention to the weather, and watch out for especially warm spring days because it can get too hot under that row cover. You may need to roll it back or raise the sides to let some heat out and let air circulate around your plants.

Remember that different weights of row cover are available, and the heavier the row cover, the more protection it provides from dipping temperatures. Your best bet is to describe what you're trying to accomplish to an experienced local gardener (at a nursery or at your local Extension office), and get advice as to the weight that best suits your needs.

Frost Cover

Frost cover is a lightweight, permeable fabric that helps protect your flowers and vegetables from frost. Frost cover and row cover are very similar. The difference is that frost cover is made to protect plants from frost, whereas row covers may not necessarily do that because row covers are generally made of a lighter-weight material.

Frost cover alone can protect plants when temperatures dip to 20°F. Of course, this will depend on the plant and the normal lowest temperature it can withstand.

Green Thumb

Frost cover can raise the temperature underneath by up to 7°F. Add a layer of clear plastic over that, and you'll get even more protection from Mother Nature's elements as well as warmer soil and a warmer growing environment.

Cloches

If you have only a few early-spring plants to protect or if you prefer old-fashioned methods, you might want to use a cloche (see Chapter 1). The principle behind a cloche is the same as that of the low tunnels. The glass or plastic cloche protects the plant from cold air. In addition, the sun heats the inside air, and the cloche holds in that heat at night. Cloches have the added benefit of protecting seedlings from pests, such as slugs and snails.

Remember it can get hot under a cloche on a sunny spring day even if the outside air temperature doesn't get that warm. But cloches are easy to ventilate. If the day is quite warm, simply remove it from the plant. If it's a bit warm but not *very* warm, set a couple of bricks or pieces of wood under its edges so cool air can enter from below.

Making a homemade cloche is quite simple. Thoroughly rinse a milk jug or a 2-liter beverage container; remove the lid; and cut off the bottom. Out in the garden, place the cloche over the plant and dig or press the edges into the ground. If you fear the wind will turn it over, you may want to tie two strings around the neck of the bottle/cloche and secure the strings with landscape pins or wrap each string around a rock or a brick.

Garden Guide

If you make a home-made cloche out of a milk jug or some other container, remember that the top must be open because the plant underneath needs air circulating around it.

Place a homemade plastic cloche, made from a milk jug, over a seedling in a pot or in the garden to protect the seedling from environmental changes.

(Donna Chiarelli Studio)

Cold Frames

A cold frame is another time-honored gardening trick that helps gardeners get an early start. Remember that a cold frame is a small, boxlike outdoor structure in which gardeners start or grow plants in pots. It has four sides made of wood, plastic, or bales, sits directly on the ground, and has a glass or plastic cover that allows light in. A cold frame is good for starting seeds, for temporarily coddling and hardening off seedlings, or for growing plants to maturity.

Now nothing new is going on here. Once again, we have a cover that protects plants from low air temperatures and a layer of air that heats up during the day. So the soil heats up, too. And at night, that air layer holds much of the heat in. Sound familiar?

The benefit of a cold frame is that it offers more protection than a row cover, a frost cover, or a cloche. Think of it this way: would you rather spend a night outdoors wrapped in a blanket or would you rather have four walls and a roof around you?

The structure of the cold frame offers that extra protection from the elements. But as with all other soil or garden covers, it can get too hot inside, and you must be able to remove or raise the top so your plants don't cook.

As a cold frame is a box, if you're making one, you must create an enclosed structure. Let's talk through the process of making the simplest one out of four bales and an old window. (For visual help, see Chapter 1.)

First, choose a location, a sunny spot because you need the sun to work for you. If you're going to plant directly in the ground, work up the soil so it's ready for your seeds or seedlings. Then place two bales on either side of the spot, long sides parallel to each other. Remember, they can only be as far apart as the width of your window. Then position the other two bales, one against each end of the first bales. Again, pay attention to the opening in the middle because your window needs to cover it completely. If you need to decrease the size of your opening, then instead of setting that fourth bale against the ends of the first two, turn it 90° and push its end *between* the first two bales.

You can make cold frames in other ways from simple to elaborate. One relatively simple type is essentially a raised bed with a cover (see Chapter 3 for making a raised bed). And again, an old window works great for the cover, but you'd want to make a fairly narrow bed as the width of whatever cover you choose will determine the width of the bed.

For those who prefer to purchase a premade cold frame, numerous sizes and styles are available in a wide range of prices. A homemade cold frame works just as well as a store-bought one, so you decide which way to go.

This wood-frame cold frame has a sunny southern exposure and is propped open so the plants inside don't get too hot.

(Donna Chiarelli Studio)

The top of this plastic-sided cold frame is just slightly vented to let a little warm air out on a sunny but cool day.

(Donna Chiarelli Studio)

As with all covers, you'll have to pay attention on warm, sunny days. If it's just a little warm, turn the window at an angle so hot air can escape or lift the top so it vents. If it's a really warm day, remove or open the cover completely. But replace it at night because the nighttime temperatures could still dip low enough to harm the plants.

If you have a heavy snowfall, brush the snow off the top of your cold frame as the plants inside still need light. And you need to remove the snow so its weight doesn't damage your structure.

Garden Guide

Your cold frame *shouldn't* need any additional help. However, in a severe cold snap, you could further insulate the contents by laying blankets, old plastic table-cloths, or tarps over your plants. Be sure to keep tarps or plastic materials from touching your plants by suspending them with tomato cages or other materials. To keep from crushing plants, set several stacks of plastic nursery pots in the cold frame. Wedged between the plant pots, the stacks will hold the insulating material off the plants.

Tunnel Houses

Let's say you need more than a box. You want to start so many plants that you need a whole room to keep them warm and safe. You need a tunnel house. Remember the low tunnels we talked about earlier? A tunnel house is the same thing, only bigger. In fact, you can make a tunnel house any size you want. Generally, they're tall enough for a gardener to stand up in.

To make one, you'll need half-inch plastic conduit and a quantity of 6 mil. plastic. Plastic conduit is tubing that electricians run wire through for safety and comes in 10-foot lengths. These lengths are going to form the hoops that hold up your tunnel house. Decide how long you want your tunnel house to be, and buy enough lengths of conduit so you can place one hoop every 2 feet.

When choosing a location, pick a sunny spot so the sun's heat can make this a warm place for your seedlings and plants. Measure out the space, and mark it with stakes. If you'll be planting directly in the ground, work up the soil. Remember, you'll probably want a pathway down the middle, and ideally, the beds on either side should be narrow enough that you can reach across without tromping on the soil and compacting it.

Push one end of your first hoop into the ground at least one foot and then the other end. Measure 2 feet and push in the next hoop. Continue until you get to the end of your tunnel. If you cannot get the end of the conduit into the ground, wet the soil to make it soft enough to push the conduit ends into it or dig a hole a foot deep and bury the ends.

The next step is to wrap the whole thing, ends and all, in plastic, and you'll need to secure the plastic around all four sides so it doesn't blow off. The easiest way to do this is to pull the plastic as tight across the hoops as you can and place a heavy object on top of the plastic about every foot or so. You can use sand bags, bricks, rocks, or any other heavy material on the loose edges of the plastic. Your goal is to make sure it is snug against the ground and that strong winds cannot lift it up.

On warm days, your tunnel house will get pretty toasty. Simply remove some of the weights, and lift the plastic to allow air into the tunnel. If it's really warm, you can roll up an entire side. Be sure to resecure your plastic around mid-afternoon so heat can build back up before night's chilly temperatures return.

Unheated Greenhouses

We met greenhouses, in general, in Chapter 1. An unheated greenhouse, or a cold greenhouse, doesn't contain a heat source but does contain windows to vent hot air. It may or may not be equipped with electric fans to help circulate air and exhaust excess warmth.

Like our other structures, an unheated greenhouse is best situated in a sunny location. It's not much different from a tunnel house when it comes to warming the interior of the structure and retaining heat during the night. However, its larger size means it won't retain heat quite as well as the smaller structures.

The difference between a greenhouse and the other structures is that most gardeners don't plant directly in the ground but either maintain plants in pots or establish raised beds. A greenhouse is also more permanent than any of the other structures.

Because of a its larger size, setting up a heat sink with containers of water is more effective than it would be in a smaller structure. Remember this technique from Chapter 1? The water warms during the day and releases the heat at night. Because it takes many gallons to make a difference in the overall temperature, this works better in a larger structure.

Other ways to warm a greenhouse include using any of the soil covers we talked about earlier. Placing black plastic on the ground—either under your pots or over your raised beds—really raises the temperature inside a greenhouse. And if you have raised beds, they'll benefit—in both nutrients and warmth— from a good layer of compost. That compost will act as a blanket, just like it would if you spread it out in the open on a garden bed.

Cooling Covers for Summer

We all sometimes need a little relief from the summer heat, and the same is true of your plants. Now the tomatoes and cucumbers and melons can take the heat. But what if you want to keep those spring crops, such as salad greens and peas, producing a little longer in June? Or what if you want to plant a second crop of those cool-loving crops in late summer? How do you get them through the August heat so they'll mature and produce for you in October? In Chapter 2, we discussed techniques for extending your harvest season, such as planting in the shade. So here, let's talk about covers you can use to keep things cool during the summer.

Covers that provide shade help cool the soil, and the cooler the soil, the more moisture it holds and the cooler the plants' roots are. Plants that have cool roots and plenty of moisture are less likely to wilt. Without the stress of wilting, your plants are more productive and, well, just happier all the way around. Most cool-weather crops prefer a soil temperature between 40°F and 50°F. So let's look at the options for cooling covers one by one.

Spun-Bonded and Shade Cloth Row Covers

Earlier we talked about using row cover to keep plants warm. To keep plants cool, we'll use the same techniques and structures, but a different kind of covering. Spun-bonded row cover is simply a row cover that is made of spun-bonded fabric, or fabric that has been spun into a swirling web-like pattern. Use it to cut down on *some* of the light—and heat—that hits your plants.

However, spun-bonded row cover is usually see-through and is used more for protecting plants from insects.

Spun-bonded row covers are generally heavier and offer a higher degree of protection from the sun's rays than non-spun-bonded row cover; but, on the downside, they exclude more light. These types of covers are better used in the summer months when there is plenty of light or for crops that can tolerate some shade.

A better way to provide a lot of shade to plants is to use shade cloth. As we mentioned in Chapter 2, this is a synthetic fabric made to allow a certain percentage of sunlight to shine through it. It's made in different percentages of shading: 50 percent shade, 70 percent, 80 percent, and so on. Sometimes you need only a small amount of shade to cool things down considerably. For example, hostas can burn up if they get too much sun. Although lettuce does just fine in summer sun, it withers under full midday sun. So offering lettuce a bit of shade will keep it from suffering. Regardless how much sunlight the shade cloth lets through, it's permeable, so rainwater and sprinkler water go right through. You can water your plants as you normally would without having to move the shade cloth.

Most shade cloth is made of synthetic fibers, but some use aluminum along with the plastic. These are very useful in hot climates because the aluminum reflects a good deal of sunlight, thus keeping it much cooler underneath.

Shade cloth also comes in two types of weaves: a knitted material and a woven cloth. The knitted variety is lighter and stronger than the woven, usually costs a bit more, and can be cut without the ends unraveling. However, the two are equal in terms of effectiveness and ease of use.

Since we can use the same techniques for shade cloth as we did for row cover, you can suspend it over hoops to make a low tunnel or lay it over the top of a tunnel house, cold frame, greenhouse, or even over the simplest of structures, such as four stakes or posts driven into the ground. Like row cover, you need to secure it so the wind won't pick it up by using rocks, bricks, landscape pins, or whatever you have available.

Garden Guide

Start a second round of cool-weather crop seeds in flats in late summer. Place the flats under shade cloth—either outdoors or inside a structure. Under shade, the flats will dry out less quickly, which helps ensure a high germination rate for your seeds.

Lattice Panels

Lattice panels are panels of criss-crossed slats that people sometimes use as trellises or dividers or even fences in their yards. Lattice panels, made of either wood or plastic, are available at garden centers or in the yard and garden departments of home improvement stores and come in standard dimensions of 4-foot by 8-foot panels. Lattice has the qualities we need in a summer cooling cover: it cuts the amount of sunlight getting to plants and lets water through. Let's think about lattice from a couple of different angles.

If you stand some lattice panels up on the south or west edge of your yard, you'll be creating mid- and late-day shade for whatever is on the ground immediately to the north or east of the panels. You'll protect those plants from the harshest light and the hottest rays during each summer day. In addition, you'd provide something for climbing plants, such as peas or ornamental vines, to climb on.

Now from another angle, think about lattice as a roof instead of a wall. Lay lattice on top of an open cold frame to shade the interior; put it on the roof of your greenhouse to keep the interior cooler; or suspend panels over stakes or posts to shade a specific section of a garden. Lean two lattice panels against each other (or cut a panel in half and lean the two halves) to make a tipi. Set the tipi—or several tipis—over a row of salad greens or peas that need to stay out of the hot sun. That's four ideas for lattice roofs, and I bet you can find more.

Lattice, by itself, can be a little flimsy, so to firm it up, nail a wooden frame around each panel. Depending on your ultimate goal, you might choose a very sturdy 2–4 frame or a less heavy, but still useful, 1–2 frame. Then nail the framed panel to posts driven into the ground. If you're making a permanent installation, you can use cement to secure the posts. Set a couple of posts and panels side by side for a lattice "wall." Or set four posts in a rectangle, and place the corners of a panel on top for a lattice "roof."

Solid Shading

Solid shading, unlike shade cloth and lattice panels, completely prohibits sunlight from reaching what's underneath. It also prohibits rainwater from penetrating, so the plants underneath solid shading will depend on you for their water. Solid shading in your yard or garden creates a completely shaded area. Why would you want a completely shaded area? Suppose you've planted some small trees in an area where you also want to put in some shade-loving ornamental plants. You can use solid shade over this space so your ornamentals will thrive. In a few years, when the trees get taller, you can remove the shade structure because the trees will take over the job of providing shade, and your ornamentals will be well established.

You can make solid shading out of materials such as metal roofing, plywood, or heavy shade cloth. Heavy shade cloth is shade cloth that shuts out at least 90 percent of the sunlight. (Or, use two layers of lighter shade cloth, if necessary, to get the amount of shade you need.) You can mount solid shading in a variety of ways. Drive posts into the ground, as with the lattice panels, and then nail metal or wood panels on top as a roof. Metal panels will cause the area underneath to heat up in the summer. The advantage of metal in the winter is that the area will remain warmer. If your material of choice is heavy shade cloth, lay it over the top of a low tunnel, tunnel house, cold frame, greenhouse, or a simple structure of posts. Whatever the structure, secure the edges of the shade cloth with weights or landscape pins.

The Least You Need to Know

- The ideal garden cover offers protection from freezing temperatures and provides a layer of air that heats during the day and then slowly releases that heat at night.

- Use soil covers such as black plastic or compost to help warm the soil sooner in spring.

- Use row cover, frost cover, and cloches in the garden to keep early-spring seedlings warm, even through spring's up-and-down temperatures.

- Start and grow plants in early spring under the protection of a cold frame, a tunnel house, or an unheated greenhouse.

- Grow cool-weather crops in summer's heat by providing cooling covers such as shade cloth or lattice panels.

Chapter 9

Maintaining Outdoor Covered Gardens

In This Chapter

- Controlling cold frame temperatures
- Watering and fertilizing under cover
- Hand pollinate plants in your covered gardens
- Synthetic and organic pest- and disease-control methods

The joy of gardening outdoors is unmatched, according to most gardeners. The fresh air, the exercise, the satisfaction of watching things grow—these are irreplaceable. But what about the bugs, the weeds, the windstorms? And let's not even talk about hail! What's a gardener to do? We certainly don't want to give up and stay indoors.

Enter the concept of covered gardens. You read all about the covers, themselves, in Chapter 8. Here, we'll tell you how to put them to work in your garden. You'll still be outside enjoying your plants and exercising. But your plants will be thriving under cover—with a little extra help from you for water, fertilizer, and maybe even some hand pollination. We'll also help you troubleshoot and solve any pest problems that crop up under those inviting covers.

Regulating Temperatures Under Cover

We talked about the soil- and plant-warming capabilities of garden covers and structures in Chapter 8, so you know it's going to be warm under there. But controlling the temperature under row cover or in a cold frame or tunnel house is as simple as opening a window. (We'll cover unheated greenhouses in Chapter 14.) Technically, I suppose we should call it "venting" because the structures don't actually have windows. But you get the idea. These structures are sealed, so unless you have an automatic vent system equipped with a thermostat, you'll need to vent them manually.

Garden Guide

The temperature under a single layer of cover can be 20°F hotter than the outside temperature, so it's important to monitor temperatures inside your structures with a thermometer (rather than just guessing) and vent when necessary to allow hot air to escape.

Venting can be as simple as raising the plastic along one edge of a row cover or tunnel. For a cold frame, you can set your cover partly to the side, lift the hinged lid and prop it open, or open a vent if you have a somewhat fancier, store-bought version.

Electric fans in a larger structure such as a tunnel house help control temperatures as well. Obviously, this requires having power available outdoors. If you have power near your covered structure, that's great. If you have to run a cord from the house or an outbuilding, be sure to use an outdoor grade extension cord for safety.

Watering and Fertilizing Under Cover

The air inside covered structures, which tends to be warmer than the outside air, dries out plants and soil. So you may need to water the inside plants more often than outdoor plants. In fact, you may need to water your under-cover plants daily, depending on the weather and your ventilation system.

Now we know that row cover is permeable—it lets rainwater through—so plants under row cover may or may not need additional watering, depending on your rainfall amounts. However, a completely enclosed structure—a cold frame or a tunnel house—obviously depends on you for moisture. For a cold frame, you can open the top to take advantage of any rain that does fall. Beyond that, you're looking at watering with a sprinkling can or hose. In a tunnel house, you can run a soaker hose through the beds and let it do the work. Or you may have to use the hose and sprinkling nozzle yourself on a daily or almost-daily basis.

Fertilization is another issue that is a bit different in a cold frame or covered garden situation. Making sure your plants receive proper nutrition is critical to your success. Because temperatures inside a covered structure are higher, the plants take up fertilizer more efficiently and may use more because they are actively growing. So though you may not need to fertilize outside plants during a growing season, your undercover plants may need a dose to continue to perform at their peak.

Pollinating Under Cover

Plants that aren't *self-fertile* are pollinated in four ways: bees and other insects, animals, wind, and hand pollination. However, with plants under cover, neither insects nor animals nor wind can get at them. So what is a gardener to do?

def•i•ni•tion

A **self-fertile** plant has flowers with both male and female parts so that it pollinates itself. This self-pollination may take place even before the flower opens.

If you're venting your low tunnel, cold frame, or tunnel house, some insects and maybe some wind could get in to do the job of pollination. But you don't want your pollination to be hit-or-miss, occurring only on those days when it's warm enough to open your structure all the way. To ensure that your plants set fruit, you can try hand pollinating using a small paintbrush. This is a labor-intensive job, but it's necessary so your plants will set fruit. (We talk about hand pollinating in Chapter 13, too.)

To hand pollinate, you must learn the difference between the male and female parts of a flower. Some flowers have both male (stamen) and female (pistils) parts. The types of plants you are most likely to hand pollinate (squash, melons, and cucumbers) have separate male and female flowers. How do you tell them apart? The male flower, with its stamen, has a straight stem at the base of the flower. The female flower, with its pistils, has a swelling at the base of the flower. That's where the fruit will form.

Select the two flowers, or the two plants, you wish to pollinate and locate a male flower and a female part or flower. With a small paintbrush or a cotton swab, gently brush the top of the male part (that's the stamen, again) where the yellow, dusty pollen is. You should see a yellow substance on your paintbrush or cotton swab. Then brush the pollen-laden brush onto the female part (those pistils, again) of the flower you wish to pollinate. If you wish to pollinate more than one plant, do not use the same tool to transfer pollen, begin with clean materials.

Some plants such as tomatoes are self-fertile, so regardless of whether you have insects or not, you'll get fruit. Other plants, such as corn, are wind pollinated, so again, insects or not, if you have wind, you'll have pollination.

Green Thumb

There are a variety of self-fertile plants that do not require hand pollination even if they are grown under cover. These plants include tomatoes, beans, lettuce, peas, and peppers.

Controlling Weeds Under Cover

Your under-cover gardens are less susceptible to weed growth because neither birds nor wind can drop seeds into your garden beds. However, the weed seeds already in the soil will benefit from the same heat, light, and moisture your desirable plants are getting. And will those weed seeds grow? You bet! However, we have ways to beat the weeds.

Suppressing Weeds

You can take a proactive move against weeds right from the start and keep those weeds from even raising their heads out of the ground.

When you establish your covered garden bed, whether it be a raised bed with row cover, a cold frame, or a tunnel house, you can lay black plastic or a thick layer of newspaper under the lovely soil you prepare for this site. Both of these suppress weed growth. Of course, the newspaper rots in time and becomes ineffective, but by that time, your covered structure may have been in place long enough that weed seeds are no longer viable. One disadvantage to using black plastic as a weed suppressor is that the plastic prevents your soil from "breathing," so sometimes the soil molds under the plastic and, generally, becomes unhealthy.

Another option is to install weed cloth, which is a synthetic fabric that is generally black in color and permeable so water can get to the plant roots below. The small holes that make the weed cloth, which is sometimes called landscape fabric, permeable are small enough so weeds cannot grow up through it from the ground below. Gardeners lay it down over the soil and cut a slit, a hole, or an *X* in it for each plant. Weed cloth allows the soil to breathe, unlike black plastic, but if a weed seed gets on top of the weed cloth, it will sprout and grow. Removing these weeds can be a real chore because the roots get entangled in the fabric, and taking up the weed cloth is also a chore because it surrounds each of your plants.

You know you can use compost as a mulch to suppress weeds among your plants under cover (see Chapter 4), and straw is also a great weed suppressor. In addition, straw helps hold moisture in the soil and makes great pathways. I already mentioned newspaper, but instead of putting it *under* the soil, you can shred it (that would be best) or spread out sheets as "mulch" around your plants.

In an established covered garden bed, you can apply corn gluten to kill weed seeds. Corn gluten is a natural substance, so it may appeal especially to organic gardeners. Corn gluten is the substance in organic Preen. If you would rather buy just corn gluten, it can be hard to find at local garden centers but is available online. It comes in three forms, unprocessed, granulated, and pelleted. Spread it by hand or by using a broadcast spreader or hand seeder. Corn gluten can be a bit on the pricey side. Note, however, that it cannot distinguish between your flower or vegetable seeds and weed seeds; it just kills all seeds. So don't apply corn gluten until your own seeds are past the sprouting and seedling stage.

Green Thumb

Remove weeds before they set seed. Weed seeds can lie dormant for up to seven years, so preventing existing weeds from dropping seeds means less weeding for you next year, and the next year, and the next year ….

Killing Weeds

If weeds do appear, then what are you going to do? You can go the old-fashioned route and pull the weeds or hoe them up, of course. That's feasible if you're reasonably fit, if your covered garden isn't too large, and if the weeds haven't gotten out of control. Or you can squirt vinegar on them, which perhaps takes as much time as pulling the weeds but is less taxing on your hands and knees. One caution, though: vinegar will kill your plants as well as the weeds, so spray or squirt with a good aim.

And finally, chemical weed killers are another option. There are many brands, many strengths, and many different kinds. Some weed killers target one kind of weed; others are less discriminating and kill them all. The best way to choose the right one for your problem is to ask advice at a local nursery or garden center. After you make a purchase, read the label and follow the instructions. Remember to use caution when using chemical weed killer near food plants. If the crop is within two weeks of harvest, let the weeds grow or pull them out by hand. Whatever you do, do not spray within two weeks of harvest! Also remember that if you spray around young food plants, the spray works its way into the soil, and the roots of your food crops may take up the chemicals. That's not good for your crop or for you, in the long run.

Whatever method you choose, you can make your covered garden areas weed-free if you remain persistent.

Controlling Pests and Diseases

In nature, pests always pick on the weakest link. Think of them as muggers: they seek out what's slow moving; they're opportunists and always go for the easiest target first. So the pests target the flowers, vegetables, trees, or vines that aren't growing fast or aren't thriving. Pests, too, always go for the easiest target first and avoid the strong and healthy plants.

Garden Guide

Gardeners who prefer natural remedies use companion planting to help ward off garden pests. For example, some strong-scented plants, such as marigolds, help keep rabbits at bay (for those days when you have the sides of your tunnels raised up to ventilate). Or some plants attract beneficial insects, which then prey on harmful insects in the next garden row. To learn more about companion planting, see the resource list in Appendix D.

So how do you combat these garden pests—these weak-plant bullies? The trick is to grow strong, healthy plants that repel insect pests and diseases because they're thriving. Ensure the health of your plants by providing the very best soil possible, making good use of compost, providing enough water when conditions are hot and windy, and being selective. If, for example, one tomato plant looks yellow and is failing to thrive, pull it up and toss it out. Always plant more than you need, and be quick to get rid of the weaklings as well as diseased plants.

Timing Is Everything

The very best gardeners use a big calendar with plenty of white space on it to keep track of their garden. So get a calendar and make notes about exactly what day you planted the petunia seeds and the tomato and pepper seeds, what day you transplanted the cabbage plants, what day you gave all the fuchsia plants a hard pinch, and when you found pests or a diseased plant and what you did about it. Make notes on pretty much everything you do in your garden. If you put your chosen insecticide product on your strawberries on May 3, make a note on the calendar about that. And when you harvest that first tomato, make a note about that. Then do a little dance of joy.

At the end of the year, don't toss that calendar! It will be your own personal guide to the correct timing for the coming year and will help you get ahead of garden pests and hopefully avoid disease. If, for example, your strawberries did better than ever this year, you'll probably want to do the same things on the same schedule next year. Fortunately, you've kept your calendar and can see that on or around May 3, you should put your insect-controlling product around your strawberries.

However, if pests ate up your strawberries this season, you'll want to make some adjustments next year. Maybe you should put the insecticide out earlier—if you are in a Southern climate, or later—if you are in a northern climate. Make a decision, and on a new calendar, put down a different date for distributing your pest-control measures.

Write down any disease problems, too. If all your tomato plants were affected by tomato wilt this year, you don't want to replant tomatoes close to the area they were in. Write it down because next spring that detail might completely slip your mind as you plan your garden.

Save all your garden calendars from one year to another, and compare them. Make little adjustments based on what you did last year or in years before to fine-tune your planting, your pest- and disease-control programs, and, in fact, all your garden activities. Eventually, if you keep and save these garden calendars or a garden journal, you'll have a record especially tailored just for you and your own garden. You'll have a blueprint for growing the very best, strongest, most fruitful, and most pest- and disease-resistant plants. For good gardening, timing really is everything.

What to Do If They Get Under the Covers

Although gardeners strive for perfection, in gardening rarely does anything work out perfectly. If you grow a lot of plants under cover, sooner or later you'll deal with insect pests. Sometimes, under row covers, where plants are protected from the elements, the insect pests are also protected. They stay warm and are out of the wind. Birds and predatory insects that might eat them can't get at them, and so the pests can suddenly overwhelm you. A call to action is necessary! With a number of different approaches to pest control available, you just choose one that's right for you.

You may want to grow everything in your garden organically, with no chemical fertilizers or chemical pesticides. Or you may choose to take a different approach and use chemical pesticides on your ornamental plants, but not your food plants. I advise you to try the organic approach before resorting to over-the-counter chemical garden sprays.

Integrated Pest Management

The buzzword in pest control for the last decade or so has been IPM or *integrated pest management*. It's all about using natural means and taking precautions to prevent pests from even thinking of visiting your garden. An IPM solution might be as simple as knocking aphids off a rose bush with a good spray from your garden hose.

def•i•ni•tion

Integrated pest management means both preventing and controlling pests with organic methods. If pests persist, however, gardeners may then look to chemical products to eradicate a problem.

Always pay attention to cultural problems—conditions within your growing environment—that might have triggered an explosion of insect pests. Knowing the cause can help you avoid a repeat of the problem in the future. And of course, knowing the cause will also help you solve the problem.

A variety of cultural problems might have weakened plants and left them susceptible to pests. Do they need more nitrogen, more phosphorus, more potassium? Could they be lacking in some important micronutrient? Could the pH of the soil be out of balance? Are the plants getting enough moisture or too much moisture? Does the soil drain fast enough? Is there enough air in the root zone? You need to address these questions to identify the source of the problem and decide on a course of action. Remember, plants that are growing in optimal conditions suffer less from insect pests in the first place. If you can identify a cultural problem, you'll have to address both that problem and the pest problem.

When your plants are pest-free again, you can abandon the chemicals and switch back to organic prevention approaches. Understand that the basic concept behind IPM is not insect pest eradication, nor is it total control. Rather, it's *management*. The goal of IPM is not to have zero insect pests; that would be unrealistic. Instead, the goal of IPM is to keep the insect pest levels low enough that they don't cause undue harm to your plants. There are billions of insect pests, and it's simply impossible to keep them out of our gardens, whether by organic or chemical means. So the best plan is to keep our plants healthy so they can withstand whatever flies or crawls past.

Safety First

When working with chemicals or even organic products, read labels carefully and follow the instructions. Remember that what is safe today, may not be safe tomorrow. Wear disposable or washable gloves and a mask during application. Immediately afterward, take the time to wash well. Remember that powders or sprays may have landed on your shoes, your legs or your pants legs, and perhaps your forearms or sleeves.

Homemade Insect Control

If something is dirty, you wash it. Right? Well, if something has bugs on it, you can "wash" that, too. Insecticidal soap is a substance that washes away insect pests. And those that manage to hang on are probably not going to be happy eating leaves that taste like soap, so they'll pose less of a threat to your plant. Okay, a few of those bugs might die or drown in the process, but for the most part, you really are just washing the pests away and discouraging them from coming back.

Here's a simple, safe, homemade insecticidal soap recipe.

To make a gallon:

> 2 TB. dish soap
>
> 1 TB. vegetable oil
>
> 1 gallon warm water

To make a quart:

> $^{1}/_{2}$ TB. dish soap
>
> 1 tsp. vegetable oil
>
> 1 quart warm water

Put the mixture in a clean spray bottle, and shake well to mix the oil and water. You'll have to experiment with this spray to see what works best for you, but you can use this basic spray to rid almost any kind of plant of insects. You'll want to spray both the tops and the bottoms of the leaves. For a persistent infestation, sometimes you may need to increase the amount of soap in the mixture. Another way to make the spray slightly more potent is to add a bit of Tabasco sauce to the basic mix.

Commercial insecticidal soaps are also available at garden centers and are generally as effective as the homemade version. As always, read the label carefully if you choose to go the store-bought route.

Now here's another homemade method: cooking spray. Really? I can use cooking spray as an insecticide? Yes, indeed you can! Go to the dollar store, and buy cans of the cheapest aerosol cooking spray you can find. Sprayed directly on the leaves of plants, cooking spray kills insects by smothering them. But wait—a word of caution: cooking spray may also kill the leaves, so test a leaf before spraying an entire plant. Too much oil on the leaves of certain plants, such as impatiens and ferns, can cause problems. However, the woody stems of most plants are not as sensitive. For very hard-to-kill insect pests, such as scale or mealy bug on the woody stems of plants, a few good blasts of cooking spray will save the day.

Sometimes the best way to kill insect pests isn't with a wet spray, but with a dry powder. Fine powder of almost any kind can immobilize insects, which have six legs, and spiders and spider mites, which have eight legs. The powder gets stuck between the pests' legs and renders them unable to move. Numerous kinds of powders have long been used as insecticides. Can you believe powdered milk works as an insecticide? That's right. Simply shake the powder on plant leaves and wait. Another choice is talcum powder, which can have mixed results. Any powdered products can cause irritation if inhaled, so wear a facemask over your nose and mouth when sprinkling or spreading any fine powder.

Finally, here's one more idea from the kitchen to help you solve a problem. If slugs or snails are eating certain plants, rinse and crush some eggshells and sprinkle them under and around the plants. Slugs and snails don't like crossing the sharp shards of eggshells, and of course, the shells also add some calcium to your soil. That's just an extra bonus for your plants.

Insect "Traps"

Gardeners, nursery folk, and truck farmers have used trap plants effectively for centuries, and you can, too. The basic idea is that certain plants are attractive to insect pests, and you can use these plants to attract or "trap" the pests. For example, watermelon and cantaloupe growers almost always battle spotted beetles known as cucumber beetles who eat the flowers of the plants and also eat small holes in the new, tiny melons, resulting in ugly, unusable melons at the end of the season. Experienced melon growers know that as much as those beetles love eating melon plants, they'd rather munch on squash plants. So for every 50 melon plants, growers plant one squash, usually an easy-to-grow zucchini. When the grower checks for insects, rather than looking at every single melon plant, he just checks the zucchini plants. If he sees cucumber beetles eating the squash, then he sprays the squash but not the melons.

Under protective cover, two insect pests, in particular, cause a host of problems: aphids and whiteflies. Both of these pests are strongly attracted to the color purple and especially to eggplants. If eggplants are growing in a row of vegetables or flowers, the pests will attack them before they attack the other plants, so planting a few eggplants under your row covers can be a great way to control pests. In this case, the eggplant is a trap plant, luring pests away from other plants. Every few days, check your trap plant for insect pests. When or if you find a good number of aphids or whiteflies, then spray only those plants with a generous dose of your homemade insecticidal soap or with a commercial product. Whatever you choose, spray the eggplant trap until the spray drips off the leaves, and this will rid the plant of aphids and whiteflies.

Several hours later, take a garden hose and wash all the spray off the trap plants, which will leave them attractive again to any new aphids or whiteflies that happen by. If you make good use of trap plants, you won't ever have to spray the main crop. Trap plants are a great, low-tech, highly effective idea for pest control.

Insect Predators

An old joke asks, how do you get rid of a bully? And the answer is: find a bigger bully. We wouldn't recommend this to your children, but we *do* recommend it as a solution for your garden pests. Always remember that all insects are not bad. Many of them are beneficial, and some of them eat the "bad" bugs that are chewing on your garden plants. So sign up some of these "bigger bullies" to keep your covered gardens pest-free.

Lady beetles are picturesque and are also one of those beneficial bugs that are good for your garden. If released in an enclosed structure, the lady beetles have no choice but to stick around and nibble on the local herds of aphids, scale, and mites. Releasing ladybugs is usually quite effective.

Green lacewings are another beneficial insect you can buy and release under your garden covers. Green lacewings are excellent killers of numerous insect pests including aphids and mites. Be sure to plant their preferred nectar plants such as carrot flowers, tansy, or red cosmos to encourage them to stay in your garden.

Green Thumb _____

Lady beetles—commonly called ladybugs—are the cute little bugs that are red with black polka dots. Both the adult beetles and the less familiar larvae feed on aphids and other insects.

Asian lady beetles, by contrast, are multi-colored. The colors can run all shades of orange, yellow, and even black. They may or may not have polka dots. These are the creatures that congregate in your windows and on the sides of your home. They are of no known benefit to gardeners.

Beneficial nematodes are available from online sources of beneficial insects, and they do work. The almost microscopic nematodes come in a powder that you sprinkle on the ground around the plants you want them to protect. These nematodes attack and eat the pestiferous kinds of nematodes that prey on the roots of your plants.

You can also buy tiny predatory wasps, which attack a number of insect pests such as the hornworm moth or the gypsy moth. You might not see immediate results, but have patience. I haven't had much luck with them so far, but do feel free to give them a try; they're safe enough.

And finally, you can purchase praying mantis egg cases. Hatch these cases in a cold frame or under your row cover so these beneficial insects will stick around. When you purchase praying mantis egg cases, ask the mail order company if they will send you a larger container that the mantis can hatch in. All you do is wash the container, which should be vented, let it dry, and set the egg case in it. Within three to six weeks, the eggs should hatch. Release them immediately. Even though they are small, it is important to remember that these praying mantis are solitary eaters and will take care of themselves. Besides being effective pest killers, it's fun to see the adult praying mantis at work in your garden. Praying mantis eat grasshoppers, wasps, houseflies, moths, spiders, small birds, and reptiles.

Garden Guide _____

It's never a good idea to use any kind of pesticide or fungicide spray, organic or otherwise, in midday when the sun is shining and the weather is hot. Spraying in the heat of the day will damage the leaves of many plants. Sprays are most likely to damage young tender plants and the newest leaves and buds on plants under these conditions. So spray in the early morning or late in the afternoon.

Store-Bought Insect Control

If your kitchen cupboards are bare or if the homemade remedies aren't doing the trick, numerous products at the local nursery or garden center may solve your problems. Before you go, take a close look at the particular insect you're trying to get rid of. Being able to tell what plant is being attached and what the bug looks like will help the store personnel help you decide which of the many products available is the right product for you.

Diatomaceous earth is fairly inexpensive, readily available at garden centers, and works as an effective insect pest-control measure. It is a naturally occurring, chalk-like rock that crumbles easily into a powder and is formed from the fossilized remains of diatoms, a type of hard-shelled algae. Sprinkle it on soil in pots, flats, or in garden rows to control those tiny, irritating little fungus gnats. And more generally, it is effective against aphids, thrips, mites, slugs, snails—even ticks and fleas. Think of the diatomaceous earth as a barrier. The tiny "grains" of powder have sharp edges. Whether the pests try to crawl through the powder or ingest the powder … well, let's just say they won't be happy.

On a preventive level, feed diatomaceous earth to farm animals in small amounts to serve as a wormer and also to kill fly eggs in their manure. If you've added fresh manure to compost heaps, sprinkle it on the tops of heaps to control flies. If you sprinkle this powder, do use a facemask as it can irritate the throat and lungs.

Pyrethrum daisy has a natural insecticide in the flowers called pyrethrum. Years ago you could buy sacks of these ground up, powdered flowers, which was used as an extremely effective pesticide that killed many species of insect pests. Now you can buy liquid pyrethrum at many nurseries, and it does make an effective insect killer when added to any of the basic soap-oil type sprays. Most pyrethrum comes in a con-centrated form so dilution is necessary. Always read and follow the label instructions. When it comes to chemicals, a little is good, but too much can be dangerous to you, your plants, and the environment. Pyrethrum is especially effective at killing flying insects, such as mosquitoes and flies. As insecticides go, pyrethrum is one of the safer insecticides, but it will kill beneficial insects, such as honeybees, as well as pests.

Another product—neem oil—is also plant-based and comes from the neem tree that grows in India. A relatively safe organic insecticide, it is often quite effective although fairly pricey.

The list of chemical inorganic insecticides is huge and still growing. And as with some of the organic products, many of these are indiscriminate—they kill both harmful and beneficial insects.

One last category of commercially available insect controls is systemic insecticides, which are applied to the leaves of plants or watered into the roots. The plant absorbs the ingredients, which make them poisonous to insect pests. Some forms of this product are combined with both fertilizer and fungicide—a substance that kills fungus diseases. These products are expensive, but they work well. However, limit their use to garden space; they're too strong to be safe for container plants.

With so many products and types of products, we could go on and on, but suffice it to say that if you have a bug eating a plant, you can find *something* to kill it at the garden center. Remember, though, that prevention is the best medicine. And perhaps the next best medicine is your garden hose. Just think how satisfying it'll be to douse that bush and scatter those bugs!

Disease Control

Some garden plants have as many problems with different kinds of fungus diseases as they do from insect pests. Black spot, mildew, and rust are all fungus diseases. To combat fungus with a home remedy, add 1 to 2 tablespoons of baking soda to the one-gallon insecticidal soap recipe; the baking soda acts as a fungicide. Crazy as it sounds, many gardeners have had good luck spraying plants with a mixture of water and skim milk. In particular, skim milk or any nonfat milk can control powdery mildew on cucumber and zucchini plants. Mix one part milk with nine parts water, shake well, and spray it on the cucumber or squash plants. Best done as a preventive measure, it's cheap, safe, and quite effective.

Growing plants under cover has some terrific advantages because the covers allow you to take control and provide the best environment you possibly can for your plants. That safe, enclosed environment is a benefit, but that same safe, enclosed environment can play host to pests or diseases that also benefit from the warmth and moisture. But now, you're better prepared to enjoy the good and deal with the bad.

The Least You Need to Know

- ◆ Water and fertilization needs are different when gardening under cover.
- ◆ The easiest way to control weeds is to suppress them.
- ◆ Healthy plants can withstand most pest or disease problems.
- ◆ Companion planting and beneficial insects are two natural ways to control insect pests in your garden.

Part 4

Gardening Under Cover: Winter

Gardening in the *winter?* Yes, that's right. We didn't use the words "year-round gardening" in our title for nothing. And we don't mean just cutting down last year's plants. We mean you can actually grow—and harvest—things in winter.

You can grow them in a root cellar; you can grow them under lights in a spare corner of your house; or you can grow them outdoors under cover. We show you how to use techniques you've already learned (in Parts 2 and 3) to grow and maintain plants throughout the winter.

Start imagining those fresh salad greens—from your garden to your plate in *December.* Or *January!* Keep reading, and you'll soon know how to make that happen.

Chapter 10

Bringing the Outside In

In This Chapter

- ◆ Characteristics of effective root cellars
- ◆ Create a root cellar
- ◆ Growing produce and flowers in a root cellar

Traditionally, root cellars are places where people store fruits and vegetables through the winter, so we'll start on that traditional plane and find out what a root cellar is and what makes a good one. And you can have one, too, no matter where you live—even if it you use a closet. Then we'll take a slightly nontraditional route and talk about actually growing things in your root cellar. And no, we don't mean icky things that grow in dark, moist places; we mean nice things such as fresh greens and sprouts. Good things *do* come out of cool, dark, moist places. Read on!

The Virtues of a Root Cellar

A *root cellar* can be beneficial in a number of ways because it makes it possible for you to eat fresh food when the only other way to have fresh produce is to go buy it at a store. Or you may buy fresh food in season and

def•i•ni•tion

A **root cellar** is a cool, dark, moist place in which to store produce or to start or grow certain plants.

store it there. Whether the fresh food in your root cellar is from your garden or purchased in season, the root cellar almost surely saves you money.

A root cellar is also environmentally friendly as it requires no energy to keep it working other than a light bulb so you can see what you're grabbing a handful of for dinner.

Root Cellar Essentials

An effective root cellar functions well and "works" properly when it has certain essential elements: ventilation, proper temperature, proper humidity, darkness, drainage, and accessibility. Let's take a look at each of these elements so you can understand their purpose when you create your own root cellar.

Ventilation

A primary need for a root cellar is adequate airflow and ventilation, as good air circulation helps prevent mold from growing on your food. Fresh air must be able to move freely around the produce, so when you set up shelves in your cellar, leave space between the shelves and the walls for air to circulate. Proper ventilation also improves the taste of your produce by allowing vegetable odors and ethylene gas to escape. If allowed to build up, ethylene gas, which is given off by stored fruits and vegetables, may cause foods to taste funny and can cause premature sprouting.

Garden Guide

To comply with building codes that exist in most areas, a root cellar must have a fresh air vent to prevent the unhealthful buildup of gasses from apples, onions, and ripening vegetables.

Remember that hot air rises and cool air sinks, so as you set up your ventilation system, put one vent near the top of the cellar to allow warm air to escape. Then put a second vent near the bottom to let the coolest air enter. Put the warm-air vent on the opposite side from the cool-air inlet as this opposition of vents promotes air circulation. And open your ventilation system at night to allow cool air into your root cellar.

Adequate ventilation is the key to having a successful root cellar operation. If the ventilation is properly set up, you can use it to control both the temperature and the humidity level.

Temperature

Keeping your root cellar at the proper temperature is just as important as providing ventilation. If your temperature is too low or too high, your produce will be affected. Produce stored under too-cool conditions will show signs of cold damage, and produce stored under too-warm temperatures will not keep as long as it would under the correct conditions.

Once you get your root cellar to the right temperature for the specific produce you're storing (see Chapter 19), you'll need to keep it there. And this is why ventilation is so important. Mount a good thermometer in your cellar; if possible get one that allows for remote reading so you don't need to open your cellar and let hot air in just to check the temperature. Remember that you can control temperatures in small areas by putting things that prefer cooler temperatures near the floor and things that prefer warmer temperatures near the top. The same with humidity. There is more humidity near the bottom of a root cellar than near the top of it.

Root cellars built indoors or in a basement may need insulation to hold the cool air in and keep the warm air out. (We'll discuss how to create a root cellar later in this chapter.)

Humidity

Humidity—the level of moisture in the air—is another critical factor in a root cellar. Produce loses water during storage, and as odd as it sounds, produce "breathes," even after harvest. If your storage area is very dry (i.e., has low humidity), the produce will shrivel. To prevent shriveling, the humidity level needs to be approximately 60 to 80 percent. You can provide this humidity by occasionally sprinkling water on the floor. To measure this humidity, you might install a humidistat—a device much like a thermometer that measures the humidity level in the air and displays it as a percent.

Darkness

Keep your root cellar dark. Leaving lights on, other than when you're in there looking for something, causes produce to deteriorate. Light can also cause some produce, such as potatoes, to begin sprouting.

Drainage

Good drainage is also essential. Though you do want the inside of the root cellar to have high humidity, you don't want standing water.

Too much water can cause a variety of problems ranging from a slippery floor to waterlogged walls that could cave in. Produce should not come into contact with water in the root cellar. Too much moisture can cause produce to deteriorate faster.

Garden Guide

Dirt in the root cellar is a necessity because it helps keep the humidity level up. You can keep the dirt floor tidy by covering it with landscape fabric or several inches of gravel. Or set stepping-stones down the middle of the floor for firm footing.

When choosing an area to make a root cellar, look for a place that has good natural drainage. If you are building a new structure outside in the ground, check to see whether the area has good drainage by digging a hole in the ground about two feet deep. Fill the hole with water and watch it. The water should disappear within 10 minutes. If it does, you have good drainage. Avoid building a root cellar where water runoff from buildings or other structures may occur.

Accessibility

And the last essential element is accessibility. After all, what good is it to have stored produce if you can't get to it? Make your root cellar easy to get to; the easier it is to access, the more you'll use it. For example, if you live in an area with heavy snowfall, an indoor root cellar may be a better choice than one outside. Who wants to shovel a path across the yard to get a few potatoes?

And here's another angle to the issue of accessibility. In addition to having a convenient location, your root cellar should be easy to use when you're in it. That means having adequate lighting so you can see what you're doing or what you're looking for. It should also be easy to clean, with enough room for you and your cleaning supplies to move around. And you should be able to reach the shelves easily to wipe them down. Finally, your cellar should be easy to get in and out of, even if you're loaded with a container of produce. It's usually best if doors open outward. All these convenience factors lend themselves to your having a happy root cellar experience.

Create a Root Cellar

Anyone can create a root cellar. Where you live is not important. What is important is that the root cellar you create remains dark, cool, and humid.

In the Basement

Creating a root cellar in the basement may be the best choice. Why? Because most basements are naturally dark and cool—two essential conditions for a root cellar. And many basements are humid—another essential element. Simply choose a corner in your basement away from the furnace and furnace ducts; wall it in; add a door, ventilation, and a drain, if necessary; and your new root cellar is ready to go.

If your basement is warmer than 50°F as a rule, you may need to insulate your walled-in corner to keep the warm air out. If your basement floor is dirt, that's great for your root cellar. Just add gravel or stepping-stones to give you good footing. If the floor is concrete, you may need to add water from time to time to keep the humidity at that desirable 60 to 80 percent range. You can add water by sprinkling it on the floor or, if necessary, by adding a humidifier to the root cellar. Keep an eye on the humidity gauge in the root cellar to know how often you need to do this. Add a little water at first, and increase as necessary. The amount of water needed will depend on the size of your root cellar and how dry it actually is.

If your basement ceiling is too low for you to stand upright, you might consider digging below the current floor level. You can do this by hand, but you need to know what you're doing. Digging in the wrong place could cause structural damage to your home's foundation.

If you position your new root cellar near an existing window, you'll have a relatively easy way to create the ventilation you need. You must block off the window (because your root cellar must be dark), but creating a vent through a window is easier than cutting a hole through the foundation or wall. If your root cellar is not near a window, you *will* have to put in a vent to the outside. You cannot just vent the root cellar into the basement space. That set-up would not create adequate air exchange, nor would it satisfy building codes with regard to venting gas buildup.

> **Safety First**
>
> Before digging in the ground, even if the area is in your basement or crawl space, call your local utility company, and tell them what you're doing. The company will send someone out to check for buried cables, wires, and pipes. This service is usually free and can be a lifesaver.

In the Garage

Creating a root cellar in your garage is yet another option. As with a basement set-up, you'd section off a corner; wall off a room the size you want; and add insulation, ventilation, and a door. Swing the door out to maximize the space inside the room.

The insulation will not only keep heat out but will also keep the produce from freezing in the winter, which is especially important if your garage is detached. Ventilation is critical in a garage root cellar because the room is susceptible to overheating during warmer months, even if you've insulated it. Installing a vent near the ceiling or roof to let out the rising warm air is vital to keeping that root cellar at the proper temperature.

Because most garages have cement floors, you'd have no natural source of humidity like you would if the floor were dirt, so you'll have to monitor the humidity level. When you choose that thermometer with a remote sensor, you may want to get one that has a humidistat built in as well.

Outdoors

If you build an outdoor root cellar, think about accessibility. Is it close enough to your house to easily get to in bad weather? How close is it to your garden?

Trash cans, barrels, covered metal cans, Styrofoam coolers, or almost any type of covered container will work as a root cellar if it's buried in the ground. Bury the container at a 45° angle. Cover it with soil on three of the four sides, but leave the side with the lid exposed. Generally, the container should be at least 2 feet deep. If you live in a very cold, northern climate, 3 feet would be better.

Green Thumb

Though some early civilizations, such as the Chinese and Egyptians, mastered preserving food and drying food, respectively, the English were the ones who apparently developed, during the seventeenth century, the process of using underground spaces to prolong the freshness of fruits and vegetables. Colonists brought root cellar knowledge with them. To see some of their handiwork, visit Elliston, Trinity Bay, in Newfoundland, Canada. Elliston, the Root Cellar Capital of the World, boasts 135 documented root cellars, some of them dating back 200 years. For a virtual visit, go to www.rootcellars.com.

A container such as a Styrofoam cooler surrounded with straw bales can serve as an inexpensive yet effective root cellar.

(Donna Chiarelli Studio)

Fill the container with your produce. For ease of access, alternate what you're storing so that *all* your apples aren't on the bottom, for example. Pack straw, hay, leaves, newspaper, or other material around the produce to insulate and cushion it. Fill the last 5 inches of the container with insulating material. Then put the lid on. Roll a large rock against the lid to keep it secure. To get produce out, roll the rock to the side, take the lid off, remove the insulation, choose your produce, and then seal it back up.

If you are really adventurous, you may want an underground root cellar. These are easier to build and easier to get into if dug into the side of a hill. Most underground root cellars are six feet deep because the temperature there remains more constant than it does closer to the surface. Underground root cellars will need a set of steps leading down into them. You could build them out of wood or out of cement. Cement steps would last longer because they would not decay like wooden steps, nor would they get as slippery as wet wood. Making a nice set of cement steps may require the help of a professional.

Underground root cellars must be well built because the soil can freeze from the humidity and they can collapse. Large beams or concrete blocks are often used to brace the walls of underground root cellars. Unless you have experience building structures, you might let a professional builder work on this type of root cellar.

Gardening in a Root Cellar

Using your root cellar as a place to grow things is not the same as gardening outside or even under cover. Because root cellars are dark, cool, and moist, most plants will rot rather than grow. However, a few plants will thrive in such an environment.

Mushrooms are a prime example. You can germinate mushrooms in a root cellar rather successfully, but once they begin to grow, they need some light. Mushrooms don't require as much light as other plants do, but they will not grow or thrive in total darkness. Mushroom kits are available online. Do not dig mushrooms out of your yard or woods. Purchase a kit that has the proper growing medium in it. There are many varieties of mushrooms available. Choose one you will enjoy eating.

Sprouts are another excellent example of plants that thrive in root cellar conditions. Sprout seeds, such as mung bean sprouts, will grow in total darkness.

Sprouting sprouts is easy; simply use a Mason jar and the "ring" part of a canning jar lid. Cut a piece of nylon window screening or cheesecloth to fit into the lid ring. Put 1 or 2 tablespoons of seeds in the jar, fill the jar half full of water, and screw on the lid-and-screen firmly. Shake the jar, and then pour off the water. Set the jar in a dark place, such as your root cellar, and repeat the rinsing daily until the seeds sprout. Use the sprouts in salads, sandwiches, stir-fry recipes, and so on.

A few crops lend themselves to being started in a root cellar. However, they need to be moved out into the light as soon as growth starts.

Asparagus is one such crop. Dig the roots in the fall, plant them in a container, and put the container in a garage or other location where they'll freeze. After a few freezes, move the container into the root cellar. When you're ready to sprout your asparagus, simply move the container to a warmer area. Light is not essential for this crop, but you'll get a better harvest if you provide light. A few weeks after moving the container into a warm spot, you'll have asparagus spears to eat. You can try growing Belgian endive, dandelion, rhubarb, parsnips, and beets in the same manner.

Microgreens, salad greens you harvest just after they sprout, are a fairly recent addition to the American menu. All you need to keep microgreens growing is a standard plastic flat of potting soil. Sprinkle the seeds thickly over the moist growing medium, cover with a damp paper towel, and leave them in the dark to sprout. When the seeds germinate, remove the towel, and set the flat in a sunny place so the sprouts will green up. Trim the sprouts off at soil level with scissors, and add them to salads and sandwiches or toss them into omelets or soups as a yummy garnish.

Suspending Growth

Many plants and bulbs will not grow until the temperature is right. Root cellars, with their cold environment, can help suspend growth, or keep plants in their dormant stage. One reason to keep a plant dormant is to keep it alive until the proper planting time. For example, if you keep some of your own potatoes to replant each year, you would not want them sprouting at the wrong time of the year. You would want to keep them dormant until the proper planting time in the spring.

When using a root cellar to suspend plant growth, first find out the lowest temperature the plant can survive. For example, if you put a plant that needs a minimum temperature of 50°F in a 40°F root cellar, you're likely to lose it because the temperature is too low. To find out what temperature a plant needs to remain dormant, you can do an online search or simply keep an eye on the plants. If you see active growth, you know the temperature is too high. Also keep an eye on the plant to make sure it does not mold or rot from the root cellar's relatively high humidity level.

Garden Guide

Extend your harvest late in the season by pulling up tomato plants and other above-ground plants—roots, soil, and all—and setting them in the root cellar. The vegetables and fruits will continue to ripen. Of course, these warm-season plants won't last through the winter, but they'll keep well for a couple months after harvest.

Overwintering Plants

You can overwinter woody, tender plants, such as bougainvillea, jasmine, and mandevilla, in a moderately warm root cellar, one that has a temperature range of 50 to 70°F and a humidity level between 50 and 60 percent. This will also work for begonia tubers; however, be sure to cut all the stems and foliage off.

Cut these plants back to a few main, sturdy stems. Keep an eye on them for mold or rot, and water them sparingly, maybe once a month at the most and then only if the soil feels dry several inches down. In the spring when you see new growth emerging, move the plants into a sunny area.

Green Thumb

A root cellar makes an excellent wine cellar as well as a place to store home-canned goods, preserves, pickles, and even eggs.

Bulbs for Forcing

Spring-flowering bulbs, such as daffodils, tulips, and hyacinths, lend themselves to forcing, or causing them to flower out of season. These bulbs need a chilling period in order to flower, and a root cellar could provide the cool, dark conditions these bulbs need.

> ### Green Thumb
>
> Forced bulbs make great wintertime gifts. Put them in a pretty pot, and let your root cellar do the work. When it's time to bring the potted bulbs into the light, you deliver to the lucky recipient. Who isn't delighted to see daffodils or tulips blooming well before spring arrives?

To "force" flowering bulbs to bloom in the winter, plant the bulbs in pots and set them in a root cellar in the fall. In the dark, cool environment, the bulbs grow roots. Then when you see green shoots start to come up—perhaps in January or February—move the bulbs to the light. Within a few weeks you'll have blooms.

When preparing containers for the root cellar, choose a good potting mix that drains well and does not hold moisture. Don't use a heavy potting mix that holds water, as this would encourage your bulbs to rot.

Don't set the containers on the floor. Instead, put them on a shelf. Don't overwater the containers; keep the soil just moist enough so the bulbs don't dry out. Learning the right amount of moisture to have in the soil may take a bit of time. You want it dry enough that it feels like it needs water but not so dry that is has no moisture. You'll have plenty of time to water once the bulbs begin to sprout.

Getting your potting mixture right is half the battle. Learning how to water and when to move plants out of the cellar into the light is the other half of the battle.

The Least You Need to Know

◆ A root cellar is a cool, dark, moist place to store produce or to start or grow certain plants.

◆ Ventilation, temperature, humidity, darkness, drainage, and accessibility are the most important elements of a successful root cellar.

◆ You can locate a root cellar inside your home or outside.

◆ A few crops, such as mushrooms and sprouts, thrive in the dark environment of a root cellar.

◆ Microgreens and asparagus are crops gardeners can start in a root cellar and then bring to the light when they sprout.

Chapter 11

Gardening Indoors Under Lights

In This Chapter

- ◆ Grow lights for gardening indoors
- ◆ How long to leave grow lights on
- ◆ Watering and fertilizing requirements for gardening under lights

Gardening indoors under lights is a great way to keep plants healthy and even flowering all winter long, as well as a way to bring winter-blooming plants into flower. And think of having fresh herbs to harvest and toss into your favorite soup or stew! All this is possible, right in your own home. In this chapter, we'll tell you how to set up a space for some plants and a grow light so you can become an indoor winter gardener. You'll learn a little bit about the light spectrum and what kind of light your plants need. And we'll also answer questions you might have about how long to leave your grow lights on.

Natural sunlight is best for your plants, but we all know sunlight is sometimes hard to come by on long winter days. So using grow lights is the next best thing. And for you garden addicts, tending to your growing plants might be just the thing to beat those winter blues.

Growing Under Lights

Gardening with grow lights lets you grow healthy plants and seedlings without a greenhouse. You can choose to put plants in any area of your home, in the basement, an unused bedroom, or right in the living room, as long as you have space for the light and adequate heating.

What does it take? You need a horizontal surface on which you can set some plants, a power source so you can plug in your grow light, and some basic hardware and perhaps a ladder so you can put a hook in the ceiling from which to suspend your grow light. Oh, and you'll need some potted plants. And you can do this anywhere in your house. If there's a window nearby for some natural sunlight, that's great. Your plants *love* light. But if not, that's okay, too; the grow light can work by itself.

As you establish your setup, keep in mind that you want your light very close to the tops of your plants. If the light is far away, the plants will reach up and get leggy and weak. Ideally, have just a few inches between the tops of your plants and your lights. I know—you have different sizes of plants, so how do you handle that? One way is to suspend the light at an angle to accommodate the tall plants on one end and the short ones on the other. Another way is to set the shorter plants up on overturned plastic containers or coffee cans that you've snatched out of the trash or recycling bin.

Artificial Lighting Options

To understand artificial light, we first need to understand sunlight. Sunlight contains all the colors in the light spectrum; think of the rainbow—remember Roy G Biv? That acronym stands for the colors of the spectrum: red, orange, yellow, green, blue, indigo, and violet. Light in the blue part of the spectrum is good for plant growth and photosynthesis, and light in the red part fosters blooming. But as sunlight has it all, your plants get what they want and need regardless of whether they're busy putting out leaves or blossoming.

Conventional incandescent light bulbs—the ones we all used until the new energy-efficient fluorescent bulbs became popular—provide light mostly from the red end of the spectrum and tend to produce a fair amount of heat. For these reasons, incandescent bulbs are not suitable for use as grow lights, but we have several other options.

There is a wide variety of grow lights on the market, ranging from LED lights to high-intensity lights to plain old fluorescent bulbs. You can invest quite a bit in whatever style of professional grow light you want, but you don't really need to. A regular 4-foot fluorescent light fixture will keep your plants healthy.

If you do choose those 4-foot fluorescent lights, use a two-tube fixture fitted with one cool white fluorescent tube (emits mostly blue-spectrum light) and one warm white one (emits mostly red-spectrum light). Using the two bulbs gives the full light spectrum to your plants. In turn, your plants will flower, fruit, and grow better. Both types of bulbs stay cool, so it's okay if the growing tips of the plants are very close to them.

Garden Guide

When choosing a light to use as a grow light, look at the box to see what colors the light projects. Sometimes you'll find a picture showing a range of colors.

Then there is a metal halide bulb, which is blue-orientated in the spectrum. It's the best type of light to use as a primary light source if you have little or no natural sunlight available. Metal halide bulbs promote strong plant growth. Note, however, that metal halide bulbs require special fixtures and are more expensive than fluorescent bulbs, but they do get high marks for energy efficiency.

A high-pressure sodium (HPS) bulb fine-tunes your lighting system to provide a broad spectrum of light that promotes vigorous plant growth. But like the metal halide bulb, HPS bulbs require special fixtures.

Both metal halide bulbs and high-pressure sodium bulbs come in many different sizes, from small to very large, and in either hot or cool varieties. Because your setup is inside your house, you'll want the cool variety. If you were using lights in an outdoor greenhouse, you might, on occasion, want the hot variety to keep young seedlings or tender exotics warm.

Reptile lights are designed to be used in cages for lizards and snakes that require high light levels and a broad spectrum of light. Because these lights emit a broad spectrum, they're good for your plants, too. Combine them with fluorescent lights or with the more advanced metal halide or high-pressure sodium light bulbs. Your plants will benefit from the broadest possible range of light coming from the different bulbs.

Garden Guide

When growing plants indoors, getting enough light to them is the key. Maximize the light you have—whether sunlight or artificial—by placing a reflective surface, such as aluminum foil or a bright white piece of paper or cardboard, in your setup. The ideal placement depends on where the light source is. If it's above the plants, then put the reflective material underneath them. If the light is shining from one side of the plants, put the aluminum foil behind them.

You can combine any and all of these types of bulbs with some extra natural light, coming in from a window or skylight. Different lights, including natural sunlight, cause your plants to respond differently. The light a plant needs depends upon what type of plant it is and what stage of growth it's in. For example, if you're growing a plant for its foliage alone, a cool bulb that emits light from the blue end of the spectrum will work just fine. If you're trying to get a plant to flower, choose a bulb that emits light from the red or orange end of the spectrum.

Timing Grow Lights

Don't leave your grow lights on 24 hours a day. Remember, all plants, even seedlings, need a dark period. Plants generally require more light to fruit or flower than in a dormant state. The best way to know what your particular plants require is to research them one by one using their botanical or Latin names.

Some growers of daylight-sensitive plants keep the lights on for most of the day, initially. Plants grown with 14 to 20 hours of light a day grow very fast, but they generally don't flower. When you want your plants to flower, cut back the number of hours of light to less than 12 per day.

Garden Guide

If there is a rule of thumb as to how long to leave the lights on, the magic number seems to be 12. At the equator, the days are all 12 hours long, and so are the nights, all year-round. In general, most plants we grow in the Northern Hemisphere will grow faster when they get more than 12 hours of light. When they get less than 12, growth slows down and the plant may initiate flowering.

Poinsettia and chrysanthemum growers have long known that if they grow their plants with more than 12 hours of light a day, the plants grow robustly but do not flower. So these growers provide long hours of light until the plants are the desired size; then they cut back to just under 12 hours of light to initiate flowering.

Whatever decision you make about the timing of your lights, it's best to do the same thing each day, and inexpensive appliance timers are perfect for this job. You designate a turn-on time and a turn-off time, plug the light into the timer, plug the timer into the outlet, and that's one thing you can cross off your daily to-do list.

Caring for Plants Under Lights

Plants grown under lights have different watering and fertilization requirements than plants grown outdoors. Your pot-grown plants cannot send roots out in search of nutrients or water the way plants in the ground can, so it's up to *you.*

In the winter, the rule of thumb for watering plants is about once a week. Their water needs depend on the amount of heat they're exposed to and the amount of light they're receiving as well as whether they're in a dormant stage or a growth stage. Many plants don't grow as rapidly in the winter, so require less water. Plants grown under lights, however, may not realize it is winter. Keep an eye on your plants as well as on the growing medium.

Green Thumb

A wide variety of tropical flowering plants benefit from being raised under grow lights. Orchids, carnivorous plants, and African violets are just a few of the choices you have, but you can encourage almost any plant to flower indoors if you give it enough light.

Don't mindlessly water once a week. If your house is a bit on the cool side, even with grow lights, you may not need to water as often. Be aware, however, that grow lights can put out some heat, so it may be warmer under your lights than in your house, which can cause your soil to dry out faster. Keep an eye on your plants; they'll tell you what they need.

When it comes to fertilizer, remember that when your plants are actively growing, they want and need lots of nutrients. But if they're not growing that actively, their nutrient requirements aren't as great.

You have various ways to fertilize potted plants. One option is to use a timed-release fertilizer. Place these granules in the pot, according to package instructions, and they slowly release nutrients. A better option is to use a combination of a three-month timed-release granular fertilizer as well as a liquid fertilizer so the plant has access to the nutrients necessary for proper growth as it needs them. Using one type of fertilizer by itself does not produce as good a result as using the combination of fertilizers. Plants absorb nutrients both through their leaves and through their roots, so using a liquid ensures maximum uptake of the fertilizer's nutrients. Mix a half-strength solution, and use it each time, or perhaps every other time, you water your plants.

The Least You Need to Know

- There are many kinds of grow lights available; however, basic fluorescent light bulbs yield satisfactory results.

- Most plants do fine if they get light 12 hours a day.

- Plants under grow lights may need more water, even in the winter.

- Plants not actively growing don't need frequent or heavy fertilization.

The Outdoor Winter Garden

In This Chapter

- ◆ Beginning a garden in fall (yes, fall!)
- ◆ Cold-tolerant and short-day food plants for winter gardening
- ◆ When to plant and how to take care of it
- ◆ Controlling weeds and pests in winter

In Chapters 1 and 2, we introduced the concept of extending your harvest beyond the conventional summer season. In this chapter, we're going to stretch the boundaries all the way to winter. You'll come to think of fall—yes, *fall*—as the end of one gardening season and the beginning of another, very interesting and quite productive one. Keep reading to find out how you can sow, grow, and harvest outdoors during the coldest months of winter.

Gardening Outdoors in Winter

Each fall, many gardeners clean up their gardens and put them to rest with a sad farewell. But the relationship doesn't have to end like that. All the effort you put into preparing the best possible garden can pay off in winter—just as it does in summer—with harvests of fresh, nutritious salad greens, herbs, and vegetables. The key to winter gardening success is choosing cold-tolerant varieties, sowing seeds at the optimum time, and using inexpensive covers to protect plants from sub-freezing temperatures.

Winter Conditions

The good news is that winter gardening is logical and easy when you understand and work with the growing conditions the winter season gives you. North of the equator, where most of us garden, winter day length is increasingly shorter, and the light levels diminish as the sun travels lower in the sky because of Earth's tilt. Fewer hours of daylight and lower temperatures are the result. But this doesn't mean you can't grow garden plants in winter. What it does mean is that you need to adjust your plant palette to include only those plants that can grow in these conditions. What are your choices? Cold-hardy herbs, greens, and root vegetables.

> **Green Thumb**
>
> Southern and southwestern gardeners are ahead of the winter-gardening curve because they have a long tradition of growing cool-season crops outdoors through the winter months.

Freezing Temperatures

Freezing temperatures are the greatest hindrance to plant growth in winter, and growth slows down gradually as temperatures drop from late fall to midwinter. In much of the country, this happens from late October to the middle or end of January.

When temperatures finally drop below the freezing point (32°F) and stay there, plants stop growing and go into a kind of frozen animation until temperatures rise and days begin to get longer. Garden plants resume growing sometime in late January or early February for much of the country. The key to making the most of your winter garden is to sow seeds early enough in fall so plants are nearing maturity when the dead of winter hits.

> **Green Thumb**
>
> Why can some plants continue to grow in winter's low light and cold temperatures when others can't? The answer lies in their ancestry. For example, tomatoes are a classic summer crop. They need long days and temperatures above 65°F to grow and bear fruit because they originated in equatorial South America. Cucumbers also demand heat and long days because they hail from Mediterranean regions. On the other hand, lettuce, which survives light freezes and as little as eight hours of daily sun, is a native of the upper latitudes of Northern Europe.

Match Plants to Growing Conditions

Vegetable plants suitable to grow from fall through winter are ones that are naturally cold tolerant and able to grow in low light levels. The two basic kinds of suitable winter vegetables are greens, which grow above ground, and root crops, which develop and stay underground until harvest.

Perennial and biannual herbs are also an option for winter gardeners, as both can be wintered over in mild climates. In cold climates, heap fluffy organic mulch, such as straw, pine straw, or dried leaves, around the base of herbs to help them through the winter, or grow them under protective row cover or in a cold frame or unheated greenhouse. In severe winters, double cover, using row cover or mulches inside the protective structure..

The following list gives you some popular, easy-to-grow crops for your winter garden.

Cold-hardy culinary herbs	**Cold-hardy leafy greens**
Chives	Arugula
Garlic	Brassicas
Parsley	Endive
Sage	Lettuce
Thyme	Mizuna
	Mustard
	Swiss chard

Leafy greens that can survive brief exposure to sub-freezing temperatures

Bok choy (or Pak choi)	Scallions	Spinach

Cold-temperature root vegetables

Beets	Carrots	Leeks
Onions	Potatoes	Radishes
Rutabaga	Turnips	

Winter Growing: Timing Is Everything

You can think of fall and winter as the backward gardening season or a mirror image of the spring and summer season. In spring, days grow longer and temperatures warmer. The opposite is true in fall as days get shorter and temperatures colder—until the growing season reaches a sort of "dead zone," and plant growth comes to a temporary standstill. This dead zone occurs in mid- to late December in colder parts of the country. You can hold mature plants in suspended animation and continue to harvest them during the dead zone, but don't plan to start new crops at this time.

> **Green Thumb**
>
> Bundle up before you go out to dig potatoes or peek under those row covers. The old warning that we lose "more heat through our heads than from any other body part" is a myth. In fact, any exposed flesh is subject to frostbite or worse, and any exposed flesh causes a loss of body heat. So put the hat on just as your mother told you; you'll just feel warmer.

When planning winter succession planting (see Chapter 6), take the dead zone into account and choose one of two schedules. Either sow seeds early enough (from August to early September) to harvest most of the produce before the dead zone, or sow seeds later than October for a harvest after the dead zone—usually from February through March when plants resume growing.

What happens if you sow seeds late in fall? If temperatures are consistently below freezing, your seeds may remain dormant in the ground until the end of the dead zone. Then they'll sprout, giving you an early spring harvest at about the same time you normally would harvest crops you started from seed indoors in late winter. No harm is done, but you'll have missed an opportunity for one last winter harvest.

Remember: young, vigorously growing plants can survive freezing temperatures better than ones at peak or slightly past peak. For winter harvests, time seed sowing carefully—sow early enough so that plants *almost* reach maturity before they enter the winter dead zone. In most parts of the country this means that your last outdoor sowings should be in late September or early October. If you sow spinach in early October, for example, you can harvest *cut-and-come-again* style from early November until December.

def•i•ni•tion

Cut-and-come-again is a technique for harvesting leafy vegetables and herbs that allows the plants to recover and produce new leaves. Use a pair of sharp scissors to trim off mature outer leaves, leaving the younger, inner leaves and growing point of the plant intact. Harvest in the same manner as each set of new leaves matures, and continue doing so until the plant naturally sets seeds and dies.

Plan succession crops of fast-growing salad greens, sowing seeds at one-week intervals, which will ensure that you can continue to harvest greens right up until winter's dead zone. Skip the dead zone and sow your last "winter" salad crop as days grow longer in early February for a couple more harvests before it's time for spring garden sowing.

Overwintering in the Outdoor Garden

Unlike shallow-rooted green vegetable plants, root crops can tolerate cold temperatures and lack of rain because they're underground, protected by the soil's relative warmth, and the plump roots store a supply of moisture. When we talk about overwintering root crops, we're not focusing on actually *growing* them through the winter but on digging up the produce periodically through the winter. But wait—digging in the ground in winter? Yes, it's possible, but you'll have to plan ahead so you can get to those carrots and potatoes and turnips when you want them.

Once again, it's all about timing. Read the directions on the seed packets for carrots, turnips, and other root vegetables. Count backward from the date of your first hard freeze (see Appendix D for an online source of last freeze dates) to get the sowing date for these crops.

When the roots are mature, you can begin to harvest them as needed for the table, protecting the rest and leaving them in the garden for future harvesting. Before your first hard freeze hits (depending on where you live, this could be in October or November), cover the growing area containing root crops with a 2-foot-thick layer of loose organic mulch, such as straw, hay, or dried leaves. Lay a waterproof tarp or sheet of plastic over the mulch and anchor it with stones or bricks to keep the mulch dry over winter. When you want to harvest a few roots for dinner, simply pull back the tarp and mulch, dig what you need, and replace the protective covering. In all but the coldest winters, this should keep the ground from freezing too hard to dig.

Maintaining the Winter Garden

Unless you're a cold-weather enthusiast, you'll probably want to spend as little time in the winter garden as possible. Happily, Mother Nature has cooperated with our natural inclinations by slowing things down in the winter garden.

> ### Garden Guide
>
> To see if winter-grown leafy greens need to be watered, stick your index finger into the soil up to the second knuckle. If the soil feels moist, keep checking daily and water only when the soil feels dry to your fingertips.

You'll need to water less frequently in winter because plants are growing slowly and need less water. Colder temperatures also mean less evaporation from the soil. It's actually healthier to water your plants less in winter because damp, cold conditions are an invitation to fungal diseases and rot. Some experts believe plants in dry soil are more likely to survive freezing than plants in moist soil and recommend you stop watering entirely during the dead zone between mid-December and mid-to-late January.

I think moderation is the key: although mulched root vegetables can fend for themselves, lift row covers daily to keep a watchful eye on your leafy plants, and if you notice them beginning to wilt, give them a sprinkling on a sunny day. Do it early enough that the foliage can dry before sundown. Leafy greens have shallow roots, and using a watering can to moisten the soil around them should suffice.

Mature root crops can overwinter without additional watering. In fact, if your area experiences cold, rainy winters, you should harvest all your root vegetables for storage before the rains begin so they won't rot in the ground. Or grow them in a raised bed filled with sandy, fast-draining soil.

Winter should also have a slow-motion effect on your fertilizing schedule. Because plants are growing slowly, they use only small amounts of fertilizer in early to mid-winter and no fertilizer at all during the dormant dead-zone months. To keep from overfertilizing, your best option is to spread a 1-inch thick layer of finished compost over the bed before sowing seeds, or apply a commercial balanced, slow-release fertilizer at planting time, using half the amount recommended on the package label, and add no more.

After the winter dead zone has passed—around the beginning of February—and plants begin growing again, apply another layer of compost or half-strength application of fertilizer as a side dressing.

Winter Weeds and Pests

You wouldn't think weeds or pests would be a problem in the winter garden, but that's not the case. Although generally fewer weeds grow in winter, weeds like henbit and chickweed are surprisingly hardy. You may see them popping up in the outdoor garden all winter in mild climates—or under protective covers even in the coldest conditions. If you pull these annual weeds up before they bloom and set seed, you should be able to keep them from coming back. If you have a big winter garden, lay black plastic sheeting, straw, or other weed-smothering mulch in the pathways.

Any time temperatures under protective covers climb above freezing, a few bugs, slugs, or other critters will take advantage of the situation. In winter, hungry rodents such as mice and voles can also be a problem. Floating row cover will exclude many bugs, and picking bugs and rodent traps are other control options for edibles, which you don't want to expose to pesticides. But weeding and pest-control measures (see Chapter 9) work the same, all year round.

Growing Plants Under Cover and in Cold Frames

You can grow your late-season crops outdoors without protection right up until the first hard freeze. Of course, if you garden in a mild climate, you can grow these crops in the ground without any protection all winter. On frosty nights, just cover them with floating row cover or an old blanket and remove it after the sun melts the frost the next morning.

When night temperatures are consistently below 32°F, you should grow plants in an unheated greenhouse or cold frame, which is really just a small unheated greenhouse. If you planted them in the garden, you can cover them with a lightweight, moveable prefab polycarbonate cold frame, or put hoops over the rows and cover the plants with one or even two layers of row cover (see Chapter 8). Row cover installation is the same, no matter what season it is.

Row cover protects winter plants in two ways. It offers mild insulation against freezing temperatures, and traps heat released from the soil (soil is slower to freeze than the surrounding air). Just as importantly, the row cover protects plants from being dried out, or desiccated, by freezing wind and spoiled by sleet and snow.

Row cover has many advantages—but also presents one problem for winter gardeners. It's fragile and can crack or tear during storms or when you remove it for harvesting. When temperatures drop below freezing and stay there, you'll need to add a second layer to protect both the row cover and the plants under it. Wait as long as possible to do this, because a second layer will block about 10 percent of the already weak winter light reaching your plants.

Adding a second protective layer, such as covering the row cover with a sheet of clear plastic or using row cover inside a cold frame, shields the row cover from the brunt of bad weather. An added benefit is that the double insulation is enough to get most winter-garden plants through subfreezing weather.

Garden Guide

Floating row covers come in several thicknesses or weights. Thicker covers provide slightly more insulation than lighter ones. Thicker ones also cost more and block more light, and they still freeze when wet. For this reason, using a sheet of heavy clear plastic over a thinner weight of floating row cover gives the best overall protection for garden crops in winter.

After giving your winter crops that bit of extra care, then you get to harvest. Winter harvesting, isn't much different from summer and fall harvesting, except you might have to wait for the frost to thaw before you can lift your garden covers and cut greens.

Overnight freezes can actually freeze leafy greens solid, even under protective covers. If you harvest leafy greens while frozen, they'll turn to inedible mush when they thaw. So if you discover that your leafy greens are frozen in the morning, postpone harvesting until the air temperature under the row cover is above freezing and there's no frost on the foliage.

To be sure they're ready to pick, reach under a cover and bend one of the leaves to see if it's pliable rather than frozen stiff. Re-cover the crops as soon as you finish harvesting because you want to preserve the heat in the soil as much as possible. And if the row cover stays in one position too long, it may stiffen up too much to drape back into place.

Green Thumb

You may think that frost-nipped salad greens and root vegetables such as carrots and turnips would be somewhat compromised in the flavor department. However, just the opposite is true. Frost concentrates the flavors and sugars in garden vegetables, making them even more delicious than when grown in the summer garden.

Mulching and covering root crops with plastic sheeting can buy a few extra weeks of harvest for carrots, turnips, beets, and other root vegetables. But before the ground freezes hard, dig all remaining roots and store them for the winter (see Chapter 19).

Ornamental Gardens in Winter

Winter gardening isn't just about root crops and salad greens. You can enjoy an ornamental perennial garden in winter, though in a much different way than you enjoy your vegetable garden. The good news is that the ornamental garden requires even less maintenance than the vegetable garden does.

Planning Ornamentals for Winter Interest

When you design or redesign your flowering perennial garden, take a moment to think about how it'll look in winter when the plants are dormant. To make a perennial garden that's attractive year-round, consider *hardscape*, color, and texture for interest in the winter months. Furthermore, plan your garden so you can see points of interest, such as a bench, an arbor, or a bird feeder, from prominent or easily accessed windows in your house.

def•i•ni•tion

Hardscape is all the nonliving elements of a garden landscape, including walkways, walls, arbors, benches, statues, fountains, and buildings.

When choosing ornamental plants for your winter garden, include both broad-leaved and needled evergreens and woody plants with interesting shapes and bark textures. These add color and shape to what would otherwise be flat field in shades of brown and gray, which is how a perennial garden looks when dormant in winter. Evergreens are especially valuable because they provide shelter for overwintering birds and small wildlife.

Green Thumb

Birds are valuable garden assets because they eat bugs and add a dimension of color, movement, and song. To keep them in your garden through the winter, put out seed feeders and fresh water. To help the birds stay warm, include high-energy foods, such as suet and peanut butter, and a tray of dried fruits, such as raisins or dried cherries.

Popular broad-leaved evergreens:

Azaleas and rhododendrons (*Rhododendron* spp.)

Boxwood (*Buxus* spp.)

Glossy abelia (*Abelia grandiflora*)

Holly (*Ilex* spp.)

Leatherleaf viburnum (*Viburnum rhytidophyllum*)

Oregon grapeholly (*Mahonia repens*)

Firethorn or pyracantha (*Pyracantha coccinea*)

Spreading euonymus (*Euonymus kiautschovicus*)

Winter barberry (*Berberis julianae*)

Popular needled evergreens:

Arborvitae (*Thuja* spp.)

Cypress (*Chamaecyparis* spp.)

Fir (*Abies* spp.)

Juniper (*Juniperus* spp.)

Pine (*Pinus* spp.)

Spruce (*Picea* spp.)

Yew (*Taxus* spp.)

Include some deciduous trees and shrubs that have colorful or textural bark, such as red- or yellow-twigged dogwoods and river birch trees. Consider a few deciduous woody plants with distinctive shapes—Japanese maple or corkscrew willow—to silhouette against a backdrop of evergreens, sky, or lawn.

Deciduous plants with interesting shapes:

Japanese maple (*Acer palmatum*)

Corkscrew willow (*Salix matsudana*)

Harry Lauder's walking stick (*Corylus Avellana* 'Contorta')

Deciduous plants with colored bark:

>   Red-twig dogwood (*Cornus sericea*)

>   Yellow-twig dogwood (*Cornus alba*)

>   Paperbark cherry (*Prunus serrula*)

Deciduous plants with textured bark:

>   Crape myrtle (*Lagerstromia indica*)

>   Paperbark maple (*Acer grisseum*)

>   River birch (*Betula nigra*)

Remember to include some flowering plants to cheer winter-weary souls. Grow a late-winter flowering, fragrant witchhazel shrub near a path or doorway for a whiff of spring every time you step outside. Hellebores are among the earliest flowering perennials, with a blooming period between late February and mid-March in most parts of the country.

And when you're bulb shopping, be sure to include some of the earliest flowering snow drops, which can open their tiny white bells as early as January, white-flowered Siberian squill, and the familiar purple or yellow crocus in your winter garden.

Late-winter flowering shrubs and perennials:

>   Witchhazel (*Hamamelis virginiana*)

>   Hellebores (*Helleborus* spp.)

Early-flowering bulbs:

>   Crocus (*Crocus vernus*)

>   Siberian squill (*Scilla siberica*)

>   Snowdrops (*Galanthus nivalis*)

Maintaining Ornamentals in Winter

After frost turns perennials brown and trees drop their leaves, rake up the remains. If you suspect foliage is harboring pests or diseases, dispose of the infected foliage and compost the rest. Use a leaf blower—or a good old-fashioned broom—to remove dry leaves and debris from decks, patios, and paths.

For visual interest—and to feed the birds—leave standing any hardy and sculptural seed-producing perennials, such as black-eyed Susans and ornamental grasses. But put an insulating layer of fluffy organic mulch four or six inches deep on top of marginally hardy perennials to protect them from frost damage or from heaving out of the soil over winter. Prune away and dispose of obviously dead tree and shrub branches. But wait to shape woody plants until after the ground freezes hard to be sure they're dormant. If you prune too soon, you may cause the wounds to "bleed" sap, which makes the plants vulnerable to disease.

Cleanup is done; now is the time to retreat to the warmth of the indoors, brew a cup of hot tea, and sit in an easy chair next to your favorite window for a little winter bird watching.

The Least You Need to Know

- ◆ You can grow perennial herbs, cold-hardy greens, and root vegetables through the winter.

- ◆ Insulate plants by growing under row cover or inside cold frames or greenhouses.

- ◆ In extremely cold weather, add extra insulation—another layer of row cover, blankets, or even a protective covering such as a portable cold frame.

- ◆ Water the winter garden sparingly to avoid freezing or rotting roots.

- ◆ Put planting on hold during the shortest days of winter from late December to mid-January or early February, but do continue to harvest mature greens.

- ◆ Succession planting and cut-and-come again harvesting ensure fresh salads all year long.

Part 5

Greenhouse Gardening: All Seasons

Greenhouse gardening is so versatile and rewarding that you can grow nearly every kind of plant in every season. Doesn't that sound *exciting*?

In these chapters, we tell you about the different kinds of greenhouses and what you can grow in each kind. We start with the basics—soil and fertilizer. Then we get into the specific types of plants: what they need in a greenhouse and how you can give it to them. You'll find a greenhouse can be simple or just *full* of gizmos to help you care for your plants.

Greenhouse gardening gives you almost unlimited choices about what to grow and when to grow it. After you read this part, you can be master of your own greenhouse environment.

Chapter 13

Greenhouse Basics

In This Chapter

◆ The right greenhouse location

◆ Optimum greenhouse temperatures

◆ An ideal growing medium for your potted plants

◆ Keeping your plants healthy in a greenhouse

This chapter will get you up and growing in your greenhouse as you discover the best exposure and which temperature range will allow you to grow your favorite plants. You'll also get the nuts and bolts of potting, repotting, and multiplying your plants. And finally, we'll tell you how to keep them healthy. If you see a bug or a wilted leaf—never fear; we'll explain how to beat the bad guys and get your plants thriving again.

Siting the Greenhouse

Sunshine is the fuel that powers a greenhouse, whether it's an unheated one, sometimes called a solar greenhouse, or has assistance from a heater. When setting up your greenhouse, orient the structure so it receives the maximum amount of life-giving sunlight from sunup to sundown. A properly sited and ventilated greenhouse makes efficient use of the sun's heat, storing it in winter and releasing it in summer.

A freestanding greenhouse is one with four walls and a ridge connecting a two-sided roof. It usually has one or two doors, plus vents in the roof, in the gable ends, or both. A freestanding greenhouse is the best design for collecting sunlight because it has two roof surfaces, which are sloped at the optimum angle (usually 45°) to collect sunlight all day long.

Garden Guide

Meet the light needs of plants by making efficient use of vertical space in a greenhouse. The more light a plant needs, the closer to the roof you hang it. Set shade-tolerant plants either on shelves or under them. This system works well for multi-use greenhouses. However, if you are growing light-demanding food plants directly in greenhouse soil, don't block light by hanging plants above them.

If possible, site your freestanding greenhouse so one side of the roof faces east and the other faces west. This orientation allows the roof to capture sunlight as the sun rises and travels over the ridge to set on the other side. This orientation also gives you the bonus of having one gable end of the greenhouse facing south, where it can collect full days of sunlight in winter, when the sun is low in the southern sky.

The north-facing gable end of a freestanding greenhouse is a good place to grow plants that tolerate lower light levels. Or some gardeners prefer to build a solid insulated wall or a potting shed on the north end of a greenhouse to protect it from the elements.

A lean-to greenhouse is usually attached to the wall of a house, garage, or shed, and is essentially one half of a freestanding greenhouse, split along the ridge with half the roof, one long wall, and two half-gabled ends. It usually has a door from outside, but may or may not have a door leading from the attached building. To collect the maximum amount of sunlight and heat in winter, attach a lean-to greenhouse to the south-facing wall of a building, with the greenhouse roof and long side exposed to winter sun. The second-best exposure for a lean-to is facing east to catch the morning sun. Avoid a west-facing exposure because the afternoon sun is too harsh for many plants, and storms often blow from the west.

Cool, Intermediate, and Warm Greenhouses

There are three recognized categories of heated greenhouses, based on interior temperature ranges. The cool greenhouse is for those of us in freezing-winter regions who want the optimum environment for growing food plants and winter-flowering ornamentals such as forced bulbs and florists' azaleas that require a cool rest before blooming. The intermediate greenhouse, which is kept warmer than a cool greenhouse, is the closest thing to an ideal environment for the widest assortment of tropical ornamental plants. If you make use of its microclimates, you can grow a few plants requiring cool temperatures, and a few of the tougher plants normally grown in a warm greenhouse. Because the intermediate greenhouse is a bit too warm for winter-season food and flowering plants, it is usually reserved for tropicals. Only warmth-craving exotics will enjoy the pricey atmosphere of a warm greenhouse. For this reason, it is for those of us with collections of equatorial plants. We discuss the actual temperature ranges and specific plants to grow in cool, intermediate, and warm greenhouses in Chapter 15.

Matching Plants to Microclimates

You can grow plants suited to slightly warmer or cooler temperatures by making use of greenhouse microclimates. For instance, the air around higher shelves and hanging-basket rods near the ceiling is usually warmer than the air at the waist-high benches. And the coolest areas are near the floor and door. Place several waterproof thermometers around your greenhouse to track the high and low temperatures in various areas so you can place plants where they'll be happiest.

Greenhouse Generalities

The special thing about a greenhouse is that it allows you to stretch your outdoor growing season and to grow plants from far-away places in an environment you tailor to the plants' needs. To grow plants successfully in your greenhouse, whether you are growing vegetables in in-ground beds or tending hanging baskets and potted plants, allow enough room for air and light to reach each and every plant. And prevent plants from touching so insect pests or diseases spread less easily.

Place each plant where it receives optimum light. If an in-ground plant is leaning or growing long and lanky, consider moving it to a sunnier portion of the bed, or make notes accordingly and change your planting scheme next season. If an overly shaded plant is potted, move the pot closer to the ceiling where it receives more light or put it where no plants hang over it to block light. On the other hand, if a plant develops dark reddish leaves or appears to be flattening out or growing downward, it may be receiving too much light. In that case, move it to a shady place, closer to the floor, or you can reduce sun exposure over an in-ground bed by hanging shade cloth or floating row cover overhead.

Your greenhouse plants are completely dependent on you for water and fertilizer. However, water and fertilize sparingly. Allow soil to dry slightly between waterings to avoid root rot. Applying a weak solution of fertilizer with each watering ensures even plant growth and protects the roots from the possibility of caustic, concentrated fertilizer burn.

Potting Your Plants

Individual containers are standard fare for many greenhouse plants, but as there is a baffling choice of shapes and materials, let me give you some advice about the types of pots available and the best use of each.

Pots are identified by the diameter of the top opening, with 4-, 5-, and 6-inch pots fitting greenhouse plants from vegetable seedlings to orchids. Just for reference, seeding pots called cells are usually 2 inches across, and nursery pots are much larger and are frequently sized by volume—as in quarts and gallons. And we have three traditional pot shapes: bulb pans, standard pots, and long Tom pots.

Bulb pans, also called azalea or begonia pots, are wide, shallow pots—about twice as wide as they are tall. This shape is good for plants such as mint, strawberries, azaleas, rhizomatous begonias, ferns, and cattleya type orchids that spread horizontally by *offshoots*, *runners*, or creeping *rhizomes*.

def•i•ni•tion

Offshoots are stems or branches that grow from the main stem of a plant and develop into new plants.

Runners are shoots that grow horizontally, usually from the base of a plant. When a runner touches ground, it roots and forms a new plant.

Rhizomes are stems that grow horizontally just below ground level and put out roots and lateral stems to form new plants.

A standard pot is as wide at the top as it is tall. Aptly named, this pot shape works for almost any plant. Simply adjust the potting medium to increase or decrease drainage to suit the individual plant.

Long Tom pots are tall, narrow, tapered pots. Used infrequently, these are best suited to deep-rooted plants, such as tree seedlings, or plants with a cascading growth habit, such as some chrysanthemums and bonsai.

Drain holes are a standard feature of all functional pots, and most pots have one hole in the center of the bottom. Orchid pots have holes in the sides as well for extra air circulation. Orchid baskets are loosely woven wire, plastic, or wooden baskets that allow aerial roots to hang out of the pot.

Green Thumb

A cache pot (pronounced "cash poe") is a decorative pot without drain holes. Use one of these as a slipcase for a functional pot when you bring a greenhouse plant into the house for temporary display. The cache pot makes a pretty accent and protects your furniture by collecting water from the pot within. Just remember to empty water from the cache pot as needed to avoid root rot.

Pots are made from many materials, including clay, plastic, ceramic, wood, fiberglass, foam, and plastic. The most popular for greenhouse plants are the traditional clay or terra cotta pots and plastic ones. One or the other will work better, depending on the plants you want to grow and your gardening style.

Clay pots have been around since the invention of pottery. They develop a lovely patina with use, and though they are breakable, they wear well, and the old ones you may find at an estate sale are just as usable as a new one. From a plant's perspective, the porous nature of unglazed clay simulates a plant's natural, in-ground growing conditions. Air and water pass through the pot walls, making them ideal for plants such as succulents and cacti that need excellent drainage and for orchids, which need both drainage and air circulation. The porosity of clay pots is also a life-saver for plants belonging to heavy-handed waterers.

Plastic pots are lightweight and may be a better choice for plants you want to hang from the ceiling. Plastic pots generally cost less than clay, but with exposure to sunlight, they eventually become brittle and break. They also don't drain as well or provide the air circulation of clay pots, but you can overcome this disadvantage by using a well-drained potting mix and reducing the frequency of watering.

Garden Guide

You can clean and reuse a pot as long as it's not cracked or broken. To clean and sterilize a used pot, scrape off accumulated crusty deposits with an old paring knife, and then use a scouring pad and scrub brush to remove dirt, and rinse well. To kill any lingering pathogens, soak the pot for at least 10 minutes in a tub containing 1 part chlorine bleach to 9 parts water. Rinse and dry the pot before reusing it.

Specialty pots include loosely woven wooden or plastic baskets designed for orchids and bromeliads that naturally grow with their roots exposed to air. Low, shallow pots are specially designed for bonsai trees. And strawberry pots have multiple openings on the sides as well as at the top and are usually planted with strawberries, herbs, or succulents.

Potting Medium

In previous chapters, we discussed creating soil mixtures for growing food plants in greenhouse in-ground beds and raised beds. These beds, which are geared to food crops, are always in contact with ground soil and contain a blend of topsoil and other ingredients. In a heated greenhouse, individual ornamental plants are generally grown in pots, with "soil" that is customized to support each plant's root and nutrient needs.

Potting medium, also called potting soil, is the growing medium gardeners use in their pots. The most important attribute of potting soil, whether a commercial brand or homemade mixture, is that it holds enough moisture to keep plant roots hydrated but drains away excess moisture that could rot roots. To stay healthy, plant roots also need oxygen, so the structure of potting soil should be open enough to allow circulation throughout the pot.

Garden Guide

Soil structure is the spacing of particles of soil as they clump together. Soil with good structure has spaces, or pores, between particles that allow air and water to circulate through the soil.

If you use soil straight from the garden in pots, you'll bring weed seeds, insect eggs, and disease organisms into a greenhouse, which could infect a valuable collection of plants. If garden soil is your growing medium of choice, review Chapter 6 where we talk about sterilizing soil, because you'll want to do that to protect your greenhouse plants.

To sterilize soil, heat soil to 180°F for a half hour, and cool before using. Because heated soil has an unpleasant odor, the best way to do this is in a heatproof pan in a closed outdoor grill. Insert a meat thermometer periodically to check the temperature.

What's the alternative to garden soil? Many gardeners use soilless potting mixes. These mixes, whether commercial or homemade, are free of soil-borne weed seeds and pathogens, which makes them suitable for growing most tender greenhouse plants. They are a blend of sphagnum peat moss, which is an organic ingredient, and inert, granular ingredients such as Perlite or vermiculite that create pores to allow water and oxygen to circulate through the mix. Soilless potting mixes may also contain small nuggets of activated charcoal to keep the mix from becoming stagnant.

Soilless mixes intended for growing orchids contain larger chunks of organic material, such as coir (ground up husks of coconut shells) or fir bark, to increase pore size. If the mix is intended for moisture-loving orchids such as moth orchids (*Phalaenopsis* spp.), they may also contain long-fiber sphagnum moss.

Soilless mixes designed for growing Alpine plants, succulents, and cacti are usually made up primarily of sand with added gravel for porosity and may contain charcoal, Perlite, or a small amount of organic matter.

Garden Guide

Cool water tends to bead up and roll off peat moss, making the growing medium difficult to moisten. For best results, use tepid water.

A major drawback of soilless mediums is that they contain few or no nutrients, so fertilize regularly, according to package directions, to keep your plants healthy, and repot every year or two when organic ingredients break down.

You can save money and customize your potting medium by making your own, and should you choose to do this, a visit to the nearest garden center will likely yield the necessary ingredients. Use the following four basic recipes to mix just what your greenhouse plants need. Each recipe caters to a different set of plants, based on humidity and drainage needs.

Basic Soil-Based Potting Mix

2 parts sterilized soil (select bagged soil labeled sterilized, or sterilize your own as directed earlier in this section)

1 part Perlite or vermiculite

1 part sand

½ part activated charcoal

Mix ingredients thoroughly, and moisten with tepid water before using.

High-Humus Potting Mix

2 parts sterilized soil (select bagged soil labeled sterilized, or sterilize your own as directed earlier in this section)

2 parts peat moss or finished compost

1 part Perlite or vermiculite

½ part activated charcoal

Mix ingredients thoroughly, and moisten with tepid water before using.

Alpine, Cacti, and Succulent Mix

2 parts Basic Soil-Based Potting Mix (see previous recipe)

1 part small, washed gravel, such as pea gravel

1 part pumice

Mix ingredients thoroughly, and moisten with tepid water before using.

Or for acid-loving Alpines, substitute 1 recipe High-Humus Potting Mix (see previous recipe) for the Basic Soil-Based Potting Mix.

Orchid Mix

6 parts medium-size fir bark chunks

1 part medium chunk activated charcoal

1 part coarse Perlite

For moisture-loving orchids, such as Phalaenopsis and terrestrials, add 1 part long-fiber sphagnum moss

Dry orchid bark repels water, so for the sake of your orchids, you must give bark a special pretreatment *before* you make this recipe. Measure out the amount of bark nuggets you need, and cook it for 8 hours, or overnight in a slow-cooker on the low setting, or simmer for an hour in a stockpot of water on a stovetop or outdoor grill. Allow the bark to cool before potting.

Strain water from bark, and mix the damp bark nuggets and other ingredients thoroughly. Pot orchids up within 24 hours, before the bark has a chance to dry out again.

Repotting Your Plants

There are three main reasons to repot a plant:

◆ You just purchased a plant and want to move it into a more attractive or long-lasting pot.

◆ The plant has outgrown its current pot. (You can tell because its growth is suffering or the soil has become crowded with roots.)

◆ The organic matter in a soilless potting medium has decomposed, blocking air circulation in the pot, putting the plant at risk of root rot.

If you've just brought a plant home from the store, it's probably young, so take into consideration the plant's mature size and shape when you choose a pot for it. Of course, if it's a slow-growing plant, plan on repotting every two or three years. Fast-growing plants may need repotting annually.

When repotting a plant that has outgrown its current container, move it to a pot one size larger than its current pot. Over-potted plants—plants in pots much larger than necessary—are more likely to contract root rot because they don't have enough roots to remove excess moisture from the pot.

Follow this procedure for repotting a plant.

1. Choose an easily cleaned work surface. Assemble the plant in its old pot, the new pot, some growing medium of your choice, a spoon or scoop, and a container of tepid water.

2. Cover the new pot's drain hole with a small piece of nylon window screen or a few shreds of long-fiber sphagnum moss to keep the growing medium from escaping.

3. Place one hand over the soil, with the main stem of the plant between your second and third fingers. Keep the soil covered with that hand as you turn the pot upside down. Rap the bottom of the pot until the root ball comes loose and lands in your hand.

4. Loosen the plant's roots to encourage new growth. (This is especially important if you are repotting a plant that has outgrown its current pot.)

5. Hold the root ball in the new pot in the position in which it should grow. Then remove it and add pre-moistened growing medium to an appropriate depth. Set the root ball on the growing medium, center it in the pot, and scoop in more growing medium to fill in between the root ball and the edge of the pot. Press the growing medium in to firm it.

6. Water the plant just enough to moisten both the old and new potting medium evenly.

7. Wipe the pot clean and set it in a bright, but not sunny place to avoid wilting. When signs of new growth appear, you can move it to its permanent home.

Newly potted plants are stressed until they establish themselves in their new pot. For this reason, do not fertilize until you see several sets of new leaves.

Fertilizing Greenhouse Plants

Outdoor plants, of course, get nutrients from the "living" soil in which they grow. But your greenhouse plants are contained and confined and so completely dependent on you for their nutrients. They start out with nutrients in the growing medium, of course, but in time, a plant depletes the medium of the needed nutrients. Some commercial brands of potting mix have fertilizer mixed in. And that's perfectly fine; your plants will probably be happy. But unless you fertilize, the plants will still eventually deplete the nutrients, so prevention is definitely the path to take.

A good rule of thumb is to fertilize your potted plants when they've been in the same pot for three months. However, if you notice leaves turning yellow, begin fertilizing before the three months are up. Use a balanced fertilizer, such as a 10-10-10 formula, at half strength with every watering or full strength every other watering, according to package directions. In general, fertilize in this manner throughout the growing season. During winter or when the plant is dormant, withhold fertilizer and water just enough to keep the plant from wilting.

Whether gardening outdoors or in a greenhouse, the same fertilizer options are available—manufactured and organic; with granular, pellet, and liquid options. They carry the same advantages and disadvantages, as we discussed in Chapter 5. My favorite way to fertilize is foliar feeding. I mix a weak fertilizer solution in a spray bottle and mist foliage with it. The foliage absorbs the fertilizer, and the roots absorb any that runs down the foliage. This method is faster acting than pouring fertilizer over the potting medium, and uses less fertilizer.

Controlling Pests

The first line of defense for controlling pests and diseases in your greenhouse is *you*. You must make sure any screens in the greenhouse are secure and intact; you must check new plants for pests and diseases before you take them into your greenhouse; and you must keep your greenhouse clean and well-ventilated, use sterile potting medium, and keep your plants healthy. If you take all of these precautions, your problems with pests and diseases should be few and far between.

If pests do appear, they are less likely to be earwigs, Japanese beetles, tomato hornworms, and others commonly encountered in the outdoor garden and more likely to be soft-bodied sucking insects, such as aphids or mealy bugs, or minute flying pests, such as white flies or gnats. Now and then a slug or snail might find its way inside. When possible, I use the totally eco-friendly method of vacuuming them up with the small wet/dry shop vac I keep in my greenhouse. For a discussion of other controls, revisit Chapters 9 and 17.

Hard-bodied scale insects are one of the worst pests of potted greenhouse plants. Adult scale look like small brown bumps, about as big as the head of a match, attached to the upper surfaces of leaves They reproduce rapidly and are difficult to kill because their hard shells repel treatments. Untreated, scale can spread from plant to plant and can slowly kill their hosts. Apply treatments every three days; eventually you'll kill the small crawlers as they hatch. In fact, the key to controlling all insects is to repeat the treatment at three- or five-day intervals, according to package directions until a couple of weeks after you have seen the last of them.

To test for the presence of flying pests and to control them to some extent, hang up yellow sticky traps—you probably call these fly paper (you can make your own by smearing petroleum jelly on pieces of yellow paper). Attracted to the yellow color, pests become trapped in the sticky coating. At least you'll be able to identify the pests and have a good idea of how big the population is.

Safety First _____

When using a pesticide in a greenhouse, follow package directions precisely. Close up and lock the door, and post a sign notifying others that the greenhouse is being treated. Leave it closed for the amount of time recommended on the package before re-entering or allowing pets, children, or others to enter.

If you don't house beneficial insects, fish, birds, or other pets in your greenhouse, you can set off a bug bomb, a powerful insecticide contained in a pressurized can, according to package direction. They come in a three-can package, to be set off at timed intervals to kill successive generations of insects as they hatch from eggs in potting soil. Reserve bombs for severe infestations or as a preventive measure at the end of summer when you bring potentially infested ornamental (do *not* use bug bombs on edible plants) plants into the greenhouse from outdoors. Bug bombs are easy to find; they're usually sold in the outdoor section of grocery stores and at hardware and garden stores.

Controlling Diseases

Plant viruses, fungal leaf diseases, and root rot are the main diseases of greenhouse plants. Viruses produce symptoms including pale streaks and dots in leaves or flowers, and infected plants weaken and eventually die. There is no cure for plant viruses, so if you suspect you have an infected plant, dispose of it before the disease spreads.

Viruses are spread from plant to plant through open wounds created by sap-sucking and leaf-chewing pests, such as aphids and slugs. If you keep these pests out of the greenhouse, you're halfway home in virus prevention. You can actually spread viruses from plant to plant if you use dirty pruners and pots. Be sure to disinfect cutting and potting tools between plants by dipping them into rubbing alcohol or flaming them with a portable torch or butane lighter. And remember to sterilize pots before reusing them by soaking them in a bleach solution.

Fungal leaf diseases cause disfigured, blotchy leaves with sooty gray, black, or fuzzy whitish growths, and sometimes rotted edges. Infected plants can drop some or all of the infected leaves, but fungal leaf diseases rarely kill a plant outright. Control fungal leaf diseases by constantly circulating air with one or two small fans, by airing out the greenhouse when weather permits, and by reducing the humidity in cold weather. Avoid wetting fuzzy-leaved plants, which hold water for a long time, and avoid watering plants late in the day because fungal spores develop in dark, cool, moist conditions. Even in freezing weather, open the door a few inches for a little while during the sunniest part of the day to admit fresh air. When you prune or divide plants, dab each cut with powdered garden sulfur or a commercial fungicide, applied according to label directions.

Garden Guide

Slatted shelves or benches deter fungal plant diseases in the greenhouse because they allow light and air to circulate freely around plants. They also allow excess water to drain away from plants. My personal favorite is rubber-coated wire closet shelving, available at discount and home centers, because unlike wooden slats, it cannot absorb moisture and pathogens.

Root rot is caused by poorly drained soil, and this, unfortunately, can kill a plant. If a plant blackens at soil level and wilts or if the soil is wet and foul-smelling, root rot is to blame. The best thing you can do is take cuttings from the healthiest part of the plant and start new plants in well-drained soil. To prevent root rot, allow the soil to dry out briefly between waterings, and don't allow pots to stand in saucers of water.

Pollinating Plants by Hand

One of the advantages of a greenhouse is that you can screen out insect pests, but the disadvantage is that you'll also screen out pollinating insects. If you want to grow vegetables in your greenhouse or if you want to pollinate flowering plants so you can collect seeds for future generations, you must become the pollinator. Happily, this is an easy and fun task, and you'll have the most success if you pollinate in the morning while the flowers are fully open.

Tomatoes are the easiest plants to pollinate. They are essentially self-pollinating because each flower has both male and female parts. Outdoors, the wind shakes the flowers back and forth, and the pollen finds its way from the male part—the stamen—onto the female receiver, or pistil. You can simulate this motion by tapping flower clusters with a small plant stake or pencil. I make a habit of shaking up my tomato flowers every time I visit the greenhouse to ensure a good crop.

To pollinate a greenhouse tomato plant, use a plant stake to tap flower clusters, distributing pollen within each self-pollinating flower.

(Donna Chiarelli Studio)

The process is a bit different for pollinating vine crops—squash, melons, and cucumbers—and other heat-loving vegetables, such as peppers and eggplants, as these plants have separate male and female flowers. (You probably remember that we talked about hand-pollinating these in Chapter 9.) To hand-pollinate these types of plants, use a small artist's paintbrush or a cotton swab. Dab the pollen-bearing parts, called stamens, in the male flowers. (You'll see the dusty pollen on the paintbrush.) Then brush that pollen-laden paintbrush against the pollen receptors, or pistils, in the female flowers. An alternative method is to pick a male flower, peel off the petals, and dab the pollen parts directly onto the pistils of female flowers.

One further note about the vine, pepper, and eggplant crops: they sometimes produce only male flowers at first. Be patient; the females will come along shortly.

Pollinate an eggplant by using a cotton swab to collect pollen from a male flower and dabbing it onto the pistil of a female flower.

(Donna Chiarelli Studio)

Garden Guide

How do you tell a male flower from a female flower? Here's one example, as a guide. A male zucchini flower has a single, pollen-laden stalk-like bit inside the flower. That's the stamen. A female zucchini flower has several smaller, shorter elements—called pistils—in the center of the flower. Also, female flowers have bulbous bases, which eventually turn into fruits.

Hand pollination is not an exact science, so your efforts may or may not produce satisfactory results. Nonetheless, we recommend you keep at it. You are, after all, the keeper of the greenhouse and therefore the provider of all good things for your plants.

The Least You Need to Know

◆ Orient your freestanding greenhouse so the roof surfaces face east and west. Orient a lean-to greenhouse so it faces south or east.

◆ Place sun-loving plants near the greenhouse roof, and protect shade-loving plants by setting them on or under benches.

◆ Match plant temperature requirements to cool, intermediate, or warm greenhouse temperature ranges.

◆ Water sparingly to avoid root rot, and apply a weak solution of fertilizer with each watering for even plant growth.

◆ Clay pots are ideal for plants with roots that need air and good drainage; plastic pots are ideal for plants that need moist soil.

◆ You can make potting medium to suit your plants' needs for drainage.

◆ Keep your greenhouse clean and ventilated, and sterilize tools and pots to prevent pests and diseases from spreading.

Chapter 14

Unheated Greenhouses

In This Chapter

- ◆ Extreme-weather plant protection with a cold frame or unheated greenhouse
- ◆ Improve greenhouse soil to keep plant roots from freezing
- ◆ Interior greenhouse covers for extra protection
- ◆ Making the most of the midwinter growth lull
- ◆ Harvest spring and summer crops up to two months early

Up to this point, we've focused on growing plants outdoors with minimal protection from the elements, which is largely possible only in the warmer months of the year or in the mildest of winter climates.

So now we want to look at growing food crops in the protection of an unheated greenhouse or cold frame, a cold frame is really just a small greenhouse, all year around. And we'll place special emphasis on the winter season, because that's when the unheated greenhouse really proves its worth.

Tender plants, such as flowering and foliage houseplants and orchids, require the protection of a heated greenhouse in winter, which is a more complicated setup. We'll explain how to grow these plants in a heated greenhouse in Chapters 15 and 16.

What Is an Unheated Greenhouse?

As you already know, greenhouses can have freestanding or lean-to styles, glass or plastic walls and roof, and windows, hinged roof panels, or other ventilation systems. They may contain potted plants or plants growing right in the ground. And they may be heated or unheated.

An unheated greenhouse has no heat source other than the sun. So during the winter, the internal temperature is completely dependent upon the external temperature. If it's sunny, it will warm up quite nicely inside. If it's cloudy, it won't benefit from any sunlight, obviously, but there will be a slight warm-up as the daytime temperatures naturally rise. And at night, there's only the warmth that built up in the air during the day, which will slowly dissipate during the dark hours, and a little warmth in the soil, left over from warmer seasons.

An unheated greenhouse or cold frame doesn't have to be big, expensive, or insulated to grow crops. Whatever the size or space you have in an unheated greenhouse, you can use various techniques to see a variety of crops through the year, even without a heater to get you through the coldest months.

Green Thumb

If you want a hobby greenhouse, don't be put off by sticker shock. You can find bargains in the classified sections of gardening magazines, local newspapers, and sometimes in a neighbor's yard.

After weeks of driving past a suburban house with an empty, cobweb-festooned greenhouse in the backyard, I summoned the courage to knock on the door and offer to buy it. The homeowner was happy to let it go, and he even helped disassemble and load it into my boyfriend's pickup. A couple of years later, I scored again: this time a one-year-old greenhouse for a third of the list price at a neighbor's moving sale.

Growing in the Ground or in Raised Beds

If the soil in your greenhouse is good garden soil (see how to improve garden soil in Chapter 3) and if it has good drainage, you can plant directly in the soil. Good drainage is especially important in winter, when wet soil or pools of standing water can turn to rock-hard ice, rupturing and killing plant roots.

If you have any doubts about drainage or soil quality, set your greenhouse on a foundation of landscape timbers at least 1 foot high. Then frame raised beds inside, with a narrow center pathway (see Chapter 3).

To help divert heavy rains around the perimeter of the greenhouse, slow the influx of water into the beds, and keep soil from washing out of the beds between the timbers, staple a lining of permeable landscape fabric to the inside of the bed walls before filling them with soil. Be sure to leave the soil floor exposed. Treated this way, the soil in the raised beds absorbs moisture from the ground and some through the timber walls, but will not be saturated by rainwater flowing in. Fill the raised beds with a well-drained mixture of equal parts compost, sand, and topsoil or good soil taken from your outdoor garden. Mound the soil slightly when filling each raised bed so that when the soil settles, it will be level with the tops of the timbers.

Garden Guide

The cutting-edge, Maine and Vermont-based market gardener Eliot Coleman rediscovered and adapted Dutch and French intensive gardening techniques to winter greenhouse growing in cold-winter areas of this country. Working with simple and cost-efficient materials, Coleman developed a unique greenhouse-within-a-greenhouse method. He began by growing winter crops in cold frames that he constructed inside unheated greenhouses, as he had seen in Holland. But he soon discovered he could more easily and economically cover his greenhouse crops with the same hoops and floating row covers he used outside in warmer seasons. Although Coleman grows winter crops in commercial-sized greenhouses, his technique works equally well in the smallest hobby greenhouse or cold frame. (For more information on Eliot Coleman, see Appendix D.)

One note about working comfortably in your greenhouse. Whether you grow in the ground or in raised beds, you'll spend a lot of quality time on your knees. So remember that when you're choosing a covering for the pathway. The softer and more water-resistant the path is, the more enjoyable kneeling will be. I put down a 2-inch layer of gravel in the path to promote drainage. Then I cut an 8-foot long by 4-foot wide, thick, rubber barn-stall mat in half lengthwise to fit, and laid the piece on top of the gravel.

Getting Through the Winter

To help crops in an unheated greenhouse get through the winter, suspend floating row cover on wire or plastic hoops above plants—just as we talked about in Chapter 1. Between the protection provided by the greenhouse and the insulation of the row cover, your plants can survive winter temperatures as low as 20°F. In other words, it will be above 32°F inside the greenhouse and under the covers where your plants are.

But what if the forecast indicates it's going to be even colder? Don't worry; you have a couple of options for coping when the temperature drops into the teens and below. You can add layers of insulation over the row cover—sheets, blankets, heavy plastic. Procedures are the same as if you were gardening outside (see Chapter 1).

If severely cold temperatures threaten and you fear your plants will freeze to death, set a portable kerosene, propane, or electric space heater in the greenhouse overnight to save them.

Safety First

If you decide to place a space heater in the greenhouse on a brutally cold night, make sure you keep the heater at least 3 feet away from any flammable substance, including row cover and plastic greenhouse walls.

If you use an electric heater, plug it into an exterior-rated extension cord and plug that into a ground-fault-circuit-interrupted (GFCI) outlet, which will cut off power if exposed to water or overheating. And just to be safe, hang or elevate the heater and the cord so that neither comes in contact with the damp ground or water.

Supplemental Light

Greenhouse plants continue to grow from fall into winter but grow more slowly as the days get shorter. During the shortest days of the year, usually from late December to late January or early February, they go into a state of suspended animation.

By checking your seed-packet instructions to determine the number of days to maturity and counting backward, you can time seed sowing so you can harvest all your plants by Christmas and let the greenhouse rest until early spring.

But if you love gardening and don't want to stop, even for two months, you can help your plants along with supplemental light. Grow lights (see Chapter 11) work in a greenhouse just as they do inside your home.

It could be expensive and complicated to run enough grow lights to light up your entire greenhouse, but one 4-foot fixture is a good idea. It'll give you plenty of light to garden by when dusk settles in on a late winter afternoon. And if you have it out there, well, you can also put it to work helping seedlings grow or ripening a plot of salad greens you started a bit too late in the fall.

The Best Plants for Unheated Greenhouses

What can you grow in an unheated greenhouse? Nearly anything! Let's put it this way: if you can grow it outside in your garden, you can grow it inside an unheated greenhouse. The only plants that will *not* work in an unheated greenhouse, unless you live in the mildest of climates, are tender tropicals that can't tolerate Northern Hemisphere winters at all.

Heat-loving vegetables, herbs, and vine fruits thrive in an unheated greenhouse in early spring. Cherry tomatoes and peppers approach ripening two months before their outdoor counterparts.

(Donna Chiarelli Studio)

The advantage to growing inside an unheated greenhouse is that you can control the environment, to some extent, and even out the seasonal extremes. Imagine getting a head start on your garden and having vegetables to harvest already in April. Or think of having fresh herbs and salad greens all the way through the autumn months. That's the beauty of an unheated greenhouse. For each season, it has its special benefits.

Spring Growing Season

The spring growing season in an unheated greenhouse can start as early as late January or early February—as soon as days are noticeably getting longer. To get an even bigger head start, you could sow seeds of cool-weather crops indoors in December so that you can set out seedlings as early as possible in late January or early February, weather permitting. You can also sow seeds directly in the greenhouse after the first of the year and, with favorable conditions, they'll quickly catch up with seedlings started the previous month indoors. Keep the seedlings covered with floating row cover until air temperatures are above freezing.

Space permitting, any early or cool-season vegetable, herb, or fruit is a candidate. Here are some early-spring favorites:

Broccoli	Cabbage
Cauliflower	Kohlrabi
Lettuce	Perennial herbs
Radishes	Spinach
Strawberries	Winter squash

Summer Growing Season

A greenhouse heats up long before the garden outside does, so start warmth-loving plants indoors in January and February, because early summer can start under glass in March or April. Time succession seed sowings of warm-loving greenhouse crops early enough so you can plant the seedlings in the greenhouse around St. Patrick's Day in mid-March and again in early April, about the same time you normally plant potatoes and onions outdoors. You'll be rewarded with ripe tomatoes, peppers, and more in late June or early July. Here are some warm-season favorites:

Annual herbs	Cucumbers
Eggplant	Melons
Peppers	Summer squash
Sweet potatoes	Swiss chard
Tomatillo	Tomatoes (choose small-fruited varieties such as cherry, grape, and paste tomatoes)

Fall Growing Season

In late summer, you'll continue to harvest from the same plants you planted in the greenhouse in early spring. You'll also begin to sow cool-season crops for winter harvest. Starting cool-season crops in July and August can be tricky because many will not germinate in hot greenhouse temperatures. For details on getting these plants off to a good start in summer, with cooling techniques, review Chapter 2.

You can grow the same cool-season plants listed previously as "early spring favorites." And of course, you can always experiment with any other plants that catch your interest.

Winter Growing Season

Early winter is still a viable growing season in the greenhouse as you can continue to sow new crops until early to mid-November in even the coldest climates. All the plants you sowed in fall and early winter will continue to mature to harvest stage. But aim to harvest as much as possible by the end of December, and then wait to set out any new seedlings until the days are noticeably longer, in late January or early February. For this last cool-weather crop of the year, choose cool-season plants that mature quickly and tolerate short days. These are some good candidates:

Arugula	Beets
Broccoli	Garlic
Kale	Lettuce
Onion family members	Perennial herbs
Radicchio	Radishes
Scallions	Spinach

Now, if you are really eager to keep things growing, here's one more gardener's trick for an unheated greenhouse. Heat your beds the old-fashioned way; create a hot bed by putting a layer of stable bedding under the bed before you sow or transplant. Like compost, nutrient-rich stable bedding—a mixture of manure and straw—gives off heat as it breaks down. It will produce enough heat for you to sow seeds, plant seedlings, and grow plants in zero-degree weather.

To create a hot bed:

Dig the soil down (or plan to build the bed up) to a 2-foot depth, setting the soil aside. Then lay in a 1-foot deep layer of fresh horse manure mixed with straw, and stomp it down firmly (wear rubber boots or stomp on a piece of plywood laid over the manure). Add a 1-foot deep layer of soil over the manure, and insert a soil thermometer midway into the soil. The manure should begin to heat up almost immediately.

When the soil maintains a temperature between 50° and 70°F, you can sow seeds or plant seedlings in it. Water as needed to keep the soil barely moist, and keep the seeds or seedlings covered with row cover when you're not tending them.

To discourage the fungal disease damping off, sprinkle a thin layer of clean sand or vermiculite over the soil after sowing. Lift the cover daily to admit fresh air and to check on sprouted seedlings.

By spring the manure will be fully composted. You can use it to enrich outdoor garden beds (if you really like digging and hauling stuff in wheelbarrows), or you can start another greenhouse crop in the now-cold bed.

Meanwhile, you can continue to harvest plants that were planted in the fall and that have gone into a cold-induced state of suspended animation. If they are frozen in the morning, just wait until they thaw later in the day to harvest them, and be sure to remember to re-cover them with row cover as soon as possible.

As you can see, we've come full circle. It's January in the greenhouse again, and we're already looking forward to that first crop of broccoli. The amazing part is that with the help of your unheated greenhouse, you've been enjoying fresh produce nearly all year long.

The Least You Need to Know

◆ A cold frame or unheated greenhouse proves its worth in extreme winter weather.

◆ Adequate soil drainage prevents freezing plant roots.

◆ Raised beds divert potentially damaging heavy rains.

◆ For ultimate cold-weather protection, cover crops inside an unheated greenhouse with floating row cover.

◆ Avoid direct seeding from late December to late January when day length is too short for plant growth.

◆ Succession planting allows spring and summer harvests inside your greenhouse up to two months earlier than outdoor crops.

Chapter 15

Heated Greenhouses

In This Chapter

- ◆ The right greenhouse for your needs
- ◆ Economical greenhouse options
- ◆ Save money heating and cooling your greenhouse
- ◆ What you should and should not grow in each type of greenhouse

In the previous chapter, we explored how unheated greenhouses can elevate your food gardening from a warm-season activity to one that you can enjoy nearly all year round. In this chapter, we focus on growing plants that require a heated winter greenhouse atmosphere to thrive.

Heated Greenhouse Basics

Plants that most require heated greenhouses are predominantly ornamental flowering and foliage plants said to be *tender*. Invariably, these plants are native to the tropics or southern regions and grow in our North American temperate climate only with extra help. Experts have grouped these plants into three recognized greenhouse temperature ranges: cool, intermediate, and warm.

Based on your personal favorites, you can match a greenhouse heat zone to the plants you want to grow. In many cases, you can grow plants from two adjacent groups—say, cool and intermediate—by making use of microclimates within your greenhouse (see Chapter 2). These microclimates are fairly predictable because they're based on that old rule: heat rises. It's warmer and brighter near the ceiling, so at waist height, approximately the level of your benches or shelves, an intermediate microclimate exists. And on the ground or under the benches is the coolest area. Note that if you want to grow plants with *widely* varying temperature preferences, your best bet is to have a cold frame or unheated greenhouse as well as an insulated, heated greenhouse so you can control temperatures according to the needs of the plants in each structure.

A heated greenhouse does have some special requirements. It needs a heat source, obviously, and a safe and reliable one, we should add. The inside of this structure is somewhat exposed to the elements, and therefore subject to freezing. You'll be using water inside the structure, and, in general, the humidity level may be fairly high. Given these conditions, you must use outdoor-grade electrical cords and equipment that's well maintained and suited to potential extremes in temperature.

To maintain temperatures and minimize the cost of heating in cold-winter areas, you'll want double or triple glazing or a translucent draft-excluding, insulated cover over your greenhouse. Anything you can do to keep the greenhouse warm that does *not* involve running electricity, is a good thing.

So let's explore each type of heated greenhouse, explaining the advantages and limitations, as well as establishing which plants are best suited to each. For the nuts and bolts on providing utilities and heat, turn to Chapter 16.

The Cool Greenhouse

In Chapter 13, we talked about how gardening in an unheated greenhouse extends the growing season of cold-tolerant outdoor plants well into freezing weather. But even with row covers or other measures, during a couple winter months days are so short and—in much of the country—temperatures are so frigid that you can't use an unheated greenhouse for much more than tool storage or overwintering potted perennials and woody plants.

With the addition of minimal atmospheric heat, you can expand plant choices for year-round gardening. If you want the coolest-weather vegetables, give them a head start by planting in early fall, then keep them alive through the coldest months of winter in a state of harvestable semi-dormancy by maintaining the air temperature at just above freezing at night and at 40° to 50°F during the day. With luck, the winter sun will help you out at least that much. We call this a cold greenhouse.

Garden Guide

To keep track of night-time temperatures in various parts of your greenhouse, use several inexpensive, water-resistant outdoor thermometers. Place one near the roof, one at waist height, one near the floor, and another near the exterior door.

But to keep those vegetables growing, to start new ones, to grow cold-tolerant winter-flowering plants, and to overwinter tender fruit trees, you need to rev up the heat, creating a cool greenhouse. The standard range of air temperatures for a cool greenhouse is a nighttime minimum of 45° to 50°F and minimum day temperature of 55° to 60°F.

Pit and Above-Ground Designs

A greenhouse doesn't have to be costly or manufactured. An economical-to-heat, intriguing homemade design called a *pit greenhouse* makes use of the earth's thermal heat in winter and its cooling effect in summer. Greenhouse-gardening pioneers Helen and Scott Nearing, spokespeople for the "back-to-the-land movement," first popularized the pit greenhouse in the 1940s. The couple worked self-sufficient farms in Vermont and Maine, and lectured and wrote from the 1930s into the 1990s (see Appendix D).

def•i•ni•tion

A **pit greenhouse** is a step-down, cellar-like structure dug into the ground to at least the frost line. Only the clear roof, or a short "knee" wall plus the roof of a pit greenhouse shows above ground.

A pit greenhouse uses the earth's residual heat as insulation. In such a greenhouse, the pit is the area in which you walk or stand as you work. The growing area remains the current ground level. To make one, dig a pit at least to the frost line to prevent the foundation from frost heaving. The ground level should be a comfortable working height of 3 to 4 feet, or from waist to chest height, depending on how deep you must dig. Make the pit, at minimum, a practical size to turn around and walk in, with enough extra room so that you can line the pit with concrete block walls. If you don't mind digging, you can make the pit wide enough to accommodate stair-step style plant shelves on one or both sides. The block walls not only hold back the earth, but also form a foundation for the roof-supporting pillars.

For a roof, frame a 45-degree pitch, which is optimum in the northern hemisphere for collecting the winter sun. Cover the roof with sections of break-resistant translucent polycarbonate or fiberglass sheets. If you prefer, you can create a hoop-style roof using galvanized steel or heavy PVC pipe covered with greenhouse-rated plastic sheeting or flexible fiberglass. Cover the dirt floor with landscape fabric, and then put down at least several inches of gravel to help drain water.

In the Nearings' lifetime, commercial greenhouse and insulating options were few and expensive. Now, however, we have ready-made above-ground greenhouses and insulating materials in all sizes to fit all budgets. If you're like me and lack a penchant for digging, a conventional free-standing or lean-to manufactured kit greenhouse will meet your cool greenhouse needs (for sources, see Appendix D).

What to Grow

When you maintain a greenhouse at above-freezing nighttime temperatures, you can begin to feed your soul as well as your stomach by venturing into the world of cold-hardy, winter-flowering plants and tender fruit trees.

Many of the same vegetables you grow in an unheated greenhouse (see Chapter 14) will prosper without risk of freezing in a cool heated one. But you'll still be unable to grow heat-loving, long-day vegetables such as tomatoes, eggplants, and peppers. Any way you look at it, your vegetable-growing season will continue to be limited by the short, dark days of late winter.

Garden Guide

When you heat a greenhouse, you can go longer without having to water the plants in winter. Why? The warmed interior greenhouse air holds more moisture than the colder outside air. Soil in pots and in-ground beds dries out more slowly in the humid greenhouse environment than they would outside.

You can grow a variety of cold-tolerant annual and perennial food plants and ornamentals in a cool greenhouse. Here are some good plant choices for the cool greenhouse:

Shrubs and trees:

Abutilon (flowering maple)

Citrus trees

Hardy palms

Jasmine

Azalea

Camellia

Heather

Norfolk Island pine

Flowering plants:

Bachelor button

Clivia

Crocus

Cyclamen

Epiphyllum (orchid cactus)

Hyacinth

Miniature rose

Nasturtium

Primrose

Snapdragon

Tulip

Bougainvillea

Cacti

Chrysanthemum

Cymbidium orchid

Hardy perennials

Geranium (*Pelargonium* spp.)

Narcissus

Pansy

Ranunculus

Sweet pea

Foliage plants:

Aspidistra (cast iron plant)

Cold-tolerant ferns

Creeping fig

Poinsettia

Saxifraga
(strawberry geranium)

Asparagus fern

Cordyline

English ivy

Rock garden (Alpine) plants

Schlumbergera (claw cactus, Christmas,
Easter cactus)

Fruits, herbs, and vegetables:

Banana tree	Bay tree
Chives	Cruciferous plants
Edible fig tree	Radish
Rosemary	Sage
Salad greens	Swiss chard
Other vegetables (see Chapter 14)	

For a complete range of choices, consult a good general gardening book or cool-greenhouse guide book (see Appendix D).

What Not to Grow

A cool greenhouse is good for many winter-flowering shrubs, perennials, cool-season annuals, and a few cold-tolerant orchids. But you won't be able to enjoy the vast assortment of warmth-loving orchids, houseplants, and tender bulbs because your cool greenhouse will dip to near-freezing temperatures at night. Don't risk your very tender, precious, or costly plants in that environment. Rather reserve those plants for the more costly, warmer greenhouse set-ups.

Garden Guide

If you have a cool greenhouse but want to grow some warmth-loving plants, subdivide your greenhouse space by stapling plastic or polycarbonate sheeting to a lumber-framed dividing wall. And use a space heater to boost temperatures in the warmer section.

The Intermediate Greenhouse

When you think of a greenhouse, do you picture a warm, fragrant, crystal-like building brimming with exotic plants gathered from the far reaches of the world by intrepid plant hunters? Well, maybe that's *my* picture, but can you relate to that? In my mind, that lush colorful mental picture of abundance most closely reflects the intermediate greenhouse, which bridges the gap between a cool greenhouse and a warm one. It has nighttime winter temperatures ranging from 50° to 60°F and sunny winter daytime temperatures from 70° to as high as 90°F.

Success in growing greenhouse plants lies in grouping plants with similar climate requirements. For example, for an intermediate greenhouse, orchids, begonias, and ferns are good choices because all have similar needs.

During the past two centuries, plant breeders here and abroad have created untold numbers of hybrid plants. A hybrid, generally, is something made by combining two different elements. In the plant world, a hybrid is a named variety of a plant that exists because a hybridizer bred two different plants to create a new one. The variety of hybrids that exists means you can choose from a nearly endless list of plants to grow in your intermediate greenhouse. You may grow a little of everything, or you may choose to collect *cultivars* of a single type of plant— for example, orchids, begonias, ferns, or amaryllis. Specializing in one type of plant ensures that your plants will have similar needs and all will be happy in the same greenhouse environment.

def•i•ni•tion

The word **cultivar** is blended from *cultivate* and *variety*. Cultivars are variations of a plant species that show characteristics that remain different from the parent plants over a number of generations. In the simplest terms, a plant breeder might breed a red daylily and a yellow daylily to come up with a new cultivar that is orange.

If you have houseplants, you already understand how to grow many of the plants that thrive in an intermediate greenhouse. In the greenhouse, however, your plants will enjoy a more natural environment, with more light and fresh air than any window can provide. You'll be amazed at how much healthier your greenhouse plants look; and healthy plants are not likely to suffer from pests, diseases, yellowing leaves, or spindly growth. In fact, you may want to invest in duplicate plants so you can rotate them in and out; keep them in the house when they're in bloom and return them to the greenhouse when they begin to look tired from their stint in the darker confines of the house.

To keep track of swings in greenhouse temperatures, invest in a maximum/minimum thermometer that records daily highs and lows. An inexpensive analog model costs under $15, or invest twice as much, or more, for a digital model that also has a remote read-out and a low-temperature alarm. (For sources, see Appendix D). Having a thermometer do this work for you saves trips out to the greenhouse to check on things and can also prevent disaster should your heater fail.

What to Grow

Utility expenses influence most gardeners to reserve the rarified atmosphere of a heated greenhouse for *exotic* ornamentals. In other words, the expense of heating a greenhouse is too great to grow ordinary plants that might just as well survive outdoors. If you are an exotic plant lover, though, the expense is worth it. Having an intermediate greenhouse is nirvana every day of the year.

def•i•ni•tion

An **exotic** plant is one that is not native to the continent on which you live, or in a narrower context, a plant not native to the *region* in which you live. An **adapted** plant, by contrast, is a plant that originated elsewhere but in a climate similar to the one in which you live.

An intermediate greenhouse insulated with a jacket of bubble wrap and a translucent storm tarp provides a warm, draft-free climate suited to a wide assortment of flowering and foliage plants in winter. Those plants that need more light and heat hang near the roof; plants that require less light and warmth occupy benches; and cool-temperature plants live under benches on the floor.

(Donna Chiarelli Studio)

Here are some favorite plant choices to get you growing in the intermediate greenhouse.

Flowering plants:

Amaryllis

Anthurium (flamingo flower)

Begonia species and hybrids—fibrous-rooted, rhizomatous, and tuberous

Big-leaf hydrangea (*Hydrangea macrophylla*)

Columnea (lipstick plant)

Fuchsia

Gardenia

Hibiscus

Jasmine

Kalanchoe

Orchid species and hybrids:

Calanthe	Cattleya
Dendrobium	Epidendrum
Laelia	Miltonia
Oncidium	Vanda
Strelitzia (bird of paradise)	

Foliage plants:

Aloe	Ananas (variegated pineapple)
Aglaonema (Chinese evergreen)	Bromeliad
Calathea	Croton
Cryptanthus (earth star)	Fiddle leaf fig
Hoya	Maranta (prayer plant)
Pepperomia	Pothos
Philodendron	Rex begonia
Sansevieria (snake plant)	Stromanthe
Succulents, many varieties	Tradescantias (wandering Jew)

Fruiting plants:

Citrus varieties   Kiwi

Papaya   Pineapple

Star fruit

For more information on selecting and growing greenhouse plants, scan the pages of houseplant and greenhouse plant encyclopedias and guide books (see Appendix D).

What Not to Grow

The relatively high nighttime temperatures of an intermediate greenhouse rule out all but heat-loving food plants, such as tomatoes, cucumbers, eggplants, peppers, and melons. You can start vegetable seeds in an intermediate greenhouse in late winter and early spring, but be forewarned—vegetable plants are insect magnets. Spare your tropical greenhouse plants from a parade of whiteflies, gnats, ants, and aphids! It's safer to grow your food plants under cover outdoors or in an unheated cold frame or greenhouse and to start your seeds under grow lights in the basement or on a sunny windowsill.

Experimenting with marginally hardy plants is fun, but don't be too disappointed if plants from the previous cool and upcoming warm greenhouse lists do not perform well in an intermediate greenhouse. You will have better luck growing plants from the cool list than the more tender beauties.

Microclimates

Remember the greenhouse microclimates we talked about earlier: the coldest are near the floor and the outside door; the warmest, near the roof; and mid-range, on the benches. If you match plant needs to intermediate microclimates, you may have success growing plants from all three greenhouse types right in the same greenhouse. Finally, we should mention that the cost of heating an intermediate greenhouse is moderate when compared to that of running a warm one. So taking advantage of those microclimates could save you a bundle.

Green Thumb _____

On sunny days, an unshaded greenhouse can reach temperatures dangerously high for both plants and gardeners. When greenhouse temperatures hit 90°F or if you see plants beginning to wilt from heat, vent the greenhouse to let out excess heat. If you have a roof vent, crack it open until temperatures drop to 80°F or even to 70°F. If your greenhouse does not have a roof vent or if the vent is covered with insulation, open the door a couple of inches.

The Warm Greenhouse

A warm greenhouse brings the equator to your doorstep, with nighttime temperatures between 60° and 70°F and daytime temperatures reaching as high as the 90s. And you must keep humidity high (above 60 percent) for the tropical plants and *epiphytes* you'll want to grow in your warm greenhouse.

def•i•ni•tion _____

Epiphytes are plants with exposed roots that absorb moisture from the air. In nature, epiphytes are nonparasitic plants that grow on damp rocks and tree branches. Many orchids and bromeliads are epiphytic, and, in the greenhouse, are commonly grown on pieces of bark or in open-weave baskets.

To increase greenhouse humidity for moisture-loving plants, wet down the floor and benches or run an electric mister during the day. Having an open water reservoir, such as a fish tank or pond, also increases humidity through evaporation. If you mist or sprinkle, allow time for foliage to dry before sundown because moist, dark conditions promote fungal leaf diseases. Install a humidity gauge, or hygrometer, so that you know exactly how much moisture is in the air—aim for between 60 and 80 percent humidity.

What to Grow

Warm greenhouses are the most costly to heat in winter, and for that reason are mostly dedicated to specialty collections and very tender plants. Here are some favorites from a vast palette of warm-greenhouse possibilities.

Flowering plants:

African violet

Episcia

Gloxinia

Orchids of Central America and Asia, such as Phaleonopsis orchid (moth orchid) and Paphiopedilum orchid (slipper orchid); for others, consult an orchid guidebook

Stephanotis

Streptocarpus

Foliage plants:

Caladium	Ceropegia (rosary vine)
Coleus	Croton
Dracaena	Dieffenbachia (dumb cane)
Fittonia	Scindapsus (devil's ivy)
Spider plant	Tillandsia (air plant)
Tropical ferns	

Also, with some care, plants from the intermediate greenhouse list, such as vanda orchids, can thrive in warm greenhouse environments.

What Not to Grow

A warm greenhouse is practical for growing only warmth-loving vegetables and herbs, because other plants will go to seed and die when exposed to excessive heat and humidity. Plus, as a warm greenhouse is not cost effective for food crops, most gardeners choose to grow these plants in unheated greenhouses, cold frames, or covered garden rows.

The warm greenhouse is also an inhospitable environment for cool-greenhouse plants. Flowering shrubs and trees that need to rest during a period of cool winter dormancy can literally grow themselves to death in a warm greenhouse environment.

Cacti, some succulents, and other arid-climate plants will not thrive in a warm, humid greenhouse. To learn about specific plants and their growing requirements, do an online search or consult a good guidebook with growing instructions (see Appendix D).

Safety First

Some plants are toxic if ingested or irritate skin when handled. If young children or pets visit your greenhouse, you should educate yourself thoroughly. Check with a pediatrician or your pet's veterinarian for a list of toxic plants, or visit the following websites for lists of toxic and nontoxic houseplants.

For lists of toxic and nontoxic plants:

The University of Nebraska Cooperative Extension:
www.lancaster.unl.edu/factsheets/031.htm

The Cincinnati Children's Hospital Medical Center:
www.cincinnatichildrens.org/svc/alpha/d/dpic/plants/poisonous.htm

www.cincinnatichildrens.org/svc/alpha/d/dpic/plants/nonpoisonous.htm

For a list of plants that are toxic to animals:

American Society for the Prevention of Cruelty to Animals:
www.aspca.org/pet-care/poison-control/plants

Microclimates

Take advantage of the cooler microclimate near the floor of your warm greenhouse to grow plants recommended for an intermediate greenhouse, such as vanda orchids, bromeliads, and tropical ferns. But stagger placement of hanging plants to be sure other plants aren't blocking the light above these floor-dwellers. Remember that in the upper regions of a warm greenhouse, the heat and light can be intense, so make sure the plants up there are suited for that zone.

Winterizing a Heated Greenhouse

Heated greenhouses are rarely used for growing food crops because the vegetables that thrive in hot conditions are also long-day vegetables, so they wouldn't thrive in the short days of winter, even if they were warm.

Instead, heated greenhouses are usually reserved for foliage and flowering plants that originated south of the equator. Because the seasons of their native lands are opposite ours, a heated greenhouse can be a flowering oasis to enjoy in winter (because the plants think it's summer). These plants often thrive in the lower light levels of winters north of the equator, because in their native habitats, they grow in the shade of the forest floor, or as epiphytes in the crotches of tree branches.

Annual Cleanup

Your heated greenhouse is a haven for growing things. And that's no surprise because you're taking good care of it for just that purpose. The bad part is that *lots* of things may grow there that you didn't invite. Algae on the glazing and spiders under the shelves and benches are the first things that come to mind. So once a year, you get to empty out your greenhouse and make it just like new. Here's how to proceed.

- Empty the greenhouse. Set the plants on a clean tarp spread on the ground under a tree. Remove all cords and electrical devices. If you have open containers, papers, or anything else that shouldn't get wet in your workbench area, remove those things as well.

- In the now-empty greenhouse, use a wet/dry vacuum to suck up dry plant debris, spilled soil, insects, and cobwebs. Be sure to stick the hose wand into the corners and under the benches, which are a favorite haunt of bugs.

- When you've vacuumed up the dirt and grit, it's time to clean the windows, or glazing, as greenhouse windows are called. And because you'll be inside the greenhouse spraying a hose overhead, I recommend donning a raincoat, old clothes, rubber shoes or boots, rubber gloves, and a water-resistant polyester baseball cap to keep your head and face dry. If you have sensitive eyes, wear goggles.

Safety First _____

Before you hose off the glazing, turn off the electric circuits for your own safety. Remove all extension cords, power strips, fans, heaters, misters, and other electrical appliances to keep from spraying them with water and ruining them.

- Use a garden hose on a gentle spray setting to wet down the inside and outside of the greenhouse.

◆ In a bucket, mix a weak solution of laundry detergent and water. Laundry detergent is a good all-around greenhouse cleanser because it's low-sudsing, kills soft-bodied insects, and is safe to use around plants because it breaks down to phosphate, a major plant nutrient. Dip a long-handled sponge mop with a scrubbing strip into the bucket, and swab it over the glazing, inside and out. If you run across algae or other stubborn dirt, scrub it loose with the scrubbing strip of the mop. Work in sections, and rinse the soap off before it dries.

◆ Check for stubborn spots of algae inside and out, and scrub them off with a little household bleach (I put some in an old spray bottle for this purpose) and a scrubbing pad or brush. Rinse again.

◆ Spray the floor with the hard stream setting of the hose nozzle to dislodge stubborn dirt. If you have mats on the floor, take them out and hose them off. Then hose off the greenhouse floor besides.

◆ Either allow the greenhouse to air dry, or run the wet/dry vacuum around the floor to remove puddles before putting the plants back inside.

While the greenhouse dries, winterize the plants you put on the tarp. Set them on a worktable, one at a time, and trim off and dispose of dead and damaged leaves. Remember to disinfect your pruners or scissors between plants to prevent spreading disease.

Rinse the plants and pots, with the hose nozzle set to gentle spray, to remove dust and insects, and they're ready to go back into the greenhouse. If you find insect pests you cannot remove with fingers or water, turn to Chapter 13 for solutions. Throw out diseased or infested plants; winter is no time for a greenhouse epidemic. You can repot plants now, if you wish. I prefer to wait until spring when longer days promote plant growth and faster recovery.

Insulating a Greenhouse

If you have a conservatory-quality greenhouse, it likely has double-pane, insulated, sealed glazing. The economy models that I and most gardeners buy come with loosely fitted single-pane glass, Plexiglas, or acrylic panels, which are drafty and offer minimal insulation. In freezing-winter climates, these are nearly impossible to heat if you don't insulate them.

Where I live, temperatures dip into the teens for days at a time in winter. After years of experimenting with various insulating materials, I've come up with an airtight, highly insulated combination of coverings that lets me heat my 6-by-8-foot freestanding greenhouse with a small electric space heater set on a low setting. You can modify my coverings, adding or subtracting layers, to suit your own climate.

Clear bubble wrap is the best insulation for greenhouse walls and ceiling—the bigger the bubble, the better the insulation. Yes, you can save scraps of bubble wrap from packaging for this purpose, but it'll take forever to piece enough scraps together to cover much glazing, the small bubbles offer little insulation, and the uncoated plastic will deteriorate rapidly with sun exposure.

Greenhouse supply and mail-order catalog companies (see Appendix D) sell 8-foot-wide rolls of large-bubble, UV light-stabilized bubble wrap designed for this purpose. The catalogs suggest you cut it to fit between the support ribs of glazing and apply it to the inside of your greenhouse. But if you do it this way, you'll end up with droopy, saggy, leaky strips of bubble wrap.

Instead, I cover the outside of my greenhouse, starting at the ground on one side, unrolling the bubble wrap up and over the ridge and down to the ground on the other side. I hold a kitchen broom under the bubble wrap, bristle-end up, to help me fish it up and over the ridge without snagging.

I use clear weatherstripping tape from the hardware store to tack the pieces to the greenhouse. Then I cut pieces of bubble wrap to fit the pointed gable ends and the door and apply them similarly. This goes pretty fast because I'm not concerned, at this point, with fastening them down tight or sealing against drafts.

Green Thumb

If you cover your greenhouse with clear plastic or bubble wrap over winter, use clear weatherstripping tape, designed to fasten plastic over house windows, to secure it. This tape has special glue that adheres even during a hard freeze. Do *not* use packing tape, duct tape, or any other kind of tape, or you'll find yourself patching and replacing tape in the cold of winter, and a drafty greenhouse with a big heating bill.

Because of the severity of our winters, I use a double layer of bubble wrap insulation, so I repeat the above process a second time. I even cover the roof vent. If you're in a warmer climate and need to open the vent on sunny days, trim around the vent and carefully fasten the bubble wrap flap to the vent window with weatherstripping tape so the vent will open. Carefully tape all around the doorframe for a secure seal.

When the greenhouse is completely covered with two layers of bubble wrap held in place with tape, I cover the bubble wrap with a single, large, translucent rip-stop greenhouse tarp called a storm tarp. These tarps, designed to protect greenhouse glass (more importantly the bubble wrap) from hail and falling tree limbs, are available from greenhouse supply companies.

Then I pull out the weatherstripping tape and cover all the tarps' seams with two layers of tape to seal out drafts. I also tape the tarp to the building, covering every loose edge. Finally, I run two horizontal bands of tape around the greenhouse, one at head height and one around the base of the building, so that strong winds can't pull the vertical taped seams loose. This is a necessary precaution; the seams of my greenhouse cover have pulled loose a few times in the past, and the worst incident resulted in my wading into a nearby icy creek to fish it out and replace it.

In winter, I insulate my greenhouse with two layers of bubble wrap covered by a translucent storm tarp and seal seams in the covering tight with clear weatherstripping tape.

(Donna Chiarelli Studio)

Over the years, I've improved on speed and ease of installation. With a helper, I can now cover the greenhouse in half an hour. In early summer, I pull the layers off, roll them up, and stash the rolls in the garage in about the same amount of time.

The cost of these coverings is more than worth the money, at about $200 for everything. Because they're protected against light degradation, they last five years or longer when you take them off and store them over summer.

The Least You Need to Know

◆ Match cool, intermediate, or warm greenhouse conditions to plants' needs.

◆ Track temperatures in various parts of the greenhouse to take advantage of microclimates for a varied plant collection.

◆ Avoid introducing insects into a greenhouse filled with valuable tropicals; don't mix in vegetable plants, which attract insects.

◆ Check with a pediatrician or veterinarian for a list of toxic plants if pets or young children visit your greenhouse.

◆ Restrict plants requiring a cold-winter dormancy to a cool or cold greenhouse; they will grow themselves to death in a heated greenhouse.

◆ Clean and insulate your greenhouse in fall to prevent disease and pest outbreaks over winter.

Chapter 16

Gizmos for Heated Greenhouses

In This Chapter

- The greenhouse of your dreams can fit your budget, too
- The most economical and efficient ways to heat, cool, humidify, or dehumidify a greenhouse
- Multitasking tools for caring for greenhouse plants
- Maintaining a healthy greenhouse environment

Now that we've focused on what plants to grow in a greenhouse and how to take care of them, let's talk about how to achieve and maintain the optimal environment for these plants and take a look at technology and equipment for heating, cooling, humidifying, and dehumidifying.

And let's also check out some useful and quirky greenhouse tools and gadgets. I am, admittedly, a gadget girl, and the lure of the garden catalog is strong. But because I have a small greenhouse, over the years I've narrowed my tool repertoire to an essential few—multitaskers all. I give you my choices, plus a few from my wish list.

Construction

Let's say you've decided you're really going to get or build that greenhouse you've been wanting, but you have so many choices to pick from! Those fantastic pictures in the gardening magazines, the greenhouse you saw down the street, and the one you sketched out on paper last year are all influencing your vision. How do you sort through these influences? Well, your budget will help you make some decisions—but you don't need me to tell you that. And your town, city, or neighborhood building codes may have a say in what you do as well. That's right. If you're planning to build a structure on your property, you'd better check with local building permit officials first. Their requirements may dictate the kind of structure you choose, its location, and the utilities, if any, you install.

Just so you're aware of the possibilities, consider this scenario. Let's say you've decided to attach a lean-to greenhouse to your home. Local building codes *could* dictate that your structure meet the same specifications as a permanent room addition. These include a permanent, load-bearing foundation; a roof that can stand up to heavy snow loads; permanent, professionally installed and inspected plumbing and electricity; plus residential-rated heating and cooling units installed by licensed professionals. As you can see, you'd be wise to find this out before you set any other plans or budgets in place.

Going High-End

If you have the budget for it, you can go high-end. And high-end *will* mean high cost. A number of manufacturers offer heavy metal-framed lean-to greenhouses—called solariums, sunrooms, or conservatories—that meet residential standards and are usually constructed onsite by the manufacturer. Another option that would meet building codes, generally speaking, is a wood-framed lean-to greenhouse put up by a professional builder who would then be responsible for getting the proper permits.

Budget-Friendly Greenhouses

If you want to test the greenhouse waters but don't have the budget or the huge ambitions for that magazine gothic-style sunroom, a freestanding model, for which many municipalities issue a less-demanding shed permit, may be what you want. Many manufacturers also offer freestanding greenhouses. Browsing your favorite garden magazine or doing an online search will yield many possibilities, and your local home store or garden center may have options as well.

Be sure to find out what type of utilities you need to install to comply with local building codes. If you go the shed route, you may be able to use "temporary" utilities and run a garden hose from a house or outbuilding spigot during the warmer months. And then, of course, in the winter you'd need to shut off the water to the spigot and drain the hose unless your winters are very mild.

Garden Guide

Run heated water to your greenhouse through a garden hose. How? Hire a plumber to connect both hot and cold water lines to a new or existing frost-proof outdoor faucet. If your winters are cold, ask for shutoff valves on the inside of the house so you can shut off water to that faucet and prevent freezing. With this setup, you turn the spigot on at the house and adjust the temperature of the water there. In eastern Pennsylvania, where I garden, I use a hose from late March until the first hard freeze, usually in November.

Utilities

Having utilities properly installed and using a few electrical gadgets will create a comfortable work space for you. And more importantly, it will minimize problems with greenhouse pests, diseases, and lost plants.

Comply with building ordinances when installing a power source, and have a city inspector sign off on the job—both for safety's sake and to avoid having to redo the job. For my little freestanding heated greenhouse, local codes allowed me to have an electrician make an inexpensive, 20-amp, direct-burial electrical cable long enough to run electricity from a ground fault circuit interrupter (GFCI) outlet on the exterior of my house to the interior of the greenhouse. A GFCI outlet, which quickly shuts off power in wet or extremely humid conditions to protect the user from electrical shock, must be used in potentially wet locations, such as kitchens, bathrooms, outdoors, and in greenhouses. The cable is essentially a heavy-duty extension cord designed to be buried, which keeps us from tripping over it or hitting it with the lawn mower.

To power the greenhouse, I attached an outdoor-grade power strip with six outlets to the legs of a greenhouse bench (above the floor to avoid contact with damp flooring) and plugged it into the cable. The strip powers a fan, a shop vacuum, a rechargeable hand-held mister, a cool-mist vaporizer, and a space heater, as needed.

Green Thumb

Shop for weather-resistant power strips from Thanksgiving through Christmas. These strips are designed for running outdoor holiday light displays and are sold in hardware and discount stores during the holidays.

If your GFCI outlet or power strip shuts down because it detects a hazard, as it's supposed to do, you'll have to push reset buttons on each tripped unit. You may also need to reset the circuit breaker in your home's electrical panel. So it's wise to keep water well away from your greenhouse's power source.

To protect the power strip in my greenhouse from dripping water, I placed a piece of heavy tempered glass on the bench directly above the strip. I also designated this area as a "dry corner" to be used for storing tools rather than plants.

The author stores electrical hookups and gadgets (including a shop vacuum and rechargeable mister), tools, and supplies in a "dry corner" of her greenhouse.

(Donna Chiarelli Studio)

Maintaining Systems

The construction is complete. Your greenhouse is up and running. Now comes the fun—maintaining your greenhouse and watching your plants grow. You're responsible for the temperature, the air circulation, and the moisture levels—in both the growing medium and in the air. How will you keep it all running smoothly? Keep reading!

Steady Temperature

We can't overemphasize the need to keep a heated greenhouse at the optimal temperature for the plants you want to grow. In winter, temperatures in the low 40s or below can cause tender plants to drop their leaves or even die. In summer, a heat wave can make plants wilt even if you water them copiously, as overheated plants simply can't absorb water through their roots fast enough to replace the moisture evaporating from their leaves.

Your options for greenhouse heat are as varied as your imagination and local building codes allow. An electric space heater is easy to install and will heat a small greenhouse in warm winter climates and a well-insulated one in colder climates (for information on insulating materials and how to install them, review Chapter 15). Our winters, in eastern Pennsylvania, have average lows in the 20s, with occasional spells of below-zero weather, and I can maintain night temperatures in the 60s in my 6½-by-8-foot kit greenhouse with a standard-sized electric space heater.

If you have a larger greenhouse or colder winters, you may need to run two space heaters. In below-zero weather, I add a second space heater that runs on a different circuit to keep from overloading one circuit. This heater is a heavy-duty model designed for use at construction sites, for example, and sits about a foot off the floor on steel legs to protect it from dampness.

Garden Guide

If you want permanent heating and cooling units in your greenhouse, consider having them professionally installed. If you purchase a maintenance contract the installer will clean, inspect, and repair the units annually.

Space heaters don't have reliable thermostats, so to keep from overheating the greenhouse during the day, I plug the heater into a grounded lamp timer that turns it off at sunup and on at sundown. I don't need it during the day because even on a cloudy day, the sun keeps the greenhouse above 70°F, and on snowy days, the snow reflects light into the greenhouse, shooting temperatures into the 80s. I adjust the heater's setting up or down, according to weather forecasts and changing day length.

A small electric space heater, which heats the author's well-insulated greenhouse, hangs from a bench to prevent contact with a potentially wet floor.

(Donna Chiarelli Studio)

If you need to provide additional heat for a small collection of tender plants, you can set them on an electric heat mat (see Chapter 6). Many of these have preset thermostats that will maintain soil temperatures at 70°F, and more sophisticated models offer an adjustable thermostat.

If you have a large greenhouse or if your local building codes require a permanent heating unit, you can buy a specialized greenhouse heater. These large units usually hang from the ceiling and have accurate thermostats you can set anywhere between 40°F to 90°F. Another electrical option is a heat pump, which will heat a greenhouse in winter and cool it in summer (for sources, see Appendix D).

A time-honored source, hot-water radiant heat, is a favorite of many commercial greenhouses because tubes that circulate hot water are installed beneath benches where they help cut costs by keeping the heat source close to the plants. For a low-end version of this kind of heat, you may be able to have a plumber install a small water heater that circulates a solution of water and antifreeze. For more heating capacity, you'll need to have a furnace company install a professional radiant heat system.

Depending on the cost of utilities in your area and personal preferences, you can also heat your greenhouse with gas, oil, or wood. I once heard a story about a hobby greenhouse enthusiast who heated his greenhouse with a salvaged house-trailer gas furnace and another who installed a vintage potbellied woodstove inside the greenhouse.

Garden Guide

To reduce the chance of furnace fumes that can harm plants, consider housing a greenhouse furnace in an insulated shed outside the greenhouse. Run heating ducts from the furnace into the greenhouse.

Cooling the Greenhouse in Summer

There is almost nowhere in the country where a greenhouse won't need some form of summer cooling. In northern, high altitude, and coastal areas, passive cooling may be enough to keep plants from being heat stressed as opening vents and/or windows is enough to keep the inside greenhouse temperature at comfortable levels. In hotter climates, passive cooling is not enough. Shading the greenhouse will help cooling units, such as greenhouse swamp coolers, misters, and in the hottest climates, air conditioners, work as efficiently as possible so that your utility bills will not go sky-high (hopefully).

Because the most basic form of passive cooling is opening greenhouse roof vents, windows, and even doors to cooling breezes, I don't know why most kit greenhouses do not come with screens, when excluding insects is so important. However, you can take measurements of your door and vents to a local window company and have them make screens to fit. You can also purchase one-size-fits-all screen curtains from garden supply catalogs (see Appendix D).

Location can make a big difference with cooling. The ideal site is beneath a deciduous shade tree, such as a maple, which is unlikely to drop limbs in storms. And when the leaves drop in fall, the greenhouse receives a full dose of warming winter sunshine. In the absence of a shade tree, the next best thing is to drape shade cloth over your greenhouse. Shade cloth is sold in varying percentages of

Green Thumb

In summer, large shade trees transpire about 30 gallons of water a day. Temperatures under the tree's canopy can be three to four degrees cooler than air above the tree.

shade, ranging from 30 to 70 percent, allowing you to choose the appropriate amount of shade for the plants you are growing.

Shade cloth cools and protects greenhouse plants from sunburn in the summer.

(Donna Chiarelli Studio)

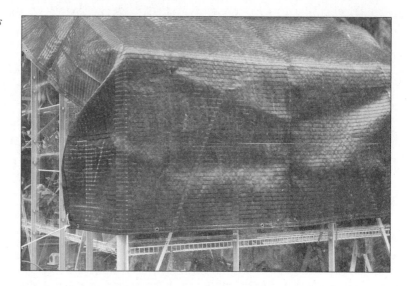

Circulating Air

Hot air naturally rises and exits through roof vents, but you can hurry the process by hanging one or more fans from the ridge to pull hot air out the vents. Either open the door or add one or two low wall vents so the fans can pull cooler air in.

A fan hung from the ridge pulls hot air out through a roof vent in summer.

(Donna Chiarelli Studio)

Humidifying and Cooling at Once

Misters can cool the surrounding air by as much as 30°F, and the moisture they add to the air also reduces wilting and dry soil. Misters with refillable water tanks range from a cool-mist vaporizer for under $30 from your local drug store to greenhouse tank misters that start around $235. Models also hook up to a garden hose and cost as much as $450. Or you can install a high-pressure misting system, similar to a patio mister, that emits cool mist from a number of small nozzles spaced out along a water line. The hotter and *dryer* the greenhouse air, the better misters work.

An inexpensive cool-mist vaporizer plugged into an electric timer is set to hydrate roots of vanda and dendrobium orchids each morning in the author's greenhouse.

(Donna Chiarelli Studio)

A venerable, pre-air conditioning cooling technology called a *swamp cooler* is still used to cool and humidify the air in large commercial greenhouses. Home greenhouse keepers can use a swamp cooler as well, though the units tend to be large and would therefore be suitable only for larger hobby greenhouses.

def•i•ni•tion

A **swamp cooler** is a simple cooling unit that fits in a window or greenhouse wall vent. The cooler's large fan pulls air from outdoors through a water-soaked nylon or excelsior pad, cooling and humidifying the air as it enters a greenhouse.

Dehumidifiers

Where summers are both hot and humid, such as southeastern and southern coastal areas, gardeners both cool and dehumidify hobby greenhouses with a window air-conditioning unit.

If humidity—not heat—is the problem, you can use a portable dehumidifier, such as those sold in home centers. Just plug it into an outlet, and select a setting that will get the humidity down to an acceptable percentage for your plants. Of course, you'll need to close the door and vents, or you'll be fruitlessly dehumidifying the great outdoors.

Garden Guide

Distilled water costs nearly $2 per gallon at the store, but you can retrieve up to 2 gallons of "free" distilled water a day from a dehumidifier with a water collection reservoir. You can use this distilled water in cool-misters, hand-held misters, and for watering plants that suffer brown leaf tips from exposure to mineral salts or chemically treated tap water. *Do not drink this water because it's not sterilized.*

Interior: Shelves, Ceiling, Floor

Greenhouse shelves and benches should have a slatted design to allow air and light to reach plants on all levels. Shelving can be of any building material—wood, aluminum, and, expanded metal, or engineered wood. Expanded metal is an open-weave metal mesh, often used as table tops for outdoor furniture. Engineered wood is a rot-proof combination of plastic and wood chips sold as a decking material.

My personal favorite is white, plastic-coated wire closet organizers because they are rustproof, easy to clean, and unobtrusive. You can even buy clever hook-on accessories, such as spice shelves, which are perfect for holding small plants, and holders and hooks for storing tools.

When using plastic-coated closet organizer shelving in a greenhouse, you can add coordinated tool organizers. Here, hooks hold pruners, a funnel, a sieve, and a butane lighter for flame-sterilizing cutting blades.

(Donna Chiarelli Studio)

Coated-wire shelves and ceiling grids attach to the greenhouse with specialized channel bolts and brackets or hooks sold through greenhouse supply catalogs. Create benches by setting shelving on unobtrusive galvanized saw-horse legs sold at hardware stores. I even found coated-wire rectangular wall grids to attach to each pitched side of the ceiling, giving me an additional 10 square feet of hanging space in my little 6 × 8-foot greenhouse. These grids support small plants such as miniature orchids, tillandsias, and Spanish moss without sacrificing head room.

Suspend wire wall organizers from the ceiling to increase space for hanging plants. Plastic-coated closet shelves hold potted plants, and a galvanized conduit pipe hung from the ridge is used as a hanging-basket bar.

(Donna Chiarelli Studio)

Traditional flooring materials include concrete or gravel over dirt. Gravel allows for excellent drainage but tends to collect debris and insects. Concrete is easier to clean, but both are poor insulators, wicking heat from the greenhouse into the ground. I found a great solution to this problem by covering my concrete floor with thick black rubber barn-stall mat cut to fit. The thick rubber mat does not conduct heat, so it stops the warmth from wicking away through the floor, and the black color absorbs the sun's heat in winter.

Greenhouse Potting Areas

The heart and soul of a greenhouse is its potting area, the place where life begins for seedlings and where old plants get rejuvenated. If your greenhouse is large enough, set up a potting bench and storage area inside. Where growing space is too precious to give up, you can find room outdoors for a proper potting shed or at least a fair-weather potting bench.

Outside my unheated vegetable greenhouse, I make do with a simple bistro table. It's big enough to support a flat of seedlings, a watering can, and a trowel while I plant and tend the adjacent garden.

Outside my ornamental greenhouse, I have a more elaborate setup. On the side where an evergreen windbreak protects the greenhouse from the harsh, western sun stands a fantastic flea-market find. The 6-foot-long stainless steel bar sink has two work surfaces and three sink basins. Its tall legs leave room underneath for buckets and a trash bin. Stainless steel is an ideal material for a potting surface because its smooth, easily disinfected surface does not harbor pathogens.

A stainless-steel bar sink serves as a potting bench outside the author's greenhouse.

(Donna Chiarelli Studio)

At one end of the sink, a galvanized double wash tub on legs holds homemade potting mix, bags of sphagnum moss, and orchid bark. A sheet of Plexiglas covers the tubs, keeping everything dry and creating another work area. In all but the coldest weather I can pot and repot, sow seeds, and let the soil fall where it may. The sink drains into the nearby vegetable garden, so I just hose everything down at cleanup time.

Essential Tools

Like gadget-collecting cooks, gardeners have their favorite multitasking tools. Some, such as watering cans and pruners, are designed by garden manufacturers to perform their appointed purposes, while others are imaginatively repurposed tools, ranging from cutlery and cookers to carpenter's helpers.

As they say in the movies, "you must have a willing suspension of disbelief" as you scan the following eclectic collection of greenhouse tools. Sometimes weird, but always useful, these are the ones I would take with me if my greenhouse and I were stranded on a desert island.

From the kitchen:

◆ Flatware—I like the pointed-handled, "mid-century modern" style because the handles make great *dibbles* for planting stem cuttings.

I use a butter knife to make planting holes, loosen pot-bound plants, and scrape lime deposits off clay pots. A spoon makes a pot-size shovel or a scoop for measuring fertilizer. Fork tines gently cultivate soil or lift seedlings from flats.

def•i•ni•tion

Dibbles are cylindrical garden tools with a pointed end used for making planting holes in soil or potting medium. In the old days, thrifty gardeners made dibbles by sharpening broken tool handles.

◆ Serrated bread knife—Nothing beats a sharp knife for cutting through crowded plant roots at repotting time.

Garden Guide

You will never have a dull knife if you keep an empty clay flowerpot handy. Gently drag each side of the cutting edge of a knife several times along the side of the pot at a 20-degree angle. As the blade sharpens, use less pressure until you are satisfied with the edge.

Green Thumb

If you have repurposed kitchen tools in your greenhouse, use a waterproof marker to label them for greenhouse use to keep them from migrating into your kitchen.

Garden Guide

Rust and UV degradation are enemies of tools kept in a humid, sunny greenhouse. For this reason, avoid plastic-handled and steel-bladed tools. Choose impervious stainless-steel and aluminum blades, and silicone and nylon handles.

♦ Kitchen shears—These are my favorite greenhouse "pruner." I also keep a pair of sharp scissors on hand for trimming delicate leaves.

♦ Sieve—When filling misters, I pour water through a stainless-steel tea strainer to make sure no debris clogs the spray mechanisms.

♦ Funnel—A funnel comes in handy for filling small-necked misters, small watering cans, and jugs.

♦ Clear plastic food containers—These make good propagators for starting seeds or rooting cuttings. Use lidless deli containers as saucers under pots.

♦ Rubber dishwashing gloves—These are a durable, waterproof improvement over garden gloves during long, gritty potting sessions that can pucker and abrade hands.

♦ Slotted stirring spoon—I use a large, nylon slotted spoon to stir fertilizer into a bucket of water.

♦ Hot pot—I can water my greenhouse plants with the warm/tepid water that protects roots from cold-water shock by stirring one hot pot of simmering water into a 3-gallon bucket of cold water.

♦ Slow cooker—Simmering hard-to-moisten orchid bark overnight in a lidded slow cooker turned to the low setting sterilizes orchid bark and helps it absorb water. Just remember to cool the bark before repotting your orchids.

Garden and greenhouse tools:

There are also some essential garden and specialty greenhouse tools I wouldn't be without (see Appendix D for sources).

♦ Soil thermometer—Use it to check temperatures in potting medium for plants that require warm or cool soil.

♦ pH gauge—This tool comes in handy for checking to see whether fertilizer, water, and potting soil are compatible with a plant's pH needs.

◆ Light meter—A good plant guide will list the foot candles of light various species of plants need to grow. A foot candle is a universal unit of measurement for light, based on how strong the light from one candle is one foot from its source. Use a plant light meter to register the light level in various areas of your greenhouse in morning and afternoon in all four seasons.

◆ Pruners and Ikebana scissors—Pruners make short work of cutting through thick or woody branches, and Ikebana scissors are durable cutters for delicate work. In a humid greenhouse, they rust easily, so use them often to keep the blades mobile, and oil all parts to retard rust.

◆ Watering cans—Get several of various sizes, including some with long spouts, which are useful for watering plants in the far corners. Pitcher-shaped ones are useful for filling misters.

◆ Rechargeable mister—With one push of a button, you can mist continuously for about 20 minutes. This makes it easy to foliar feed and to water plants with exposed roots.

The author uses a battery-operated, rechargeable mister, which can run continuously for about 20 minutes, to mist and water orchids, bromeliads, Spanish moss, and tillandsias.

(Donna Chiarelli Studio)

From the pharmacy:

Some drug-store staples make perfect sense in a greenhouse setting.

- Antibacterial soap—This keeps your hands clean and reduces chances of having minor nicks and scratches get infected. You can also clean tools and pots with it.

Green Thumb

Small things make a big difference. Include these useful little greenhouse helpers in your tool kit:

Waterproof markers

Plastic or wooden plant labels

Twist ties

Green garden Velcro on a roll

Kneeling pad

- Disposable latex gloves—Waterproof, formfitting gloves stand up to hours of potting and greenhouse cleanup chores. Afterward, just toss them.

- Aspirin—In Chapter 17, we give instructions for an insecticide made by dissolving aspirin in water.

- Baking soda—Mix 1 tablespoon baking soda into 1 gallon water, and spray on foliage weekly to deter, but not cure, powdery mildew, a fungal leaf infection.

- Rubbing alcohol—Sterilize cutting tools and dab or spray on plants as an insecticide.

From the hardware store:

Browse the shelves of your local automotive supply or hardware store for these helpful greenhouse aids.

Green Thumb

Include these hardware-store extras in your greenhouse tool kit:

Disposable razor blades or a razor knife

Pliers

Screwdriver

S-hooks

Small paintbrushes for dusting leaves and pollinating flowers

Small trash can with disposable liners

- Drywall saw—This heavy-duty serrated hand saw can cut through the toughest woody root divisions.

- Waterproof outdoor thermometers—Place several around the greenhouse to register microclimates.

- Humidity gauge, or humidistat—This is essential to keep track of greenhouse humidity.

- Trouble light—This tough, weather-resistant light, encased in a protective hooded cage with a hook on top, is perfect for night gardeners needing some light in the greenhouse. And you can unhook and shine it on plants or under benches for closer inspection.

◆ Shop vacuum—This powerful wet/dry vacuum comes in a compact size. Outfitted with a crevice tool, it can collect fallen leaves, bugs, and debris in tight corners.

◆ Grabbing tool—Either one designed for reaching into cabinets or a mechanic's tool with small grabbing prongs will help you reach between pots and under benches to pick up dead leaves or up to the ceiling to adjust hanging plants.

◆ Step stool—This comes in handy when you need to reach plants hung high or to clean greenhouse roof glazing.

◆ Propane torch or butane lighter—Flaming for a few seconds is the best way to sterilize cutting blades.

Keep It Running Smoothly

As much as we would love to, we can't spend every hour hovering over our greenhouses. We work all day, sleep all night, and occasionally go on extended trips. So who watches the greenhouse when we can't? Our options include some automatic and remote-control gadgets, and the old standby—your friendly neighborhood plant sitter.

Gadgets That Watch the Greenhouse When You Can't

You can install a "greenhouse cam" or create a "smart greenhouse" you can check on from any computer. And who knows, you can probably even check in from a smart cell phone. But gadgets that help you keep an eye on your greenhouse from afar don't have to be particularly high tech or expensive. These are some of my favorites.

◆ Grounded lamp timers—Use these inexpensive timers to turn heaters, misters, grow lights, and other essential electrical equipment on and off during the day and night, as needed. You can reset the times to accommodate the season's shorter and longer days as well as colder and milder temperatures.

◆ Remote mini/max thermometer—These units include a remote sensor to place in the greenhouse. The sensor sends continuous temperature, and in some models humidity, readings to a base unit you place inside your house. If the greenhouse heat fails and the temperatures drop below a preset temperature (usually 37°F), an alarm alerts you so you can take action to keep your plants from freezing.

◆ A night light—Plug this into a greenhouse outlet, and when you glance out from the house at night, you can rest assured the electricity is on.

The Backup Plan

As the old saying goes, "an ounce of prevention is worth a pound of cure" when it comes to protecting your valuable greenhouse plants. So keep a portable space heater on hand in case your main heater breaks down. A lightweight propane heater, such as campers use, will heat a small greenhouse for eight hours on a 1-pound propane canister. If your greenhouse is larger, you can find a more powerful, longer-lasting propane unit at a farm supply store.

Safety First

Kerosene heaters have historically been used as backup greenhouse heaters. But they're not the best option because inefficient heaters or dirty wicks can leak kerosene fumes that are toxic to plants and humans, too.

If you go away for a few days, you can purchase an automatic plant-watering device that uses a pump set into a bucket of water to water valuable plants through drip tubes. Another option is to purchase water-wicking capillary fabric from a greenhouse catalog. Place capillary mat in trays of water and set plants on it. (The pots, of course, need to have holes in the bottoms.) The soil in the pots wicks up moisture from the trays. You can also plug a mister into a timer; maintaining high humidity helps plants go longer between waterings.

If you're unable to water your plants for extended periods, you can purchase more sophisticated automatic watering devices that hook up to city or well water. Or you can always go the traditional route and arrange for a greenhouse sitter to care for your plants when you're away.

The Least You Need to Know

◆ Avoid expensive delays and mistakes by checking your local building codes before building a greenhouse.

◆ Attached greenhouses usually must be built to the same codes as permanent residences; detached greenhouses usually have fewer code restrictions.

◆ To avoid electrical shock, only use GFCI outlets in a greenhouse, and keep all electrical appliances in a designated dry area off the floor.

◆ On hot, sunny summer days, use vents, fans, humidifiers, and/or shade cloth to cool your greenhouse environment.

◆ Open-mesh greenhouse shelving allows light and air to reach plants on all levels.

◆ Maintain a potting area stocked with tools and pots in or near the greenhouse.

Chapter 17

Maintaining a Heated Greenhouse Ecosystem

In This Chapter

- ◆ Living creatures create a greenhouse ecosphere and benefit plants
- ◆ The right animals or beneficial insects for your greenhouse
- ◆ Circulating water and air improve the air quality and deter diseases in a greenhouse
- ◆ Misting your greenhouse for happy plants and animals
- ◆ A clean greenhouse environment deters disease

When you create your own greenhouse ecosphere, you won't need to travel to exotic lands for adventure. You can step right outside your door and delight in birding in a tropical rainforest or spotting a lizard basking lazily in an arid landscape.

Inviting living creatures into your greenhouse infuses it with motion, color, and the spark of life. And they'll earn their keep by snacking on bugs they discover in their greenhouse explorations.

We took you halfway to this paradise in Chapters 13 and 15 by helping you establish an environment that meets the needs of your favorite warmth-loving plants. In this chapter, we'll tell you how birds, fish, amphibians, reptiles, and other beneficial creatures can benefit your greenhouse and how best you can match these creatures to your heated-greenhouse climate.

The Rainforest Greenhouse

Life itself depends on fresh, buoyant air in a greenhouse as plants "breathe in" carbon dioxide and "exhale" oxygen. The oxygen-rich air is one reason we feel so good when we visit the greenhouse. However, we can't always be there to use up the excess oxygen, especially in winter when it's closed. So full-time animal residents are a perfect solution because they breathe in oxygen and exhale the carbon dioxide that the plants need.

Garden Guide

There are large and miniature versions of many greenhouse plants on the market today, making it easy to match the size of your plants to the size of your greenhouse. If your greenhouse is small, you can focus your collection on miniature orchids, miniature African violets, or begonias, just to name a few. Pass up big plants such as the aptly named monstera, a decorative vine with dinner-plate–size leaves.

A rainforest greenhouse requires fresh, moving air combined with high humidity. And if you grow the beautiful little cloud-forest orchids, plants with exposed roots such as vanda orchids, orchids and bromeliads growing on pieces of bark or tillandsias, you'll need a mister or a cold-mist vaporizer to bathe their roots in clouds of cool water droplets. Amphibians such as anoles (chameleons), salamanders, colorful tree frogs, and toads are a perfect complement to these conditions. These little critters drink by lapping up dewdrops in their natural environment, and a greenhouse mister also keeps their skins hydrated. Small birds such as finches and canaries also enjoy hopping through the mist and lapping up the water droplets that accumulate on greenhouse glazing and plant leaves.

The Desert Greenhouse

If your plant passions lean toward cacti, succulents, and other arid-climate plants, you'll need a greenhouse with low humidity, warm daytime temperatures, and cool nights. In many areas of this country, you'll need to both heat and dehumidify your greenhouse. If you do, you'll be making an environment that is just right for lizards and other reptiles.

Green Thumb

Cacti are native only to the Americas and are among the largest and most diverse plant families. The characteristic that sets cacti apart from all other plants is the spine cushion. Some cacti don't have spines, but all cacti have spine cushions.

Lower the humidity by running a dehumidifier. (Review details on running a dehumidifier in Chapter 16.) A garden book focused on your plants of choice will include advice about the proper humidity levels.

Providing Negative Ions and CO_2

Plants, animals, and people breathe easier in air rich in *negative ions*. Because closed houses and greenhouses can become stuffy and negative-ion depleted, a water feature can help rectify this situation. A fish tank or small pond outfitted with an air pump and air-stone aerator or small fountain produces a pleasing sound and is a natural way to generate negative ions. Or install a negative-ion generator. Some models of air purifiers contain negative-ion generators, and you can also buy a negative-ion producing fluorescent screw-in light bulb at discount and home center stores.

def•i•ni•tion

Negative ions are oxygen particles that lose an electrical charge near moving water or in vigorously circulating air. In nature, negative ions are plentiful near large bodies of water, waterfalls, and in the mountains. The air is also filled with negative ions after a thunderstorm or on a crisp, breezy autumn day. Negative ions are also produced by a home's shower and in water sprayed from a garden hose nozzle. Negative-ion charged air makes us feel clear-headed and energetic.

Fans and Air Exchange

When plants exhale in unmoving air, oxygen collects and hovers over the foliage like a little cloud, "suffocating" plants. Greenhouse fans running at a low setting are essential because they simulate outdoor breezes, blowing oxygen away from foliage and replacing it with a fresh supply of carbon dioxide and negative-ion-charged air.

Moving air also hinders fungal plant diseases. Fungal spores are ever-present in the air but take hold and grow on foliage only in stagnant, damp conditions. I learned this the hard way. When my greenhouse was new, I postponed installing fans until my rex begonias and miniature roses developed gray mold and lost all their leaves. After I hung a couple of small, personal-size fans near the ridge to circulate air down and around the greenhouse, healthy new foliage grew back on the same plants.

Since installing fans, I haven't had fungal plant diseases in my greenhouse for 10 years, even though the humidity is always between 80 and 90 percent. If you have a large greenhouse, a commercial-size greenhouse fan may serve you better. See Appendix D for commercial greenhouse supply sources.

Keeping the Greenhouse Clean

One of the easiest ways to maintain a healthy greenhouse environment is to clean up spilled soil and fallen leaves as soon as you see them. Also, don't allow plants to sit in saucers of water. In addition to becoming smelly eyesores, decaying leaves, stagnant water, and damp soil spills are breeding grounds for insect pests and fungal diseases.

Wet/Dry Vacuum Speeds Cleanup

My favorite cleanup tool of all time is a small wet/dry shop vacuum I keep plugged in and ready to go. Using its long crevice tool, I easily probe corners and between pots to pick up debris and puddled water without sucking up living plant leaves. The wet/dry vacuum is also a fantastic nontoxic bug-control tool. I can pick up the odd slug or pill bug before it knows what happened. And here's one last tip: add a small handful of powdered garden lime to the reservoir of a wet/dry vacuum to keep it smelling sweet. The caustic lime also kills any insects and slugs you may vacuum up.

Safety First _____

If you want to control stinging insects, do so *only* in the early morning when these cold-blooded insects are sluggish and inactive. If you are allergic to stinging insects or if you have doubts or concerns, call a professional exterminator. If honeybees, which are endangered, are a problem, have a professional relocate them.

Controlling Algae

After a while, green algae will no doubt grow on humid greenhouse glazing and perhaps on the floor. It's not actually harmful to plants, and your greenhouse birds and amphibians may get some nutrients from nibbling on it. But if you let it build up, it will reduce the amount of light that reaches your plants. And on the floor, algae can be a safety hazard because it becomes slippery.

Cleaning the walls, ceiling, and floors in spring and fall when you air out the greenhouse is usually enough to keep algae under control. If you have animals or fish in the greenhouse, you can either remove them and the plants while you clean, or use a cleaner that's labeled safe for use around the animals you have.

I've had good results by covering my large fish bowl with plastic sheeting and using nothing more than plain water from the garden hose. I work on a small section at a time, wetting the glazing with the soft-spray setting, scrubbing the algae loose with a long-handle, long-bristle brush, and rinsing it off with the same soft-spray setting. My greenhouse finches are curious, but they stay away from the water spray.

If you have hard-to-remove algae, you should remove animals from the greenhouse and then use an ammonia-based window cleaner on the glazing and chlorine bleach on the floors. Ammonia is a concentrated form of the plant nutrient nitrogen, so when diluted, won't harm plants. Bleach is not good for plants, and you wouldn't want it dripping from the glazing onto them, so reserve it for floor use. If you do use bleach, allow 24 hours for it to evaporate before moving animals back into the greenhouse.

Garden Guide

A clean, new plastic toilet brush does a great job of cleaning algae off greenhouse glazing. The long, soft bristles reach all the nooks and crannies and between overlapping panes of glazing. And the long handle will keep you from scraping your knuckles like you would if using a scrub brush.

What do you do about all the water that accumulates on the floor after rinsing your greenhouse? If the floor is gravel over dirt, the rinse water will help clean the gravel as it drains away. If you have a solid floor, you can mop it up. But I like to suck it up with the wet/dry vacuum because it does a better job of removing muddy water than mopping does.

Keeping Plants Clean

Clean plants grow better and are less attractive to insects and diseases than neglected ones. Pick off and dispose of yellowing or dead leaves whenever you see them, and clean leaves so leaf pores don't become clogged with dust. To clean the leaves of smooth-leaved plants, gently rinse them with the soft shower or mist setting from a hose nozzle. If you have plants with fuzzy or hairy leaves, such as African violets, dust leaves with a soft, natural-bristle paintbrush. Avoid wetting the leaves because fuzzy leaves are slow to dry, which makes them vulnerable to fungal diseases.

Beneficial Creatures

The right animals are a beneficial addition to your greenhouse because they add beauty, use excess oxygen, eat bugs, and, in the case of fish ponds, can even charge the air with healthy negative ions. And if all this weren't enough, the fish water you remove when you refresh the water is a superb fertilizer that you can spray on foliage or pour into pots.

So choose animals or birds that are comfortable in your greenhouse's temperature range and level of humidity, and select those that won't eat or tear up your plant collections. If you have your heart set on chewers such as parrots or turtles, they can live happily in a greenhouse, but put them in a roomy cage or habitat. If you want small animals but worry they may escape when the door is open, keep them caged, put them in a roomy terrarium, or carefully screen all escape routes. I blocked the escape route for my free-flying pair of African green singing finches by hanging a screen curtain inside the greenhouse door to act as a vestibule. Magnets pull it closed behind me, forming a soft bird barrier when I open or close the door.

Birds

Two kinds of birds can live happily in a greenhouse: parrots and finches. Parrots, even little ones such as love birds and parakeets, are notorious chewers, but they can live happily in large cages if you have the room for them.

There are many types of finches. Some are hardier than others, and these hardier ones are better suited to greenhouse living. Society finches are a good choice because they all pile into a closed nest basket to stay warm at night. Zebra finches and green singing finches are also tough little birds. Probably the best thing about finches is that they're too small to make much of a mess. I keep their seed in a roofed outdoor type feeder; the roof keeps the seed dry and clean. I hang the feeder over the aisle so spilled seed goes on the floor and not into pots where it would sprout into a weedy tangle. If your greenhouse is fairly large, you could house canaries, which are also pretty cold hardy.

The brilliant yellow color and lyrical songs of a pair of green singing finches enliven the author's greenhouse.

(Donna Chiarelli Studio)

By cold hardy, I mean they could survive in a warm or intermediate greenhouse. If your greenhouse temperatures drop below 50°F, you should put your birds into a cage and take them into the house until warmer weather.

If you need to catch free-flying birds to remove them from the greenhouse, do it at night as birds are not active in the dark. After they go to sleep, it's relatively easy to pick them off their perches and put them into a cage.

Amphibians

A warm, humid greenhouse can house amphibians and turtles. If you want small, colorful tree frogs and the little 3- or 4-inch chameleons called anoles, it might be best to construct a secure habitat to keep them from hiding in a potted plant and inadvertently being transported outside. You may also need to set up a turtle habitat if yours develops a taste for your plant collection.

Place a mister near their habitat, or buy a small one at a pet shop to place inside the habitat to provide water droplets for them to drink. And provide them with a plug-in basking "rock." A real rock placed in a shallow bowl of water creates a swimming pool with an island.

Green Thumb

Don't collect animals from the wild, because they aren't adapted to living in captivity. And some, such as the eastern box turtle, are protected by law in many states. Know your state's laws, and get your pets from reputable dealers or rescues.

Even though these creatures happily devour any flying or crawling insects they encounter, you'll need to buy crickets and packaged food at the pet shop to supplement their diet.

Some amphibians and turtles commonly available at pet shops and rescues include:

Anoles and chameleons   Salamanders

Tree frogs   Turtles

Reptiles

Lizards and nonpoisonous snakes will be at home in a humidity-specific greenhouse once you give them a warm place to bask, fresh water, and a supply of appropriate food. If you allow them to roam, they'll bask on the warm ballasts of fluorescent lights, on a plant-heating mat, or near the greenhouse heater and greedily snap up any stray insects they encounter.

If you worry they may escape or develop a taste for your plants, keep them in an appropriately sized habitat terrarium or cage. A terrarium is an ecosystem in miniature. Terrariums intended to house small animals, such as lizards or chameleons, and are usually constructed in a roomy aquarium. On top is a screen, which keeps the animal in, but admits light and air.

Reptiles commonly available from pet shops and rescues include these:

Basilisks	Water dragons
Girdle-tailed lizards	Iguanas

Fish

An aquarium is a fully contained system, complete with an air supply and heater, making it possible to outfit your greenhouse with a fresh- or salt-water setup stocked with any kind of exotic fish your heart desires.

A large Asian goldfish bowl with bubbling fountain and young fantails creates a serene corner in the author's greenhouse.

(Donna Chiarelli Studio)

If you prefer a more natural setting, you can add a large oriental fish bowl or a small pond populated by mosquito fish or fancy goldfish. Small koi are a possibility, but they grow quite large, so you'll eventually have to find a home for them in an outside pond. Pond fish like these are quite cold hardy, making a pond heater unnecessary in a heated greenhouse.

Garden Guide

If your greenhouse is cool in winter, switch to a winter fish food formula and reduce feedings. Because the water is colder, the fish assume a semi-hibernating state.

Fancy gold fish, good candidates for greenhouse pets, include these varieties:

Black Moor	Comet
Fantail	Lionhead
Oranda	Shubunkin

Butterflies

Called nature's jewels, butterflies are a source of iridescent beauty that makes them a favorite of children. These gentle beauties are becoming increasingly endangered around the world, but you can provide them with a sanctuary all year-round in the greenhouse and help support the breeders who work to perpetuate these jewel-like insects.

Butterflies and their caterpillars make good greenhouse inhabitants because they're selective eaters. Technically, they are host specific, meaning they'll eat only one species of plants or closely related ones. You'll need to do a little research before ordering larvae (for butterfly guide books and informative websites, see Appendix D) to make sure you order a species that won't snack on your valued greenhouse plants. For example, the caterpillar of the beautiful swallowtail butterfly is called the parsleyworm for good reason. It devours parsley, carrot tops, fennel, and dill, making this one butterfly you wouldn't want to turn loose in your vegetable greenhouse. But it might be a possibility for an ornamental greenhouse where you could supply pots or bouquets of its favored foods.

> **Green Thumb**
>
> A host plant is a food plant used by a specific species of insect. Butterflies and moths lay their eggs on host plants that their caterpillars eat.

Butterflies have unique behaviors that are entertaining to watch. They have a unique way of drinking, called puddling. They land on patches of mud and decaying vegetation and lap up nutrients and moisture with their long, curling proboscis—a hollow tube through which they take in nectar. If you have butterflies in your greenhouse, set a fresh butterfly feeder in a sunny spot every few days. To make one, fill a shallow saucer with damp garden mud topped with a few slices of over-ripe fruit, such as strawberries, bananas, grapes, or apples.

After the sun rises, observe these cold-blooded insects as they perch on a plant stem and bask in the sun to warm their bodies and wings enough to allow flight. They'll sit motionless with their wings spread wide or sometimes with wings folded toward the sun. They also curiously taste plants with their feet, drumming on leaves to stir up scents.

You can order inexpensive, reusable butterfly kits and additional caterpillars starting at around $15 online (see Appendix D) that come complete with larval food. When the adults hatch—if they're native to your area and if they mature during the summer, you can enjoy them for a day or two and then release them outside.

Butterflies are compatible with certain birds. Just make sure the birds you choose don't include live butterflies or caterpillars in their normal diets. One conservatory and butterfly sanctuary I visited with a large butterfly population solved the problem of natural butterfly mortalities by introducing a flock of tiny, ground-dwelling button quail, which continually patrolled the conservatory's undergrowth for fallen butterflies.

Green Thumb

A butterfly's life span is typically about three to four weeks. That breaks down to 3 to 5 days as a caterpillar, 5 to 10 days as a chrysalis, and a week or two as a butterfly.

As a greenhouse host or hostess, it's your job to provide for the specific needs of each stage. Supply the right host plants for caterpillars to feed on, nectar plants for butterflies, and water for both the caterpillar and butterfly stages.

Some butterflies and larvae you can order online include the following:

> Bright white
>
> Fritillary
>
> Painted lady

Ladybugs and Other Beneficial Bugs

Beneficial insects are predator bugs that eat the insect pests that eat your plants. Many are pest-specific, preferring to eat the larvae of various plant pests or the soft-bodied adults. Based on the pest you need to control, you'll want to do a little research to find out which beneficial insect to release in your greenhouse. You can learn more about beneficial insects online or from books on the subject (see Appendix D).

Released in a greenhouse, these beneficial insects will destroy a pest population and then either move outside in search of more food or live out their lifecycle in your greenhouse. Chances are you'll need to order anew if you have future problems with the same pests. Beneficial insects perform equally well in unheated greenhouses and in the outdoor garden (see Chapter 9). Pest outbreaks tend to happen with some regularity, so you may want to keep a pest journal so you can get a head start on ordering beneficials right before you expect an outbreak.

Garden Guide

Beneficial insects are very sensitive to pesticides, so do not use pesticides in your greenhouse for at least a month before releasing beneficials.

These are some commonly available beneficial insects and the pests upon which they prey.

Beneficial Insects	Insects Upon Which They Prey
Lacewing larvae	aphids, mealybugs, scale, thrips, mites
Ladybugs	aphids, scale
Praying mantis	many kinds of insect pests
Syrphid fly larvae	aphids
Wasp larvae:	
Braconid spp.	tomato hornworms
Trichogramma pretiosum	many kinds of insect eggs

Disease and Pest Control

Remember that where animals, fish, and other beneficial creatures live, we should avoid using pesticides (for manufactured controls to use for plants only, see Chapter 13). If a plant does develop a problem, you can remove it from the greenhouse and treat it with a product that's labeled for that plant and that specific problem. And be sure to wait the specified time for the product to dissipate before you put it back into the greenhouse.

Tight Screens and Wiping Feet

The best control, of course, is prevention, and one great line of defense is screens. Although many greenhouse kits do *not* come with screens, having some made to fit your greenhouse vents, windows, and doors is worth the investment. You can also track pests and diseases into the greenhouse on your shoes, so place a bristled door mat or boot scraper outside the door, or keep a dedicated pair of greenhouse shoes on hand.

Safety First _____

Greenhouses are attractive nuisances, which means that they, along with swimming pools, can tempt young children to stray into your yard to investigate. If you have children in your neighborhood, lock your greenhouse, or lock potentially toxic greenhouse treatments in a cabinet, including home remedies. Never store plant treatments in empty soda or juice jars.

Quarantine New Plants

Many old-time gardening books recommend quarantining plants you bring home—whether from a garden center or a friend's garden—for a few weeks, and it's still a good idea. Observe the newbies during this time for creepy crawlies, fine webs, and yellowing or blotched leaves. To protect your collection, treat the plants until cured, or dispose of them in the trash.

Greenhouse-Friendly Home Remedies

Untold numbers of home remedies for garden and greenhouse exist. Some work; some don't. We talked about some in Chapter 9. I rely on just a few tried-and-true, least-toxic remedies, one of which is the aspirin-water preventative.

Researchers at Cornell University, The University of Arizona, and others have discovered that plants, when under attack by diseases and possibly insects, produce a natural-defense hormone chemically similar to the salicylic acid in aspirin. Researchers who sprayed vegetable plants with a solution of aspirin dissolved in water discovered that the plants responded by producing their own salicylic acid, and the beneficial effects lasted from several days to several weeks.

A recipe for aspirin-water spray appeared in the January 4, 2004, issue of the gardening newsletter *The Avant Gardener.*

> 3 adult-strength (80 mm) aspirins
>
> 4 gallons water
>
> Dissolve aspirins in water; spray on plant foliage.

This recipe is the closest thing to a magic bullet that I've ever used. I've sprayed plants in my greenhouse with aspirin water for several years and no longer see insects or diseases on my plants. If you want to try aspirin-water spray on your valued plants, test it on a few to make sure there are no adverse reactions before using it wide-scale.

Sterilizing Tools

One of the best things you can do to prevent the spread of plant diseases is to use a sterile work surface and sterilize your cutting tools between plants when pruning and trimming. Sterilizing pruners, scissors, and knives is standard practice for orchid growers because these valuable plants are vulnerable to plant viruses, but these safe practices make sense for any plant you value.

Newspaper, which is manufactured under high heat, is sterile. So cover the table with a thick layer of newspapers when you repot or prune plants, and peel off and dispose of a sheet after working on each plant.

Garden Guide

A soldering torch can be a bit heavy and awkward to hold in one hand while sterilizing blades. So instead, try one of the tiny chef's torches sold at kitchenware shops for crisping crème brûlée. Or try a long-snouted butane lighter made for lighting grills.

A time-honored method of sterilizing tools is to dip your cutters into a glass of rubbing alcohol between each use. And that doesn't mean between today's use and tomorrow's use. That means you snip two leaves off one plant; dip the tool; snip two leaves off a different plant.

Recently, orchid growers have found that flaming the cutting edges with a hand-held soldering torch to be more effective.

To sterilize the blade, run the flame back and forth across the edge of each blade for about five seconds, and allow the blade to cool before using it on a plant.

The Least You Need to Know

♦ By controlling the temperature and humidity, you can create a rainforest-like environment or a desert-like environment in your greenhouse.

♦ Animals and beneficial insects convert excess oxygen into carbon dioxide, which plants need.

♦ Birds, amphibians, reptiles, fish, and butterflies all add interest to greenhouse environments.

♦ Moving water contributes healthy negative ions to greenhouse air.

♦ Misting the greenhouse hydrates exposed plant roots and provides water droplets for small beneficial creatures to drink.

- Circulating air hinders fungal greenhouse diseases.

- Quarantine new plants and sterilize pruning tools to keep from spreading infectious plant diseases.

Part 6

Gardening Basics: After the Harvest

And we saved the best for last! This small section is big on information. We tell you how to get the ultimate head start on next year's garden—by saving seeds from *this* year's plants. There's nothing more satisfying than growing plants from *free* seeds! Next, we tell you how to keep your garden healthy—by cleaning it up, of course. We explain how to clean it, when to clean it, what to do with your soil (if anything), and when to do it.

Then after the work, bring on the rewards. We tell how to store just about everything you grew in your garden in a root cellar. And you don't have to spend long hours steaming, sterilizing, or canning. Just pack up your produce (we tell you how), and take it to the root cellar. What a perfect end to a whole *year* of gardening!

18

Next Year's Garden

In This Chapter

- ◆ How to select plant candidates for seed collecting
- ◆ Collecting and storing seeds from your plants
- ◆ Garden cleanup to aid winter gardening and give you a head start on spring
- ◆ Overwintering tender perennials, herbs, and outdoor container plants

Seeds for many of next year's plants are yours, free for the taking, when you collect and save them from your own garden. In this chapter, we tell you how to collect and store seeds for next year's garden. And to perpetuate plants that aren't good candidates for seed saving, we explain how to take cuttings. We also give you techniques for cleaning up your garden in the fall to keep it healthy and to prepare it for winter gardening with cold frames and greenhouses.

Seeds and Plants for Next Year

Commercial seed packets cost only a couple of dollars each, but that adds up over time—especially now that you're gardening year-round. So save yourself some money, and collect seeds. In addition to the money, you'll have the satisfaction of starting plants from your own seeds. If you grow heirloom varieties or save seeds from plants you acquired from your Aunt Helen's garden or from Grandpa's backyard, then the satisfaction factor is all the greater.

When it comes to perennials, the cost of nursery-grown, potted plants is certainly more of a consideration than the cost of a seed packet. Perennials run anywhere from $5 to $25 or more per plant. If you raise your own perennials from seeds, cuttings, or offsets, your savings on plant purchases can run from the hundreds into the thousands over the years.

Seed Collecting

In Chapter 6, we talked about starting the seed-saving process by buying and sowing seeds of open-pollinated plants (see Appendixes B and C for sources). So now, let's find out how to select parent plants, how to protect their fruits while they set seed, and how to collect and store the seeds for next year's garden.

> **Green Thumb**
>
> Although many perennials are not difficult to grow from seed, some perennial seeds do not store well and should be sown soon after you collect them. To learn how to grow different types of perennials from seed, invest in a good seed-starting guide (see Appendix D).

In choosing prospective seed-parent plants, you might choose a plant because it bore fruit early, tolerated frost well, had especially flavorful or good-sized fruits, didn't seem susceptible to pests or disease, showed fabulous flower color or size, or for any other reason you value. And don't stop with one set of parent plants; choose several of each variety to diversify the gene pool and ensure against future crop failures. (Remember how the famous Irish potato famine came about because farmers were growing only one disease-susceptible variety of potato?)

When you choose a parent plant, mark it by tying on a bright-colored scrap of fabric. This will serve as a visual reminder to allow these plants to go to seed so you can save their seeds.

Most garden plants you collect seeds from will be annuals. To collect from biennial herbs, such as parsley, and from flowering biennials, such as foxglove (*Digitalis purpurea*), leave them in your garden over the winter and collect seeds after they bloom the following summer.

Now root crops are another story. To save seeds from carrots, potatoes, sweet potatoes, or other root crops, harvest and store the best-looking or best-tasting (it's okay to sample a few) ones over winter (for storing root crops see Chapter 19). In spring, plant these parent roots in your garden and allow them to go to seed for collection.

Do not harvest seeds too early. If they don't fully ripen before you pick them, they won't germinate after you plant them. If you grow plants with seeds you can cook and eat, such as corn, beans, and other legumes, leave the seeds on the plant to dry. When you collect them, knock the seed heads against the inside of a bucket so the seeds break loose and fall to the bottom of the bucket.

Garden Guide

Some plants pollinate themselves; others require pollen from nearby plants in order to set seed. To keep all your bases covered, remember to plant several of everything.

Seed-setting plants such as lettuce, onions, and many flowers scatter their tiny, ripe seeds over the ground. To catch these seeds before they fall and are lost, tie a paper bag over seeding flowers. Shake the bag occasionally to see if it contains loose seeds. The best time to collect seeds is on a sunny afternoon when the seeds are naturally dry. Choose a collecting day before the first frost because frost dampens seeds, just as dew and rain do, and damp seeds spoil in storage.

Green Thumb

Drying seeds may stick to paper towels. Smooth, clean office paper makes a better surface for seeds to dry on. When dry, you can roll the paper into a funnel shape and easily pour the dried seeds into a storage envelope.

Preparing seeds of melons, squash, and similar large-seeded fruits is straightforward. Scrape the seeds from the ripe fruit, put them in a kitchen sieve or colander, and rinse off the pulp. Then spread the seeds on a piece of clean, white paper to dry for a week before storing.

Allow edible, seed-containing fruits such as tomatoes, peppers, and cucumbers to remain on the plant until they are a little overripe, but pick them before they spoil. Extracting seeds from soft fruits like these is a multi-step process.

Here's what you do:

Day 1:   Scrape the pulp and seeds out with a spoon, and toss the rest of the fruit on the compost pile. Drop the pulp and seeds into a clean, clear jar half filled with water, screw on the cap, and let it stand overnight at room temperature. The pulp and bad seeds will float. The viable seeds will sink.

Day 2:   Skim off and dispose of anything that floats. Leave the good seeds in the jar, fill it with water, swish to rinse, and then pour off the water along with any new particles that float. Refill the jar with clean water and let it stand overnight.

Day 3: Repeat what you did on Day 2.

Day 4: Drain the seeds, spread them out on a sheet of clean white paper, and dry them indoors for a week. When they are dry, store them in labeled paper envelopes.

Seed Storing

Because exposure to heat and humidity damages stored seeds, your refrigerator is the perfect place to store them because its temperature hovers above freezing and the air is dehumidified.

Garden Guide

Seed packets usually contain between 30 and 100 seeds. If you don't have space in your garden for that many plants, start what you need and save the rest in a resealable plastic bag in the refrigerator. Seeds keep for about five years, although with each passing year, fewer will sprout.

To determine seed viability, try this simple test. Moisten a paper towel and space out 10 seeds on it. Roll the towel, place it in a resealable plastic bag, and set it in a warm (80°F) place for the length of time the seed packet lists for germination.

At the end of the germination period, unroll the paper towel and count the seeds that sprouted. This gives you the percentage of viability. If 6 of 10 seeds sprouted, that's 60 percent viability. So if you want 6 plants, sow 10 seeds. If you want 12 plants, sow 20, and so on.

Here's how to prepare your seeds for refrigerated storage:

- Seal dried seeds in paper envelopes, and write the name of the variety and the current date on each envelope.

- Put paper envelopes containing all seeds *except corn and legumes* into an airtight jar with a screw-on lid or in a resealable freezer bag. Store corn and bean seeds in labeled, breathable paper bags or envelopes.

- Add one quarter cup of a desiccant, such as dry powdered milk or silica gel (available at craft stores) to each jar or bag. Label the containers with the year (this process goes for leftover commercial seed as well), seal them up, and store the jars or bags in the refrigerator until you need to sow the seeds.

I dedicate one crisper drawer in my fridge to seeds, but you can also keep bagged seeds corralled in a plastic or cardboard shoebox.

Dedicating a refrigerator crisper drawer to garden seeds provides ideal storage conditions and easy access for year-round seed starting.

(Donna Chiarelli Studio)

One additional note: save the original seed packets for your purchased seeds as they contain valuable planting and growing instructions. When you package their offspring—your own garden-grown seeds—fasten the original packet to the envelope containing your saved seeds.

Bring Tender Plants Indoors

As the nighttime temperatures dip in autumn, pay attention to the forecast. Before it freezes, move tender potted plants (perhaps your hanging baskets), tender perennials in patio pots, and houseplants that have summered outdoors into the house or garage.

Store pots containing plants such as cannas, New Zealand flax, purple heart, and other tender perennials over winter in a breezeway, mudroom, basement, or garage that stays above freezing. Wait until frost nips the foliage; the roots will survive. Trim the frost-wilted foliage away, and move the plants indoors. These plants will assume a semi-dormant state and can survive without light for a few winter months, but water the pots once a month—just enough to keep them from completely drying out. After your last spring frost in April or May (or June in really cold climates), move them to their outdoor homes. When you see some growth, resume a regular summer watering and fertilizing routine.

def•i•ni•tion

A **stem cutting** is a piece of a plant's stem, which includes the growing tip of the stem and three or four leaf joints, called nodes.

Herbs small enough to pot up and bring indoors will continue to produce edible leaves well into winter. If a plant is too big to move, take a *stem cutting*, and keep it in a glass of water for a week or two in the refrigerator, or pot it up and try to root it. Herbs don't get enough sun indoors in winter to thrive, but you can enjoy fresh leaves until they gradually yellow and have to be tossed.

Taking Cuttings

To start a stem cutting, cut a 6-inch piece of stem, including the growing tip and three or four leaves. Remove the bottom two leaves, and insert the stem, up to the bottom remaining leaf, into a 4-inch pot of moist growing medium. Do several for insurance. Cover each potted cutting with a clear plastic bag and set it in a warm, light place out of direct sunlight, such as near a window with a sheer curtain or partially closed blinds.

Check the soil daily, and water as needed to keep the soil barely moist. After four weeks, tug the stems slightly each time you do a moisture check. When the cuttings offer some resistance, they are rooted. Remove the bags, and grow the potted cuttings on a sunny windowsill. Move cuttings to bigger pots if the roots fill their 4-inch pots before spring.

Garden Cleanup

After you pot all the plants you want to shelter indoors for the winter, it's time to clean up and winterize the garden. Both vegetable and perennial garden beds benefit from some late-fall attention.

Northern gardeners should do garden cleanup before the ground freezes too hard to dig. Southern and West Coast gardeners can clean up at a more leisurely pace, aiming to finish before winter rains make the soil too muddy to work.

Begin your garden cleanup in both perennial and vegetable garden beds by raking up and removing dead plant material. Do this in a somewhat organized way by starting with any plants that show signs of insect infestation or disease. Gather this material, and dispose of it somewhere other than your compost pile. Then rake up the healthy plants and compost them.

Now is a good time to take a pH test of your garden soil and adjust soil acidity or alkalinity (see Chapter 5). Fall is also the best season to add slow-acting lime, which is used to increase soil alkalinity (raise the pH), or wood ashes, which supplies the major plant nutrient potassium, to your garden. These caustic amendments can damage living plants but break down safely in an empty garden.

Prune deciduous shrubs and trees after the leaves drop and they go dormant. We prune when plants are dormant because if we prune when plants are actively growing, the wounds "bleed" sap, which depletes the tree's natural juices. The fresh wound is also open and vulnerable to pests and diseases.

But wait! Before you wield those pruning shears, remember that we do not prune spring-flowering shrubs, such as lilacs, forsythia, and some types of hydrangeas, in the autumn. These shrubs have already begun to develop next spring's buds. If you prune this summer's growth, you'll also be pruning next spring's flower show. So unless you want to skip a year of flowering, don't prune these spring bloomers until immediately *after* they bloom next spring.

Just as when you prune in the greenhouse, disinfect your pruners between plants to avoid spreading plant diseases. The fastest and most effective method is flaming the pruner blade for five seconds using a portable butane torch or fireplace lighter.

Winterizing Outdoor Gardens

When you garden year-round, you go a step beyond simple garden cleanup in the fall. You'll want to amend, fertilize, and protect empty beds against weeds so they're ready to plant with early spring crops. Also, prepare one or two beds for one last fall crop, and get out protective covers to prolong the harvest of some favorite summer crops.

To Till or Not to Till

It's healthier for your garden if you can avoid tilling because it destroys earthworms and soil structure—the spaces between the particles in your soil. If you've been careful not to walk on your planting beds, the soil should be fluffy and loose, and you won't need to till.

Sprinkle a high-nitrogen, slow-release fertilizer on the soil, according to package directions. Then cover your garden beds with a 3- or 4-inch deep layer of organic mulch—the thicker, the better. If you are improving a flowerbed, distribute mulch around existing plants, taking care not to let mulch touch plant stems. Piling mulch up against plant stems is an invitation for rot, nesting insects, and fungal diseases.

Garden Guide _____

Winter mulch suppresses weeds around perennials. When you apply it over the top of dormant perennials *after* a hard freeze, it also provides insulation against freeze-and-thaw damage, which can heave the plants out of the ground.

You don't need to dig organic amendments and mulches into the soil. Earthworms using it as a food source will pull it into their underground tunnels over winter, improving both soil structure and fertility.

Put That Garden to Work!

If there is a mantra for gardening year-round, it's that every few weeks you must start a batch of seeds either indoors or outdoors. Here is a list of some frost-tolerant plants to set out as seedlings or to direct sow in summer for fall harvest. You can start fast growers again in the fall for a second harvest in early winter:

Plant	Summer	Fall
Beets	Direct Sow	Direct Sow
Broccoli	Direct Sow	
Bush beans	Direct Sow	
Cabbage	Start Indoors	Set out seedlings
Endive	Direct Sow	
Flower bulbs		Set out (overwinter)
Garlic		Set out cloves (overwinter)
Lobelia	Start indoors	Set out
Pansies	Start indoors	Set out (overwinter)
Peas	Direct Sow	
Lettuce	Direct Sow	Direct Sow
Radishes	Direct Sow	
Shallots		Set out cloves
Snapdragon	Start Indoors	Set out
Spinach	Direct Sow	Direct sow

Think of the end-of-season activities we covered in this chapter as the dessert course of your gardening year. Perhaps it's even saving the best for last. Because when you garden year-round, you actually begin anew with fall garden cleanup. You'll be amending, fertilizing, and protecting empty beds against weeds so they're ready to plant with early spring crops, but you will also prepare some outdoor beds for one last fall crop, and use your protective covers to extend the harvest of your favorite summer crops. Most importantly, you will perpetuate future garden generations by collecting and saving your own seeds and multiplying your own perennials. With this book, and this chapter, we have shown you how to stop thinking in terms of "the garden season," and to start gardening year-round. Refer to it often and you will be rewarded by the fruits of a never-ending season.

The Least You Need to Know

- You can save hundreds of dollars by starting your own perennials from seeds, cuttings, or offsets.

- Choose several sets of parent plants to diversify your seed gene pool for healthy future generations.

- Harvest seeds when fruits are overripe, but not rotten.

- The cold, dry air in a refrigerator provides an ideal environment for seed storage.

- Prune flowering shrubs immediately after they bloom, no matter what time of year, to avoid trimming off next year's flower buds.

Chapter 19

Storing the Bounty

In This Chapter

- ◆ Storing crops in a root cellar
- ◆ Choosing the best crops to store
- ◆ Preparing crops for storage

You know what a root cellar is because you read Chapter 10—we're just sure of it! Storing crops for winter use in a root cellar is nothing new. In fact, it was one of the first ways people stored their crops—long before electricity or the development of modern food-preservation methods.

Using root cellars to store some types of crops, such as potatoes, carrots, apples, and pears, is still popular today and with good reasons. Storing produce in a root cellar doesn't require electricity, nor does it take as much work as other methods of storage, such as freezing or canning. All you have to do is remove the produce from the garden or field and put it into storage. Nothing could be simpler!

Once you've learned the old ways of root cellaring (by reading this chapter!), you'll be amazed at what you can store and how long produce will keep under the proper storage temperatures. And in this chapter, we'll tell you what those storage temperatures are. You'll be eating fresh from the garden most of the winter after you begin storing your fresh fruits and vegetables in a root cellar. So let's learn how to preserve those crops you spent the season growing!

Storing Crops in a Root Cellar

Storing crops in a root cellar is not rocket science; anyone can do it, even if you live in an apartment. As we told you in Chapter 10, root cellars can be as small or as large as you wish. They can be in a tiny closet or in an elaborate underground chamber. Whatever your situation, you can create a root cellar that will be perfect for you.

Green Thumb

Keep an eye on the produce in your root cellar, and use what has blemishes or is getting soft spots first. As produce spoils, it releases gasses. Produce touching the decaying items will be the first to go bad. Eventually, if you don't remove the spoiled produce, it will ruin all of the items you have stored.

The main thing a root cellar must do to keep your produce at its optimal freshness is to hold the temperature within a certain range and remain moist enough to keep your crops from drying out. Maintaining appropriate temperature and humidity levels takes some trial and error because changing external environmental conditions affect your root cellar, as does the activity going on inside. The temperature and humidity in an empty root cellar behave differently than in a full root cellar. And a root cellar being used to grow things (again, see Chapter 10) acts differently from a root cellar being used for storage.

In general, a root cellar's temperatures should stay somewhere between 40° and 55°F. Cooler temperatures—those closer to 40° than to 55°—are generally better in a root cellar but not always, as some crops prefer extra coolness and some prefer a little more warmth.

Humidity is another factor to consider. Most crops are happy with 90 percent humidity. However, other crops—for example, garlic, onions, soybeans, dried peppers, pumpkins, squash, sweet potatoes, and green tomatoes—prefer their humidity to be between 60 and 70 percent. Keeping these crops in a high-humidity root cellar is an invitation to mold.

How does one keep the preferences of each type of produce straight? It takes experience and practice. And a little table like this one helps, at least to get you started.

Root Cellar Preferences

Cold, Moist Conditions	Cold, Not-Quite-So-Moist Conditions	Cold, Dry Conditions	Cool, Moist Conditions	Warm, Dry Conditions
32°–40°F, 90–95% Humidity	32°–40°F, 80–90% Humidity	32°–50°F, 60–70% Humidity	40°–50°F, 85–90% Humidity	50°–60°F, 60–70% Humidity
carrots, beets, winter radishes, Brussels sprouts, broccoli	potatoes, cauliflower, apples, oranges	garlic*, onions, green soybeans in the pod *Garlic is even happier at 50% humidity.	cucumbers, watermelon, eggplant, ripe tomatoes	dried peppers, pumpkins, squash, green tomatoes, sweet potatoes

The containers you use to store crops in a root cellar are important, too. The best containers are wooden baskets or boxes made for this purpose. These containers allow air to circulate so the fruits and vegetables in storage can breathe. Plastic bread crates and milk cartons work as well.

Don't set containers or lay any produce directly on the floor, especially if you have a concrete floor. Put everything on a shelf or bench. For produce such as garlic or grapes, hanging them is really the best method of storage.

Garden Guide

If your root cellar doesn't have enough humidity for the crops you're storing, simply sprinkle a bit of water on the floor. But don't add too much water. A little at a time is all you need; then check your humidity level after half an hour or so. If it's still not high enough, add more water.

Which Crops Store Best

When planning which crops to plant, think about what you'll eat in the coming months, how much of each item you'll need, and then what will survive the storage season in your root cellar. (For starters, look back at the table of Root Cellar Preferences to see some possibilities.) Some varieties of vegetables store better than others.

Seed catalogs or seed packets may indicate whether a particular variety "stores well" or not. Also, when cultivating crops you'll store at home, don't use a fertilizer high in nitrogen.

Some vegetable crops that store especially well in root cellar environments include the following:

beets	kale
broccoli	kohlrabi
Brussels sprouts	leeks
burdock	onions
cabbage (including Chinese cabbage)	parsnips
	potatoes (sweet and white)
carrots	winter radishes
cauliflower	rutabaga
celeriac	salsify
celery	squash
colbaga	tomatoes
collards	turnips
eggplant	melon squash
endive	muskmelon
escarole	watermelon

Green Thumb _____

When choosing specific varieties of produce for winter storage, read seed packets and seed and garden catalogs as they usually indicate which ones are known for their storage capabilities. Here are some of our favorites: beets 'Long Season,' broccoli 'Waltham 29,' Brussels sprouts 'Long Island Improved,' cabbage 'Krautman' or 'Savoy Langedijker Winterkeeper,' Chinese cabbage 'Wong Bok,' carrots 'Autumn King,' cauliflower 'Andes,' onions 'Copra,' sweet potatoes 'Allgold,' white potatoes 'Kennebec' or 'Yukon Gold,' tomatoes 'German' or 'Burpee's Long Keeper,' and watermelon 'Yellow Storage' or 'Christmas Melon.'

For those of you who want to store fruit, a wide variety will work. Apples, crabapples, cranberries, dried fruit, grapes, grapefruit, oranges, tangerines, pawpaws, pears, plums, and quince are all fruits that will last longer in a root cellar than if kept at room temperature.

Remember to do your research before you plant—or before you purchase the produce at a farm or farm market. Some varieties keep well, and others keep only a few weeks. Always try to plan ahead. Think about what you'll do with the crops you store and how fast your family will eat the produce.

Harvesting for Storage

For best results, harvest produce at the "right" time. In addition, handle the produce gently so you don't bruise it.

Harvest soft fruits such as tomatoes and peppers as late as possible but before frost hits them. Leave hard-shell fruits, such as pumpkin and squash, in the field until a hard frost occurs.

Leave root crops in the ground until their foliage is completely blackened by frost. However, if any part of the plant itself is above ground, then heavily mulch that part so the frost doesn't damage it.

Depending on where you live, your harvesting may take place in October, November, or December. Don't wait too long or the ground could freeze, making it impossible to get your crop dug without significant damage—to the produce and perhaps to yourself.

It's best to harvest your vegetables during a dry spell. Vegetables exposed to recent rains may be plumped up and have more soil clinging to them. Do not wash the produce after you remove it from your field or garden; leave it just like you harvested it.

Keep your crops as cool as possible as you harvest. In other words, don't leave them lying in the sun on a warm afternoon. Harvest early in the morning or just before night falls. The cooler the produce is when you harvest it, the longer it will last.

Preparing for Storage

After you harvest your crops, examine each item. You should have about one inch of the stem on the produce right above the crown, which is the area on top of the produce where the stems are attached; clip off any excess. If you leave too much foliage, it will wilt, draw moisture, and turn slimy. And you want no wilting, slimy stuff in your root cellar! It's also a good idea to hustle produce from most above-ground crops right into the root cellar.

Some produce, however, needs to cure prior to being stored. Curing means to let the produce dry and develop a hard rind. Potatoes, onions, garlic, sweet potatoes, squash, and pumpkins are the produce that require curing. Let them sit in a cool, dark, not-too-humid place for about two weeks.

The next step is to learn how to keep your produce fresh in storage, because different crops have different preferences or requirements. Some prefer the open air of your root cellar while others prefer to be buried in a material such as sawdust, plastic such as freezer or storage bags, sand, and moss. Each crop has a specific storage preference, and the closer you can come to this preference, the longer the crops will keep. Let's look at some specifics.

Storage Medium	How to Use It	Crops That Prefer This Storage Medium
Sawdust	Pack vegetables in a single layer in damp sawdust, making sure there is an inch of sawdust between layers and that vegetables do not touch.	Beets, carrots, horse-radish, potatoes, sweet potatoes, rutabagas
Sand	Pack vegetables in a single layer in damp sand, making sure there is an inch of sand between layers and that vegetables do not touch.	Beets, carrots, horse-radish
Plastic bags	Poke holes in the bag with a pin. Sprinkle one vegetable with just enough water to keep it damp, and bundle it inside the plastic bag. Pack plastic-wrapped fruits in a bin or crate with mesh or slatted sides so the produce can breathe.	Turnips, winter radishes
Moss	Pack vegetables in a single layer in damp moss, making sure there is an inch of moss between layers and that vegetables do not touch.	Beets

Beets are a good choice for storage because they last through most of the winter—and even into March if you store them correctly. For best results, pack the beets in damp sawdust in single layers in wooden containers. Plastic milk containers would work, too. Some sawdust may fall out of the sides as you work. Choose containers with small openings to help prevent this. If you don't have access to sawdust, try leaves, sand, or put them into plastic bags with a few air holes in the bags so the gases can be released. It is also a good idea to put just a sprinkling of water in the bags so there is some moisture available to the produce. A good rule of thumb is to put about a teaspoon of water in a plastic bag, shake it up well, then turn it upside down and shake. You want the excess moisture out but you want enough in there so the bag has moisture drops on it.

Garden Guide

Did you know vegetables breathe? And they continue breathing even after you pick them. As produce breathes, it changes; it continues to mature and ripen. That's why it is important to store each item properly. Moist, cool air slows the respiration rate of your fruits and vegetables. The less water they lose and the slower they breathe, the longer your produce will last.

When storing items in damp storage medium such as sawdust, be sure the material is not too wet. You want the material damp enough to keep the produce plump, but not so wet the produce tries to sprout—or worse, rot.

Carrots are a popular root cellar crop you can store in sawdust, as well. If you keep them under ideal conditions (see the table earlier in this paragraph), they can last into the following May. It's best to wait until June to sow seeds of carrots you wish to store so that they are ready to harvest late in the season along with other crops meant for the root cellar. Remember that a root cellar will be too warm in the summer to begin storing crops in it.

You can also store carrots right in the ground where they're grown. Simply put a two-foot layer of mulch over the plants as insulation. As long as the ground is workable, you can continue to harvest the carrots. Sometimes, mice or other critters may find your plants, but you can deter these gnawing critters by placing a layer of hardware cloth under the mulch.

Some gardeners prefer to store carrots in damp sand, but the author prefers to pack her unwashed carrots in dry, clean "play sand" for storage.

(Donna Chiarelli Studio)

Potatoes are another staple crop for root cellar storage. Choose potatoes from a second crop or ones that mature later in the season. You should keep potatoes dry once their tops die down, or they may resprout. When you dig potatoes, it's important to properly cure them before you store them. Just a quick review on curing: put the produce in a dry area for at least two weeks, and make sure they're not exposed to rain, wind, or sun during this time. They should not touch, and the temperature in the area where they are curing should be between 60° and 75°F. Once the produce is cured, move it to the root cellar. The normal storage time for properly cured potatoes is four to six months. Avoid storing the varieties "Cascade" and "Norchip" because they're poor keepers.

Garden Guide

Do not store apples and potatoes near one another. Apples give off ethylene gas, which promotes ripening, maturation, and therefore, sprouting of potatoes. If you must store them in the same room, ventilate it well so the ethylene gas can escape.

Apples are one of the more popular fruits that people store in root cellars. A single apple tree can produce several bushels of fruit. When picking apples for storage, let them mature on your tree before removing them because apples harvested before they're ready tend to shrivel in storage. Choose apples that mature late in the season as summer-harvested ones don't keep as well. Also, leave the stems on the apples. Some good storage varieties are "Jonathan," "Rome Beauty," "McIntosh," "Winter Rambo," and "Spitzenburg."

When putting apples into storage, keep them in single layers. Bruising can be a real problem with apples when they're stacked. Some people prefer to wrap their apples in paper and cover them with straw. While this isn't necessary, it doesn't hurt anything.

Pears are another popular item to store in a root cellar, but picking them at the right time is essential to their keeping ability. Pick pears before they ripen, just as the skin changes from green to yellow-green. The fruit should easily lift from the tree. As with apples, leave the stems on the fruit.

Wrap pears in newspaper or any similar type of paper individually and keep them in a single layer. To ripen the pears for eating, move them into a warmer room. Be careful here because if the room is too warm, the pears will spoil instead of ripen.

Choose unblemished fruits and vegetables for storage. Do not toss, tumble, or roll vegetables or fruits you plan to store for the winter. Bruising can cause a lot of unnecessary spoilage, and sadly, one bad apple *can* spoil the entire cart!

The Least You Need to Know

- Storing crops in a root cellar is one of the easiest ways to preserve your harvest.

- Choose crops that store reasonably well, and check for specific varieties that have been bred for longer storage.

- Regulate the temperature and humidity levels for the particular type of crop or crops you wish to preserve.

- Put only unblemished fruits and vegetables into storage.

Appendix A

Glossary

annuals   Plants that grow, flower, and set seed in one season.

balanced formula   A fertilizer that contains equal parts of the three plant macronutrients—nitrogen (N), phosphorus (P), and potassium (K)—such as a 10-10-10 formulation.

biennials   Plants that produce leaves and roots the first year, and then flower or produce fruit and go to seed and die at the end of their second season.

bolt   To quickly send up a tall flower stalk and set seed.

bottom watering   The process of putting water in an outer tray into which you place potted seeds and seedlings.

browns   Compost materials that are high in carbon and provide energy, such as leaves, woodchips and sawdust, hay and straw, paper and cardboard, eggshells, coffee grounds, tea bags, and soil.

bulb pan   A wide, shallow pot—about twice as wide as it is tall.

capillary mat   A method of bottom watering in which a mat of synthetic fabric is placed inside an outer tray holding a small amount of water to absorb moisture and then release it slowly to potted seeds or seedlings that sit directly on it.

clay soil   Soil, characterized by very small particles, which packs together tightly and does not drain well.

cloche A bell-shaped cover, historically made of glass, that is put over a plant to protect it from frost, heavy rain, or hail.

cold frame A small, box-like outdoor structure in which gardeners start or grow plants in pots.

complete fertilizer A fertilizer that contains all three of the primary macronutrients—nitrogen, phosphorus, and potassium.

composting The process of allowing formerly living materials to decompose, or break down.

cool greenhouse A greenhouse that has a nighttime minimum temperature of 45° to 50°F and a minimum daytime temperature of 55° to 60°F.

cover crop A crop such as field peas, vetch, or clover planted in a garden area over the winter to suppress weeds, then till under to add nutrients to the soil.

cultivar A word blended from *cultivated* and *variety*. Cultivars are variations on a plant species that show characteristics that remain different than the parent plants over a number of generations.

cultivate To prepare soil for crops and gardening by breaking it up with a hoe, garden fork, or tiller.

cure To let produce such as onions, potatoes, garlic, sweet potatoes, squash, and pumpkins stand for about two weeks to dry and to harden the skin.

cut-and-come-again A technique for harvesting leafy vegetables, herbs, and flowers using a pair of sharp scissors to trim off flowers or mature outer leaves, leaving flower buds or the younger, inner leaves and growing point of the plant intact.

diatomaceous earth A naturally occurring, chalk-like rock that crumbles easily into a powder and is formed from the fossilized remains of diatoms, a type of hard-shelled algae. Works as an effective insect pest control measure.

dibble A cylindrical garden tool with a pointed end used for making planting holes in soil or potting medium.

direct sow The process of sowing seeds directly into soil outdoors where you want the plants to grow.

epiphyte A plant with exposed roots that absorb moisture from the air. In nature, epiphytes are non-parasitic plants that grow on damp rocks and tree branches.

exotic   A plant that is not native to this continent, or in a narrower context, is not native to the region in which you live.

fallow   A field or garden area not being used, usually to allow nutrients to restore themselves in the soil.

fast compost   Compost made within a season or so by turning the pile weekly to speed decomposition of materials within the pile.

forcing   The process of causing plants to flower out of season, most typically done with bulbs.

freestanding greenhouse   An unattached greenhouse with four walls and a ridge connecting a two-sided roof.

friable   Easily crumbled; used to describe a desirable soil that neither packs together nor sifts through the fingers.

frost cover   A lightweight polyester or polyethylene fabric that lets some water and light through, but insulates plants from extreme cold temperatures.

furrow   A long, shallow trench dug to proper depth for seed sowing.

genus   A group of closely related plant species form a genus, or plant family. In botanical names, the genus is the first, capitalized word.

germination   The process of a dormant seed sprouting and growing into a seedling.

green manure   A crop such as clover or alfalfa that is planted in a fallow garden area in spring or summer, allowed to mature, and then turned under in the autumn to add organic matter to soil.

greenhouse   A structure at least the size of a small room, with plastic or glass walls and roof.

greens   Compost materials that are high in nitrogen and provide protein for micro-organisms that aid decomposition. Green materials include grass clippings, hedge trimmings, kitchen scraps, and livestock manure.

hardening off   The process of setting indoor-started seedlings outdoors in a protected place so the seedlings can gradually adjust to outdoor weather conditions.

hardiness zone   An area characterized by a certain climate that supports certain types of plants. In the United States, each hardiness zone differs by 10°F in terms of the average coldest winter temperatures.

hardscape   The nonliving elements of a garden landscape, including walkways, walls, arbors, benches, statues, fountains, and buildings.

heat sink   A method of collecting and retaining heat in an unheated greenhouse, cold frame, or tunnel house. Containers of water absorb heat from the sun during the day, then slowly release it at night.

heirlooms   Varieties of flowers, vegetables, and small fruits selected over many generations for superior traits. Seeds from heirlooms produce plants like the parent.

humidity   The level of moisture in the air.

humus   The organic matter in the soil; humus is the result of the natural decomposition of leaves and other plant material that takes place in the soil.

hybrid   A named variety of a plant created by breeding or "crossing" two different plants. Hybrids are generally sterile or do not produce offspring like the parents. Contrast *heirlooms*.

incomplete fertilizer   A fertilizer that contains only one or two of the three primary macronutrients: nitrogen, phosphorus, and potassium.

insecticidal soap   A homemade or commercial substance sprayed on plant leaves to rid plants of insect pests.

integrated pest management   A method of both preventing and controlling pests first by organic means, then by chemical means if other measures fail.

intensive garden   A garden laid out in squares, which are densely planted with vegetables, herbs, or flowers, with a path running around each side of every bed.

intermediate greenhouse   A greenhouse with nighttime winter temperatures from 50° to 60°F and sunny winter daytime temperatures from 70° to as high as 90°F.

last frost date   The average date of the last winter frost in a given area, when temperatures dip below freezing and harm plants.

lattice panels   Wood or plastic panels of criss-crossed slats that gardeners use as trellises or dividers or even fences in their yards.

lean-to greenhouse   A greenhouse that is essentially half of a freestanding greenhouse—with one roof surface, one long wall, and two half-gabled ends. It is attached to the wall of a house, garage, or shed.

loamy soil   Soil, characterized by medium-sized particles, that has high organic content and is friable; considered the best type of soil.

long Tom pot   A tall, narrow, tapered pot suited to deep-rooted plants, such as tree seedlings, or plants with a cascading growth habit, such as some chrysanthemums and bonsai.

low tunnels   Garden structures created by securing row covers over hoops that span a single crop row. Typically, such a structure is just high enough to accommodate the height of the crop plants within the tunnel.

macronutrients   Nutrients that plants need in large quantities. The primary macro-nutrients are nitrogen, phosphorus, and potassium. The secondary macronutrients are calcium, magnesium, and sulfur.

microclimate   The climate of a small or restricted space.

microgreens   Salad greens harvested just after they sprout.

micronutrients   Nutrients essential for plant health but needed in only small quan-tities. The seven micronutrients are boron, copper, iron, chloride, manganese, molybdenum, and zinc.

negative ions   Oxygen particles that lose an electrical charge near moving water or in vigorously circulating air. Negative-ion charged air makes us feel clear-headed and energetic.

nitrogen   One of the three macronutrients all plants need; promotes rapid leaf and stem growth. Chemical symbol: N.

offshoots   Stems or branches that grow from the main stem of a plant and develop into new plants.

open-pollinated plants   Plants that are pollinated naturally by wind, birds, or insects.

overwintering   Keeping vegetable plants alive and producing through autumn and into winter.

passive cooling   Cooling a structure with naturally circulating air entering through windows, doors, or roof vents.

perennials   Plants that live from 3 to 50 years or more. They reproduce by seed, by underground or ground-hugging stems called runners, or by sprouting plantlets that sprout at the base of old plants.

pH   The measure of a soil's acidity, based on a scale of 0 to 14. On the pH scale, 0 is extremely acid, and 14 is extremely alkaline. The number 7 is considered neutral.

phosphorus   One of the three macronutrients all plants need; promotes blossoming and fruit production. Chemical symbol: P.

photosynthesis   The process in which plants use energy from the sun to turn water and carbon dioxide into starches and sugars. The plant releases oxygen, a by-product of photosynthesis.

pistil   The female part of a flower, which receives the pollen from the male part.

pit greenhouse   A step-down, cellar-like greenhouse structure sunken into the ground below the frost line. Only the roof of a pit greenhouse shows above ground.

potassium   One of the three macronutrients all plants need; promotes strong stem growth and imparts some extra winter hardiness to plants. Chemical symbol: K.

presoaking   A method of softening hard-coated seeds by steeping them overnight in warm water—about 80°F—before planting.

presprouting   A method of giving difficult-to-sprout seeds a head start by sprouting them on a damp paper towel before planting.

propagation heat mat   A waterproof plastic or rubber mat that encases thermo-statically controlled heating cables. When plugged into an outlet, the mat provides consistent, gentle bottom heat to seed flats and pots to aid germination.

raised beds   Areas for growing plants that have been mounded up or contained within timbers, rocks, or landscaping stone.

rhizome   A stem that grows horizontally just below ground level and puts out roots and lateral stems to form new plants.

root cellar   A cool, dark, moist place, either indoors or outdoors, in which to store produce or to start or grow certain plants.

row cover   A lightweight polyester or polyethylene fabric that lets some water and light through, but protects plants from insects, harsh weather, and temperature extremes.

row garden   A traditional food-garden style in which plants are laid out in rows alternating with paths.

runner   A shoot that grows horizontally, usually from the base of a plant. When a runner touches ground, it roots and forms a new plant.

sandy soil   Soil, characterized by large particles, that sifts through the fingers easily and drains quickly.

scarification   The process of scratching away a small amount of a seed's hard outer coat so moisture can reach the embryo within to induce sprouting.

seed   A dormant, embryonic plant, complete with root, stem, a kernel of nutrition called an endosperm, and seedling leaves called cotyledons.

self-fertile   A self-fertile plant has flowers with both male and female parts so that it pollinates itself.

shade cloth   A synthetic fabric manufactured to block a certain percentage of sunlight.

side dressing   A method of safely applying fertilizer between rows of crops or in a circle around individual plants, avoiding contact with plants.

slow compost   Compost material that takes up to two years to decompose because the pile is neither turned nor stirred.

soil heating cable   A plastic-coated electric wire attached to a thermostat. Placed under soil in a bed and plugged into a grounded outlet, it warms the soil to the ideal temperature for germination.

soilless potting mix   A sterile blend of sphagnum peat moss and inert, granular ingredients such as Perlite or vermiculite and charcoal that create pores to allow water and oxygen to circulate through the mix.

species   A group of plants with common characteristics that set it apart from other plants of the same genus.

spectrum   The full range of colors in light.

square-foot garden   A garden laid out in a series of squares, usually 4 square feet each, with each square being subdivided into 1-square-foot sections for planting.

stamen   The male part of a flower, which produces pollen.

stem cutting   A piece taken from a growing plant stem, including the growing tip and two or more leaf nodes.

stratification   A process of placing seeds in a moist growing medium and refrigerating them for a specified length of time, depending on the type of seed. Seeds of plants requiring a cold winter dormant period require stratification to initiate germination.

succession planting   The practice of starting a batch of seeds every other week in order to space out crops throughout the growing season and lengthen the harvest.

swamp cooler   A term for a simple cooling unit that fits in a window or greenhouse wall vent. The large fan of the cooler pulls air from outdoors through a water-soaked nylon or excelsior pad, cooling and humidifying the air as it enters a greenhouse.

systemic insecticides   Substances applied to the leaves of plants or watered into the roots to make the plants poisonous to insect pests.

tender   A tender plant is one that will not survive exposure to frost or freezing temperatures.

tile (v)   To lay perforated pipe beneath the surface of the soil to promote the drainage of excess water.

top dressing   A method of safely spreading fertilizer during the growing season across the surface of the garden as mulch, avoiding contact with plants.

transplant shock   The condition sometimes caused by transplanting a seedling or plant, characterized by wilting and failure to thrive. Usually due to root damage, transplant shock can stunt or kill a plant.

trap plant   A plant that attracts a particular insect pest, planted next to a row of crop plants.

true leaves   The first set of adult-like leaves that develop on a seedling *after* the initial set of seedling leaves.

tunnel house   A plastic tunnel-shaped covering constructed over rows of plants growing in the ground; usually tall enough for a gardener to stand upright in.

unheated greenhouse   An unheated greenhouse, or a cold greenhouse, doesn't contain a heat source but does contain windows or vents to vent hot air.

vermicompost   Waste excreted by earthworms; also called worm castings. An extremely fertile and desirable substance.

vermiculite   A lightweight, tan, granular material created by heating mica chips until they expand. Vermiculite is light in weight and improves drainage, air circulation, and fertilizer retention in soil.

warm greenhouse   A greenhouse with nighttime temperatures between 60° and 70°F, and daytime temperatures reaching as high as the 90s.

water breaker   A wide garden hose nozzle with many small holes that delivers a gentle shower; useful for watering seedlings and delicate plants.

weed cloth   A synthetic fabric used to suppress weeds in garden areas. Weed cloth is permeable so water can get to the plant roots below.

wintersowing   The method of planting seeds in covered (but not sealed) containers in winter and setting them out to endure the elements, just as seeds do in the wild.

Appendix B

Fruits, Vegetables, Herbs

When should I plant seeds? Can I start a second crop of this? What do I do with these seedlings that someone gave me? The information in these tables will answer many of your questions. We hope it's easy for you to figure out when to do what—and where to do it—with many different types of plants.

Remember this: start all seeds at 70°F, and set them out according to the timing recommended here or on the seed packet. In these tables, we list temperatures only for those plants that require growing temperatures other than 70°F. Also note that entries that say simply "Direct sow" mean to direct sow *in the garden*.

The abbreviation *UC* stands for "under cover" and refers to an under-cover gardening situation—either an unheated greenhouse or an outdoor bed protected by covers in both freezing and above-freezing temperatures.

Fruits

Plant	Spring	Summer	Fall	Late Winter
Melon	Sow indoors for garden; grow UC	Set out in garden		Sow UC
Strawberry	Set out in garden 60°F		Move offshoots UC 60°F	Hand pollinate UC

Vegetables

Plant	Spring	Summer	Fall	Late Winter
Arugula	Direct sow		Direct sow in garden or UC	Sow UC
Beans (bush or pole)	Direct sow		Direct sow	Sow UC
Beet	Direct sow			Sow UC
Broccoli	Sow indoors; set out in garden		Sow indoors for UC	Sow indoors; set out UC
Broccoli rabe	Sow indoors; set out in garden		Sow indoors; Set out UC	Sow indoors; set out UC
Cabbage	Sow indoors; set out in garden	Sow indoors	Set out in garden	Sow indoors; set out UC
Carrot	Direct sow	Direct sow	Direct sow	Sow UC
Cauliflower	Sow indoors; set out in 50°F–60°F soil		Sow indoors; set out in garden	Grow UC
Cucumber	Sow indoors; set out UC	Set out in garden	Sow indoors; set out UC	

Plant	Spring	Summer	Fall	Late Winter
Eggplant	Sow indoors; set out or grow UC	Direct sow		
Endive	Direct sow		Direct sow in garden or UC	Sow UC
Kale	Direct sow		Direct sow in garden or UC	Sow UC
Kohlrabi	Direct sow; grow at 50°F–60°F		Direct sow; grow at 50°F–60°F	Sow UC
Lettuce	Direct sow	Start indoors; chill seeds; set out in shaded garden	Direct sow	Sow UC
Mizuna	Direct sow		Direct sow	Sow UC
Mustard	Direct sow; grow at 50°F–60°F		Direct sow; grow at 50°F–60°F	Sow UC
Onion family	Direct sow seeds or set out starts		Direct sow seeds or set out starts	Sow UC; overwinter
Bok choi	Sow indoors; set out in garden	Sow indoors	Set out in garden	Sow indoors; set out UC
Pea	Direct sow		Direct sow	Sow UC
Pepper	Start indoors		Set out in garden	Start indoors; set out UC
Potato	Set out in garden		Harvest	Set out; harvest
Raddichio	Direct sow		Direct sow	Sow UC

continues

Vegetables   (continued)

Plant	Spring	Summer	Fall	Late Winter
Radish	Direct sow		Direct sow	Sow UC
Rutabaga	Direct sow		Direct sow	Harvest; overwinter; grow UC
Spinach	Direct sow		Direct sow	Sow UC
Summer squash	Direct sow	Direct sow	Sow UC	
Sweet potatoes	Direct sow	Direct sow	Direct sow	
Swiss chard	Direct sow or set out seedlings		Sow UC	Sow UC; harvest
Tomato/ tomatillo	Start indoors	Set out seedlings		Start indoors; grow UC
Turnip	Direct sow	Direct sow	Direct sow	Overwinter; harvest
Winter squash	Direct sow	Direct sow		Sow UC in 60°F soil

Herbs

Plant	Spring	Summer	Fall / Winter
Basil	Sow indoors	Direct sow	
Chive	Sow indoors	Set out	Overwinter
Cilantro	Sow indoors		
Dill	Sow indoors	Set out	

Plant	Spring	Summer	Fall / Winter
Fennel	Sow indoors	Set out	
Garlic			Set out cloves; overwinter
Marjoram	Sow indoors	Set out	
Oregano	Sow indoors	Set out	
Parsley	Sow indoors or direct sow		Sow indoors or direct sow
Rosemary	Set out seedlings	Set out	Overwinter in cool greenhouse
Sage	Set out seedlings	Set out	Overwinter outdoors or in cool greenhouse
Thyme	Set out seedlings	Set out	Overwinter outdoors or in cool greenhouse

Ornamental Plants

The following list of ornamental plants includes favorites for the outdoor garden and for the three heated greenhouse climate zones.

If you match plant needs to your greenhouse microclimates (coolest temperatures near the floor and outside door, warmest near the roof, and mid-range on the benches), you can grow a few plants from all three greenhouse types in just about any greenhouse.

Cool Greenhouse Plants

(Nighttime temperature: 45° to 50°F minimum; minimum daytime temperature: 55° to 60°F)

Shrubs and trees

Azalea (*Rhododendron obtusum, R. simsii*)

Camellia (*Camellia japonica*)

Citrus trees, various species

Flowering maple (*Abutilon hybridum*)

Hardy palms (various species)

Heather (*Calluna vulgaris*)

Jasmine (*Jasminum* spp.)

Miniature rose (*Rosa* spp.)

Norfolk Island pine (*Araucaria heterophylla*)

Flowering plants

Bachelor button or cornflower (*Centaurea cyanus*)

Bougainvillea buttiana

Clivia miniata

Cacti, various species

Chrysanthemum hybrids

Cyclamen spp.

Cymbidium orchid spp.

Flowering bulbs, corms, and tubers

Hardy perennials

Geraniums (*Pelargonium* spp.)

Nasturtiums

Orchid cactus (*Epiphyllum* spp.)

Pansies (*Viola tricolor*)

Primrose (*Primula* spp.)

Ranunculus spp.

Snapdragon (*Antirrhinum majus*)

Sweet peas (*Lathyrus odoratus*)

Foliage plants

Asparagus fern

Cast iron plant (*Aspidistra* spp.)

Cold-tolerant ferns, various spp.

Cordyline (*Cordyline fruticosa*)

Creeping fig (*Ficus pumilla*)

English ivy (*Hedera helix*)

Poinsettia (*Euphorbia pulcherrima*)

Rock garden (alpine) plants, various spp.

Schlumbergera (claw cactus, Christmas, Easter cactus)

Strawberry begonia (*Saxifraga stolonifera*)

Intermediate Greenhouse Plants

(Nighttime temperature: 50° to 60°F; sunny winter daytime temperature: from 70° to as high as 90°F)

Flowering plants

Amaryllis (*Hippeastrum* spp.)

Begonia species and hybrids

       fibrous-rooted

       rhizomatous

       tuberous

Big-leaf Hydrangea (*Hydrangea macrophylla*)

Bird of paradise (*Strelitzia* spp.)

Flamingo flower (*Anthurium* spp.)

Fuschia spp.

Gardenia spp.

Hibiscus spp.

Jasmine (*Jasminum* spp.)

Kalanchoe spp.

Lipstick plant (*Columnea* spp.)

Orchid species and hybrids:

       Calanthe spp.

       Cattleya spp.

Dendrobium spp.

Epidendrum spp.

Laelia spp.

Miltonium spp.

Oncidium spp.

Vanda spp.

Foliage plants

Aloe spp.

Begonia rex

Bromeliad spp.

Calathea spp.

Chinese evergreen (*Aglaonema* spp.)

Croton spp.

Devil's ivy (*Scindapsus* spp.)

Earth star (*Cryptanthus* spp.)

Fiddle leaf fig (*Ficus lyrata*)

Hoya spp.

Pepperomia spp.

Philodendron spp.

Prayer plant (*Maranta* spp.)

Snake plant (*Sansevieria* spp.)

Stromanthe spp.

Succulents, various species and hybrids

Variegated pineapple (*Ananas comosus*)

Wandering Jew (*Tradescantia* spp.)

Fruiting plants

Citrus, various species

Kiwi (*Actinidia* spp.)

Pineapple (*Ananas lucidus*)

Star fruit (*Averrhoa carambola*)

Papaya

Indoor and Warm Greenhouse Plants

(Nighttime temperature: 60° to 70°F; daytime temperature: as high as the 90s)

Flowering plants

African violet (*Saintpaulia ionantha*)

Begonia spp.

> fibrous-rooted
>
> rhizomatous

Cape primrose (*Streptocarpus* spp.)

Episcia spp.

Gloxinia spp.

Orchids

> Moth orchid (*Phaleonopsis* spp.)
>
> Slipper orchid (*Paphiopedilum* spp.)
>
> For others, consult an orchid guidebook

Stephanotis spp.

Foliage plants

Air plant (*Tillandsia* spp.)

Caladium (*Caladium hortulanum*)

Devil's ivy (*Scindapsus* spp.)

Rosary vine (*Ceropegia woodii*)

Coleus blumei

Dracaena spp.

Dumb cane (*Dieffenbachia* spp.)

Fittonia spp.

Spider plant (*Chlorophytum comosum*)

Tropical ferns (various species)

Resources

Books

Bubel, Nancy. *The New Seed-Starters Handbook*. Pennsylvania: Rodale, 1988. This is an excellent resource for growing food and flowering plants, herbs, wildflowers, trees, and shrubs from seed.

Bubel, Mike and Nancy. *Root Cellaring: Natural Cold Storage of Fruits & Vegetables*. Vermont: Storey Books, 1991. This long-standing reference tells you how to choose food plants with long-storing fruits and how to build and stock root cellars.

Coleman, Eliot. *The New Organic Grower's Four-Season Harvest: How to Harvest Fresh, Organic Vegetables from Your Home Garden All Year Long*. Vermont: Chelsea Green Publishing, 1992. This, the precursor to Coleman's *Winter Harvest Handbook*, covers material on growing under cover that's not included in the newer book.

Coleman, Eliot. *The Winter Harvest Handbook: Year-Round Vegetable Production Using Deep-Organic Techniques and Unheated Greenhouses*. Vermont: Chelsea Green Publishing, 2009. Here is a guide to extending growing seasons for food plants from a market gardener's perspective. Home gardeners should adapt the information to small-scale gardens.

Crockett, James Underwood. *Greenhouse Gardening as a Hobby*. Garden City, New York: Doubleday & Company, 1961. This enjoyable read is a great introduction to hobby greenhouse gardening by a seasoned expert—the original host of *The Victory Garden* television program.

Damrosch, Barbara. *The Garden Primer*. New York: Workman, 2008. The ultimate reference for garden planning and growing food and ornamental plants.

Foster, Catharine Osgood. *Plants-a-Plenty: How to Multiply Outdoor and Indoor Plants Through Cuttings, Crown and Root Divisions, Grafting, Layering, and Seeds*. Emmaus, Pennsylvania: Rodale Press, 1977. This is a reliable source of information for propagating plants vegetatively.

Franks, Eric, and Jasmine Richardson. *Microgreens: a Guide to Growing Nutrient-Packed Greens*. Utah: Gibbs Smith, 2009. Market gardeners tell how to grow and use microgreens.

Freeman, Mark. *Gardening in Your Greenhouse*. Pennsylvania: Stackpole Books, 1998. This is a good basic guide to growing herbs, flowering, and food plants in the greenhouse.

Gershuny, Grace. *Start with the Soil: the Organic Gardener's Guide to Improving Soil for Higher Yields, More Beautiful Flowers, and a Healthy, Easy-Care Garden*. Pennsylvania: Rodale Books, 1993. A classic guide to garden-soil improvement.

Heffernan, Maureen. *Burpee Seed Starter: a Growing Guide for Starting Flower, Vegetable, and Herb Seeds Indoors and Outdoors*. New York: Macmillan, 1997. This comprehensive collection of plants provides detailed seed-starting information.

Logsdon, Gene. *The Gardener's Guide to Better Soil*. Pennsylvania: Rodale Press, 1975. This gives a thorough discussion of improving soil fertility, correcting soil pH, adding amendments, and irrigating.

McCullagh, James C. *The Solar Greenhouse Book*. Pennsylvania: Rodale Press, 1978. This book, covering gardening in an unheated greenhouse, includes information on how siting and weather affects greenhouse efficiency and plans for homemade greenhouses.

Murphy, Wendy. *Gardening Under Lights*. Virginia: Time-Life Books, 1978. This is a timeless guide to growing plants indoors under lights.

Nau, Jim. *Ball Culture Guide: The Encyclopedia of Seed Germination, 3rd ed.* Illinois: Ball Publishing, 1999. This professional seed-starter's guide gives detailed information on germination methods, temperatures, and times for individual seeds of ornamental and food plants.

Nearing, Helen and Scott. *The Good Life.* New York: Schocken (a division of Random House), 1990. Here is a firsthand account of homesteading by early proponents of organic farming. This one-volume edition is a combination of the authors' lauded earlier words, *Living the Good Life* (1954) and *Continuing the Good Life* (1979).

Ogren, Thomas Leo. *Allergy-Free Gardening.* Berkeley, California: Ten Speed Press (a division of Crown Publishing Group at Random House), 2004. If you have allergies to pollen, you should read this book. It's full of information on plants that cause allergies and what allergy sufferers can do to deal with these plants in their local environment.

Ogren, Thomas Leo. *Safe Sex in the Garden.* Berkeley, California: Ten Speed Press (a division of Crown Publishing Group at Random House), 2004. This book contains lots of information on organic pesticides.

Pleasant, Barbara, and Deborah L. Martin. *The Complete Compost Gardening Guide.* Vermont: Storey Publishing, 2008. This is a comprehensive, contemporary composting book, covering all aspects of composting, including several methods of vermicomposting.

Reader's Digest. *Garden Problem Solver.* Pleasantville, New York: The Reader's Digest Association, Inc., 2000. A comprehensive guide to controlling garden pests, diseases, and environmental problems, this gives an integrated pest control approach.

Reader's Digest. *Success with Houseplants.* Pleasantville, New York: The Reader's Digest Association, Inc., 1979. This is a timeless guide to growing tropical ornamental plants in home or greenhouse.

Richerson, Sheri. *101 English Garden Tips.* Massachusetts: LifeTips.com, Inc., 2009. This tip book is full of advice on growing an English garden with a section on greenhouse gardening.

Rogers, Marc. *Saving Seeds: The Gardener's Guide to Growing and Storing Vegetable and Flower Seeds,* Vermont: Storey Communications, Inc., 1990. This is a useful guide to raising flowering and food plants and harvesting and storing seeds.

Salt, Bernard. *Gardening Under Plastic: How to Use Fleece, Films, Cloches and Polytunnels.* London: B.T. Batsford, Ltd., 2001. Here is excellent coverage of gardening under protective covers, but American readers should account for climate differences when reading this British book.

Smith, Edward C. *The Vegetable Gardener's BIBLE: Discover Ed's High-Yield W-O-R-D System for All North American Gardening Regions.* Massachusetts: Storey Publishing, 2000. This is a thorough food-gardening grower's guide.

Smith, Shane. *Greenhouse Gardener's Companion: Growing Food & Flowers in Your Greenhouse or Sunspace.* Colorado: Fulcrum Publishing, 2000. This comprehensive guide to cool greenhouse growing covers some flowering plants but focuses on growing food plants.

Taylor, Kathryn S., and Edith W Gregg. *Winter Flowers in Greenhouse and Sun-Heated Pit.* New York: Charles Scribner's Sons, 1969. Here is a timeless look at growing ornamental plants in a cold or cool greenhouse.

Equipment, Supplies, and Tools

◆ **Ace, The Helpful Place**
www.acehardware.com

This national hardware chain carries lawn and garden supplies, including weatherstripping tape. Check the website to find the store nearest you.

◆ **A.M. Leonard**
www.amleo.com
1-800-543-8955

This catalog and online source of quality garden tools includes drop spreaders, power equipment, and greenhouses.

◆ **Charley's Greenhouse and Garden**
www.charleysgreenhouse.com
1-800-322-4707

Here is a one-stop catalog and online shopping for greenhouse kits, equipment, and gardening supplies, including UV-stabilized bubble wrap greenhouse insulation, translucent storm tarps, polycarbonate panels, soil thermometers, minimum/maximum thermometers, remote thermometers with low-temperature alarm, rechargeable misters, greenhouse fans, heat mats, rooting hormone, and much more.

◆ **Fungi Perfecti**
www.fungi.com

This supplier has gourmet and medicinal mushroom kits, books, cultivation tools, and other supplies as well as information on growing mushrooms.

◆ **Gardens Alive!**
www.gardensalive.com
513-354-1482

This is a catalog and online source of beneficial insects and other environmental garden and lawn-care aids.

◆ **Gardeners Supply Company**
www.gardeners.com
1-888-833-1412

Find earth-friendly gardening supplies including screen curtain, composters, water barrels, and garden fertilizers, amendments, and pest control products here.

◆ **Harmony Supply**
www.harmonyfarm.com
707-823-9125

This source supplies lab services, tools, fertilizers, and other garden supplies.

◆ **Tractor Supply Company**
www.tractorsupply.com

This farm and garden supplier's inventory includes rubber barn stall mats. Check the website for the store nearest you.

◆ **Wind and Weather**
www.windandweather.com
1-877-255-3700

This catalog and online supplier of electronic weather-watching equipment includes remote sensor thermometers, rain gauges, and garden accessories.

Plants and Seeds

◆ **Bountiful Gardens**
www.bountifulgardens.org
707-459-6410

This catalog and online source provides heirloom, untreated, open-pollinated seeds; books; and gardening supplies.

◆ **Johnny's Selected Seeds**
www.johnnyseeds.com.
877-564-6697

This is a catalog and online source of food and flowering plant seeds, as well as other gardening supplies.

◆ **Renee's Garden Seeds**
www.reneesgarden.com

This is an online source of gourmet vegetable, kitchen herb, and cottage garden flower seeds.

◆ **Seeds of Change**
www.seedsofchange.com
1-888-762-7333

Here is a catalog and online source of certified organic food and flowering plant seeds as well as other gardening supplies.

Societies, Websites, and Blogs

◆ **AHS Heat Zone Map**
www.ahs.org/publications/heat_zone_map.htm

The current version of the American Horticultural Society's heat-zone map.

◆ **American Association of Poison Control Centers**
www.aapcc.org
1-800-222-1222 (Poison Help hotline)

Locate the poison control center near you for information on potential toxins, first aid, and emergency treatment.

◆ **Cooperative State Research, Education, and Extension Service**
www.csrees.usda.gov

An online resource for locating your local Cooperative Extension office.

◆ **Hobby Greenhouse Association**
www.hobbygreenhouse.org

Nonprofit organization of hobby greenhouse growers, with local chapters, newsletter, and magazine.

◆ **Seattle Tilth**
www.seattletilth.org
206-633-0451

A gardener and composter's hotline and source of home-gardening information.

◆ **USDA Hardiness Zone Map**
www.usna.usda.gov

Follow the link at the bottom of the page to find the current version of the U.S. Department of Agriculture Plant Hardiness Zone Map for North America and Hawaii.

◆ **U.S. Environmental Protection Agency Hotlines and Clearinghouses**
www.epa.gov/epahome/hotline.htm

A cooperative effort of Oregon State University and the Environmental Protection Agency, this website lists contact information for agencies that can answer questions about product toxicity, application guidelines, air quality, endangered species, antimicrobial information, poison control, and more.

◆ **Victory Seed Company**
www.victoryseeds.com/frost

This online list gives first and last frost dates for the United States and Canada.

◆ **Wintersowing**
www.wintersown.org

Comprehensive online source of information about how to wintersow and what you can wintersow, plus extensive seed-saving information.

Index

Check out the
BEST-SELLERS

Grammar and Style
SECOND EDITION

978-1-59257-115-4
$16.95

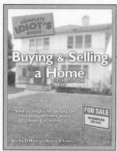

Buying & Selling a Home
FIFTH EDITION

978-1-59257-458-2
$19.95

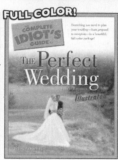

FULL COLOR!

The Perfect Wedding

978-1-59257-566-4
$22.95

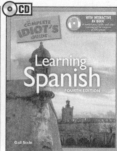

CD

Learning Spanish
FOURTH EDITION

978-1-59257-485-8
$24.95

Investing
THIRD EDITION

978-1-59257-480-3
$19.95

Baby Sign Language

978-1-59257-469-8
$14.95

978-1-5

$

89-9

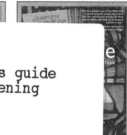

Calculus
SECOND EDITION

978-1-59257-471-1
$18.95

CD

Music Theory
SECOND EDITION

978-1-59257-437-7
$19.95

The Perfect Resume
FOURTH EDITION

978-1-59257-463-6
$14.95

CD

Playing the Guitar
SECOND EDITION

978-0-02864-244-4
$21.95

Manga Illustrated

978-1-59257-335-6
$19.95

Knitting & Crocheting
THIRD EDITION
Illustrated

978-1-59257-491-9
$19.95

More than **450 titles** available at booksellers and online retailers everywhere

ALPHA

www.idiotsguides.com